Boundary Issues in Counseling

MULTIPLE ROLES AND RESPONSIBILITIES

**Barbara Herlihy, PhD
and Gerald Corey, EdD**

American Counseling Association
5999 Stevenson Avenue
Alexandria, VA, 22304

BOUNDARY ISSUES IN COUNSELING

10 9 8 7 6 5 4 3 2 1

American Counseling Association
5999 Stevenson Avenue
Alexandria, VA 22304

Director of Acquisitions
Carolyn Baker

Director of Publishing Systems
Michael Comlish

Copyeditor
Lucy Blanton

Cover design by Coryell Douglas

Library of Congress Cataloging-in-Publication Data

Herlihy, Barbara.
    Boundary issues in counseling: multiple roles and
responsibilities/Barbara Herlihy and Gerald Corey.
        p. cm.
    Includes bibliographical references and index.
    ISBN 1-55620-167-2 (alk. paper)
    1. Counseling   2. Counseling—Moral and ethical aspects.
I. Corey, Gerald.   II. Title
BF637.C6H415   1997   97-1331
361'.06—dc21   CIP

To our colleagues who struggle with the issues explored in this book.

Table of Contents

About the Authors

Barbara Herlihy, PhD, NCC, LPC, is professor of counselor education at the University of New Orleans. She is a National Certified Counselor and a licensed professional counselor whose work experience has been primarily as a school counselor, counselor educator and supervisor, and private practitioner. She has served as chair of the American Counseling Association (ACA) Ethics Committee, as co-chair (with Madelyn Healy) of the Association for Counselor Education and Supervision (ACES) Ethics Interest Network, and as a member of the ethics committees of the Association for Specialists in Group Work (ASGW) and the Southern Association for Counselor Education and Supervision (SACES).

Dr. Herlihy has authored or coauthored numerous articles on ethical issues in counseling. She is the coauthor with Larry Golden of the AACD *Ethical Standards Casebook* (fourth edition, 1990); and with Gerald Corey of both *Dual Relationships in Counseling* (1992) and the *ACA Ethical Standards Casebook* (fifth edition, 1996). She is a frequent presenter of ethics seminars and workshops across the United States, including ACA professional development workshops in 1995, 1996, and 1997.

Gerald Corey, EdD, ABPP, NCC, is professor of human services and counseling at California State University, Fullerton. He is a Diplomate in Counseling Psychology, American Board of Professional Psychology, and is a National Certified Counselor and a licensed counseling psychologist. He is a fellow of the American Psychological Association (APA) and a fellow of the Association for Specialists in Group Work. He is the recipient of the California State University- Fullerton Outstanding Professor of the Year

Award in 1991 and an honorary doctorate in humane letters from National Louis University in 1992.

Dr. Corey has authored or coauthored numerous articles and has 13 books in print in the field of counseling, including *Issues and Ethics in the Helping Professions* (fifth edition, in press, coauthored with Marianne Schneider Corey and Patrick Callanan) and *Becoming a Helper* (third edition, in press, coauthored with Marianne Schneider Corey). Along with his daughters Cindy Corey and Heidi Jo Corey, he coauthored *Living and Learning* (1997). He has a special interest in teaching courses in ethical and professional issues, group counseling, and theories and techniques of counseling. Over the past 20 years he has conducted workshops for mental health professionals at many universities in the United States as well as in Canada, China, Germany, Mexico, and Scotland.

Guest Contributors

Our guest contributors have enriched this book immensely. They have provided a diversity of perspectives, including those of student, counselor educator and supervisor, practitioner, and specialist. They have shared their thoughts and opinions and have raised issues that are well worth considering. These contributors (and the chapters in which their contributions appear) are as follows:

L. DiAnne Borders, PhD, is professor and chairperson, Department of Counseling and Educational Development, University of North Carolina at Greensboro (chapter 5).

Hal Cain, MS, CRC, is graduate associate and doctoral candidate in rehabilitation services, College of Education, Ohio State University (chapter 9).

A. Michael Dougherty, PhD, is associate dean of the College of Education and Allied Professions, Western Carolina University, Cullowhee, North Carolina (chapters 5 and 10).

Holly Forester-Miller, PhD, is associate professor and counselor education program coordinator, North Carolina Central University, Durham (chapters 6 and 7).

Harriet L. Glosoff, PhD, is assistant professor of counseling psychology, University of Southern Mississippi, Hattiesburg (chapter 8).

Robert Haynes, PhD, is psychology internship director, Atascadero State Hospital, California (chapter 9).

Craig D. Kain, PhD, is assistant professor and co-chair, Graduate Program in Psychology, Antioch University Southern California, Marina del Rey (chapter 9).

Rod Merta, PhD, is associate professor of counseling, Department of Counseling and Educational Psychology, New Mexico State University, Las Cruces (chapter 6).

Michelle C. Muratori is a graduate student in counseling psychology, Northwestern University, Evanston, Illinois (chapter 4).

Thomas A. Parham, PhD, is an assistant vice chancellor for counseling and health services at the University of California at Irvine (chapter 7).

Les J. Powell is a graduate student in counseling, Fort Hays State University, Kansas (chapter 9).

Sue Spooner, PhD, is professor and program coordinator, College Student Personnel Administration, University of Northern Colorado, Greeley (chapter 10).

Holly A. Stadler, PhD, is professor and head, Department of Counseling and Counseling Psychology, Auburn University, Alabama (chapter 4).

Derald Wing Sue, PhD, is professor of psychology, California School of Professional Psychology–Alameda and California State University, Hayward (chapter 7).

Susan L. Walden, PhD, is assistant professor of counseling, University of Houston–Clear Lake, Texas (chapter 3).

Preface

Dual or multiple relationships may be one of the most controversial of all issues in the counseling profession. They have been the subject of extensive debate, which has produced many questions and few answers. We hope that this book will be useful to others who share our interest in dual or multiple relationships and who struggle, as we do, to find a clear personal stance on the issues involved. We intend it to be a resource that reflects the current thinking of our profession on the topic. We also want it to represent a diversity of opinion and perspectives. To that end, we have invited several guest contributors to present their positions on various topics.

We have organized the book to begin with a general introduction and overview of dual relationships. In the first three chapters, we define the issues and areas of concern (chapter 1), then focus on sexual dual relationships (chapter 2) and present the client's perspective (chapter 3). The next three chapters (chapters 4, 5, and 6) examine issues in the preparation and supervision of counselor trainees. Chapters 7 through 10 focus on how dual relationships affect practitioners in various settings and aspects of their work. In chapter 7, we discuss issues that confront counselors in the community as they work with a diverse client population. In the next three chapters (chapters 8, 9, and 10), we focus on unique boundary issues that arise in specialty areas of practice including private practice, group and family counseling, substance abuse counseling, working with clients who are living with HIV, rehabilitation counseling, forensic work, school counseling, and higher education. In the final chapter (chapter 11), we identify key themes, ask questions to encourage integration and reflection, and offer a decision-making model.

We make no claim to having discovered answers to complex and difficult questions. Rather, it is our aim to raise issues, present a range of viewpoints, and discuss our own positions. We hope that you will use this material as a springboard for further reflection and discussion. We invite you to think about the issues that are raised, apply them to your own work, and discuss them with colleagues.

This work focuses on a specialized topic in counselor preparation and counseling practice. Because dual and multiple relationships are pervasive in the helping professions, this book can be used as a supplement to any of the textbooks that are used for courses in ethical and professional issues. It can also be used in practica, fieldwork, and internship seminars. We hope that counselor educators and students will find this book useful for getting a current view of the potential problems and solutions that are associated with dual or multiple relationships. Finally, we hope the book will be useful to practitioners who struggle with dual and multiple relationship issues in their work.

1 Boundary Issues in Perspective

Dual or multiple relationships occur when professionals assume two or more roles simultaneously or sequentially with a person seeking their help. This may involve taking on more than one professional role (such as counselor and teacher), or combining professional and nonprofessional roles (such as counselor and friend or counselor and lover). Another way of stating this is that helping professionals enter into a dual or multiple relationship whenever they have another, significantly different relationship with one of their clients, students, or supervisees.

Multiple relationship issues exist throughout our profession and affect virtually all counselors, regardless of their work setting or the client population they serve. Relationship boundary issues affect the work of helping professionals in diverse roles, including counselor educator and supervisor, agency counselor, private practitioner, school counselor, college or university student personnel specialist, rehabilitation counselor, and practitioners in other specialty areas. These issues can impact the dyadic relationship between counselor and client, and they can also emerge in complex ways when relationships are tripartite (as in client/supervisee/supervisor or client/consultee/consultant) or involve families or group work. No professional remains untouched by the potential difficulties inherent in dual or multiple relationships.

This book is a revision of the 1992 *Dual Relationships in Counseling* book, but with an expanded focus. Since 1992 there have been many changes in how helping professionals think about multiple relationships, power issues, managing multiple roles and responsibilities, and boundary issues in counseling. In many respects, this is a new book rather than a simple revision.

The term *dual relationships* is now a bit simplistic, and it really no longer adequately describes the complexity of issues that mental health practitioners, counselor educators, and supervisors face in trying to determine the appropriate boundaries of their relationships with those they counsel, teach, and train. Professionals sometimes need to manage multiple roles, and there is an inher-

1

ent duality even in some roles that are supposedly singular. Although we use the terms *dual relationships* and *multiple relationships* somewhat interchangeably, this new edition is based on the assumption that counseling professionals must learn how to manage multiple roles and responsibilities effectively. This entails dealing effectively with the power differential that is inherent in counseling relationships and training relationships, balancing boundary issues, and striving to avoid using power in ways that might cause harm to clients, students, or supervisees. This book rests on the premise that we need to develop ethical decision-making skills that allow us to weigh the pros and cons of multiple roles.

Over the past two decades, the counseling profession has become increasingly concerned about multiple relationships and appropriate boundaries as ethical issues. Much has been written about the harm that results when counseling professionals enter into sexual relationships with their clients. Throughout the 1980s, sexual misconduct received a great deal of attention in the professional literature, and the dangers of sexual relationships between counselor and client, professor and student, and supervisor and supervisee have been well documented. Today, there is clear agreement that sexual relationships with clients, students, and supervisees are unethical, and prohibitions against them have been translated into ethics codes and law. In the next chapter, we examine in detail the issue of sexual dual relationships.

In the 1990s, nonsexual dual and multiple relationships have been getting more attention, and the topic has been appearing more frequently in our professional journals. Recent revisions of the codes of ethics of the American Counseling Association (ACA, 1995), the American Psychological Association (APA, 1992), the National Association of Social Workers (NASW, 1996), and the American Association for Marriage and Family Therapy (AAMFT, 1991) have dealt more specifically and extensively with topics such as appropriate boundaries, recognizing potential conflicts of interest, and ethical means of dealing with dual or multiple relationships.

Nonsexual dual or multiple relationships are often complex, which means that there are few simple and absolute answers that can neatly resolve dilemmas that arise. It is not always possible for counselors to play a singular role in their work, nor is it always desirable. It is likely that they will have to wrestle with balancing multiple roles in their professional relationships. Examples of problematic concerns include whether to barter with a client for goods or services, whether it is ever acceptable to counsel a friend or social acquaintance, how a counselor educator should manage dual roles as educator and therapeutic agent with students, how ethically to conduct experiential groups as part of a group counseling course, whether it is acceptable to date a former client, and how to manage the budget for a caseload of clients in rehabilitation counseling.

In this chapter, we focus on nonsexual dual relationships that can arise in all settings. These questions guide our discussion:

- What guidance do our codes of ethics offer about dual relationships?
- What makes dual relationships so problematic?
- What factors create the potential for harm?
- What are the risks inherent in dual relationships, for all parties involved?
- What important but subtle distinctions should be considered?
- What safeguards can be built in to minimize risks?

Ethical Standards

The codes of ethics of all the major professional associations of mental health professionals address the issue of multiple relationships. Following are excerpts from the codes of ethics for counselors, psychologists, social workers, and marriage and family therapists:

- Counselors are aware of their influential position with respect to clients, and they avoid exploiting the trust and dependency of clients. Counselors make every effort to avoid dual relationships with clients that could impair professional judgment or increase the risk of harm to clients. (Examples of such relationships include, but are not limited to, familial, social, financial, business, or close personal relationships with clients.) (ACA, 1995, A.6.a.)

- Psychologists must always be sensitive to the potential harmful effects of other contacts on their work and on those persons with whom they deal. A psychologist refrains from entering into or promising another personal, scientific, professional, financial, or other relationship with such persons if it appears likely that such a relationship might impair the psychologist's objectivity or otherwise interfere with the psychologist's effectively performing his or her functions as a psychologist, or might harm or exploit the other party. (APA, 1992, 1.17)

- Social workers should be alert to and avoid conflicts of interest that interfere with the exercise of professional discretion and impartial judgment. Social workers should inform clients when a real or potential conflict or interest arises and take reasonable steps to resolve the issue in a manner that makes the clients' interests primary and protects clients' interests to the greatest extent possible. In some cases, protecting clients' interests may require termination of the professional relationship with proper referral of the client. (NASW, 1996, 1.06)

- Marriage and family therapists are aware of their influential position with respect to clients, and they avoid exploiting the trust and dependency of such persons. Therapists, therefore, make every effort to avoid dual relationships with clients that could impair professional judgment or increase the risk of exploitation. (AAMFT, 1991, 1.2)

As can be seen, these regulations address dual relationships quite extensively. The careful attention given to the issue in the newer codes is one reflection of the fact that dual relationships have been a problematic ethical issue for mental health professionals. Other evidence is offered by studies such as that conducted by Gibson and Pope (1993), who surveyed a large national sample of counselors regarding their beliefs about a range of behaviors. Respondents were asked to indicate whether they believed each of the behaviors was ethical or unethical. Fully 42% of the items that were found to be controversial (with at least 40% of the participants judging the behavior ethical and at least 40% judging it unethical) described some form of nonsexual dual relationship. This study clearly indicated that there is little consensus among counselors around nonsexual dual relationship issues.

What Makes Dual Relationships So Problematic?

Dual or multiple relationships are rarely a clear-cut matter. Often, counselors need to make judgment calls and to apply the codes of ethics carefully to specific situations. Dual relationships are fraught with complexities and ambiguities. They are problematic for a number of reasons, including that

- they can be difficult to recognize;
- they can be very harmful, but they are not always harmful;
- they are the subject of conflicting views; and
- they are not always avoidable.

Dual relationships can be difficult to recognize. Dual relationships are relatively easy to define but much more difficult for us to recognize in our daily practice (Pope & Vasquez, 1991). They can evolve in subtle ways. Some counselors, counselor educators, or supervisors may somewhat innocently establish a form of extraprofessional relationship. They may go on a group outing with clients, students, or supervisees. They may agree to play tennis with a client, go on a hike or a bike ride, or go jogging together when they meet by accident at the jogging trail. Initially, this social encounter may seem to enhance the trust needed to establish a good working relationship in therapy. If such events continue to occur, however, eventually a client may want more. The client may want to become close friends with the counselor and feel let down when the counselor declines a request. Or if a friendship does begin to develop, the client may become cautious about what he or she reveals in counseling for fear of negatively affecting the friendship. At the same time, the counselor may avoid challenging the client out of reluctance to offend someone who has become a friend.

It can be particularly difficult to recognize potential problems when dual relationships are sequential rather than simultaneous. Yet "the mere fact that the two roles are apparently sequential rather than clearly concurrent does not, in and of itself, mean that the two relationships do not constitute a dual relationship" (Pope & Vasquez, 1991, p. 112). A host of questions present themselves: Can a former client eventually become a friend? How does the relationship between a supervisor and supervisee evolve into a collegial relationship once the formal supervision is completed? What kinds of posttherapy relationships are ever acceptable? These questions are explored in later chapters.

Dual relationships are not always harmful. A wide range of outcomes to dual relationships is possible, from harmful to benign. Some dual relationships are clearly exploitive and do serious harm to the helpee and to the professional involved. Others are benign; that is, no harm is done. To take two examples:

- *A high school counselor enters into a sexual relationship with a 15-year-old student client.* All professionals agree that this relationship is exploitive in the extreme. The roles of counselor and lover are never compatible, and the seriousness of the violation is greatly compounded by the fact that the client is a minor child.

- *A couple invite their marriage counselor to attend a social occasion. The couple plan to renew their wedding vows and host a reception after the ceremony. The counselor attends the ceremony, briefly appears at the reception to offer her best wishes to the couple, and leaves. The couple are pleased that the counselor came, especially because they credit the counseling process with helping to strengthen the marriage.* Apparently, no harm has been done. In this case the counselor's blending of a social role with her professional role could be argued to be benign or even beneficial to the counseling relationship.

Dual relationships are the subject of conflicting views. The topic of dual relationships has been hotly debated in the professional literature. Some writers have taken a conservative stance, maintaining that codes of ethics will be of little value if professionals take great latitude in interpreting them. These writers have tended to focus on the problems inherent in dual or multiple relationships and to favor a strict interpretation of ethical standards that are aimed at regulating professional boundaries. Pope and Vasquez (1991) asserted that counselors who engage in dual relationships are often skillful at rationalizing their behavior as a means of evading their professional responsibility to find acceptable alternatives to dual relationships. Pope (1985) and Pope and Vasquez (1991) identified the following problems in dual relationships:

- Entering into dual relationships with clients, or even considering entering into them after termination, can drastically change the nature of therapy. Counselors could begin using their practices unconsciously to screen clients for their likelihood of meeting the counselor's social, financial, or professional needs.

- Dual relationships create conflicts of interest, and thus compromise the objectivity needed for sound professional judgment.

- There is a danger of exploiting the client because the counselor holds a more powerful position.

- Dual relationships distort the professional nature of the therapeutic relationship, which needs to rest on a reliable set of boundaries on which both client and counselor can depend.

- Dual relationships affect the cognitive processes that benefit clients during therapy and help them maintain these benefits after termination.

- If a counselor were required to give testimony in court regarding a client, the integrity of the testimony would be suspect if a dual relationship existed.

Bograd (1993) noted that the power differential between the helper and the helpee undermines truly equal consent to a relationship outside the professional boundary. Even when practitioners have good intentions, they may unconsciously exploit or harm clients who are vulnerable in the relationship. If the professional boundaries become blurred, there is a strong possibility that confusion, disappointment, and disillusionment will result for both parties involved.

St. Germaine (1993) made the point that, although dual relationships are not damaging to clients in all cases, counselors must be aware that the potential for harm is always present. She mentioned that errors in judgment often occur when the counselor's own interests become part of the equation. This loss of objectivity is one factor that increases the risk of harm.

Other writers have believed that codes of ethics should be viewed as guidelines to practice rather than as rigid prescriptions, and that professional judgment must play a crucial role. Corey, Corey, and Callanan (1993) reminded us that ethics codes are creations of humans, not divine decrees that contain universal truth. They did not believe that all dual relationships are always unethical, and they have challenged counselors to reflect honestly and think critically about the issues involved.

Bograd (1993) noted that some professionals celebrate multiple connections that cross boundaries among teaching, supervision, therapy, collegiality, and friendship. These helping professionals tend to view multiple relationships as an inevitable and potentially beneficial complexity of interpersonal relationships rather than as evidence of professional indiscretion. For example, Tomm

(1993) believed that codes of ethics, in expecting practitioners to maintain their professional distance, imply that all dual relationships are wrong. According to Tomm, actively maintaining interpersonal distance focuses on the power differential and promotes an objectification of the therapeutic relationship. He suggested that dual relating invites greater authenticity and congruence from counselors and that, in fact, counselors' judgment may be improved rather than impaired by dual relationships, which can make it more difficult to use manipulation and deception or hide behind the protection of a professional role.

Hedges (1993), who presented a psychoanalytic point of view, believed that there is an essential dual relatedness in psychotherapy. He argued that transference, countertransference, resistance, and interpretation de facto rest upon the existence of a dual relationship. He urged practitioners to remember that, when viewed in this light, all beneficial aspects of therapy arise as a consequence of a dual relationship.

Whatever stance one takes, Tomm made an excellent point that it is not duality itself that constitutes the ethical problem. Rather, the core of the problem lies in the counselor's personal tendency to exploit clients or misuse power. Thus simply avoiding multiple relationships does not prevent exploitation. Counselors might deceive themselves into thinking that they cannot possibly exploit their clients if they avoid occupying more than one professional role. In reality, there are many ways that counselors can misuse their therapeutic power and influence and many ways they can exploit clients even though they are not engaging in dual or multiple relationships.

> The diversity of perspectives summarized here indicates that the debate over dual relationships has been extensive. At this point, we ask you to consider for a moment What is your stance toward dual or multiple relationships? With which of the perspectives do you most agree? How did you arrive at this stance? What do you see as its risks and benefits?

Some dual relationships are unavoidable. One consensus that seems to be emerging from the controversy over dual relationships is that not all dual relationships can be avoided. The recent revisions of the codes of ethics of the American Counseling Association and the American Psychological Association acknowledge this reality:

- When a dual relationship cannot be avoided, counselors take appropriate professional precautions such as informed consent, consultation, supervision, and documentation to ensure that judgment is not impaired and no exploitation occurs. (ACA, 1995, A.6.a.)

- In many communities and situations, it may not be feasible or reasonable for psychologists to avoid social or other nonprofessional contacts with persons such as patients, clients, students, supervisees, or research participants. (APA, 1992, 1.17)

Perhaps the clearest example of a situation in which dual relationships may be unavoidable is that of the rural practitioner. In an isolated, rural community the local minister, merchant, banker, beautician, pharmacist, or mechanic might be clients of a particular counselor. In such a setting, counselors may have to play several roles and are likely to find it more difficult to maintain clear boundaries than do their colleagues who practice in urban or suburban areas.

Some Subtle but Important Distinctions

Dual relationships have not always been clearly defined in the literature, which has compounded the confusion surrounding this complex issue. As we mentioned earlier in the chapter, dual relationships have been a frequent topic in our professional journals. The debate has been extensive, and much of it has been enlightening and thought provoking. However, it seems to us that we have sometimes "painted with too wide a brush" in cautioning against dual relationships.

Some roles that professionals play can be combined without creating a problematic dual relationship. Individuals who choose to enter the helping professions are not expected to sacrifice the multiple roles in which people naturally engage, nor are they expected to restrain themselves from acting as friends, neighbors, relatives, or employers (Glosoff, Corey, & Herlihy, 1996). Ethical questions that arise around the issue of whether it is ever appropriate to assume any of these roles with a *client* need to be framed somewhat differently when a counseling relationship is not involved. For instance, mentoring a student is often mentioned by counselor educators as one type of "beneficial dual relationship." Although serving as a mentor to a student involves playing a multiplicity of roles (perhaps including thesis or dissertation adviser, course instructor, encourager, collaborator in research projects, and coauthor of a professional publication), the mentor does not serve as the student's counselor. Problematic dual relationships arise from the simultaneous taking on of the role of *counselor* and another distinctly different role (such as friend, lover, relative, employer, or business partner) with a client, student, or supervisee, but other types of role blending, in which professionals play more than one *noncounselor* role (such as the roles involved in mentoring), need not be routinely discouraged. Nonetheless, *any* relationship (including mentoring) that involves a power differential carries with it a potential for exploitation, and the person in the more powerful position must remain alert to possible problems. The mentor and student need to discuss in advance any issues that might arise, such as who gets what type of credit for any research or publication, or whether conflicts of interest could occur when the mentor is in a position to evaluate the student. Some leaders in the profession are now making mentoring arrangements with graduate students at other institutions rather than with their own students. Although this type of arrangement may require more effort because of the distance involved, it seems to us to be an excellent way to provide the benefits of mentoring while avoiding many of the pitfalls.

Some behaviors in which professionals may engage from time to time have a *potential* for creating a dual relationship but are not, by themselves, dual relationships. Some examples might be accepting a small gift from a client, accepting a client's invitation to a special event such as a wedding, going out for coffee with a client, accepting goods rather than money as payment, or hugging a client at the end of a particularly painful session. Some writers (Gabbard, 1995; Gutheil & Gabbard, 1993; Simon, 1992; Smith & Fitzpatrick, 1995) have suggested that these incidents might be considered *boundary crossings* rather than boundary violations. A *crossing* is a departure from commonly accepted practice that might benefit the client, but a *violation* is a serious breach that causes harm. Crossings occur when the boundary is shifted to respond to the needs of a particular client at a particular moment. Interpersonal boundaries are not static and may be redefined over time as counselors and clients work closely together. Nonetheless, even seemingly innocent behaviors such as those just described can, if they become part of a pattern of blurring the professional boundaries, lead to dual relationship entanglements with a real potential for harm.

Some roles that professionals play involve an *inherent duality*. One such role is that of supervisor. Supervisors often find that supervisees experience an emergence of earlier psychological wounds and discover some of their own unfinished business as they become involved in working with clients. Ethical supervisors do not abandon their supervisory responsibilities by becoming a counselor to a supervisee, but they can encourage their supervisees to view personal therapy with another professional as a way to become more effective as counselors and as persons. At the same time, it needs to be recognized that although the supervisor and therapist roles differ, personal issues arise in both relationships, and supervisors need to give careful thought as to when and how these issues should be addressed. As another example, counselor educators serve as teachers, as therapeutic agents for student growth and self-awareness, as supervisors, and as evaluators, either sequentially or simultaneously. There is always the possibility that this role blending can present ethical dilemmas involving conflicts of interest or impaired judgments.

None of these roles or behaviors actually constitutes an ongoing dual relationship of the type that is likely to lead to sanctions by an ethics committee. Nonetheless, each does involve two individuals whose power positions are not equal. Role blending is not necessarily unethical, but it does require vigilance on the part of the professional to ensure that no exploitation occurs. One of the major difficulties in dealing with dual relationship issues is the lack of clear-cut boundaries between roles. Where exactly is the boundary between a counseling relationship and a friendship? How does a counselor educator remain sensitive to the need to promote student self-understanding without inappropriately acquiring personal knowledge about the student? How can a supervisor work effectively without addressing the supervisee's personal concerns that may be impeding the supervisee's performance? These are difficult questions, and any answers must include a consideration of the potential harm to clients, students, or supervisees when a dual relationship is initiated.

The Potential for Harm

Whatever the outcome of a dual or multiple relationship, a potential for harm almost always exists at the time the relationship is entered. To illustrate, let us revisit the example given earlier of a behavior that was identified as benign. As it turned out, no apparent harm was done when the marriage counselor attended the renewal-of-wedding-vows ceremony and reception. But what might have happened if the counselor had simply accepted the invitation without discussing with the couple any potential problems that might arise? What if the counselor had been approached at the reception and asked how she knew the couple? Had the counselor answered honestly, she would have violated the privacy of the professional relationship. Had she lied or given an evasive answer, harm to the clients would have been avoided, but the counselor could hardly have felt good about herself as an honest and ethical person.

One of the major problems with dual relationships is the possibility of exploiting the client (or student or supervisee). Borys studied a variety of possible nonsexual dual relationship behaviors and concluded that they were all related to the same principle: Do not exploit (Borys, 1988; Borys & Pope, 1989). Kitchener and Harding (1990) contended that dual relationships lie along a continuum from those that are potentially very harmful to those with little potential for harm. They concluded that dual relationships should be entered into only when the risks of harm are small and when there are strong, offsetting ethical benefits for the consumer.

How does one assess the potential for harm? Kitchener and Harding (1990) have identified three factors that counselors should consider: incompatibility of expectations on the part of the client, divergence of responsibilities for the counselor, and the power differential between the parties involved.

First, the greater the incompatibility of expectations in a dual role, the greater the risk of harm. For example, John, a supervisor, is also providing personal counseling to Suzanne, his supervisee. Although Suzanne understands that evaluation is part of the supervisory relationship, she places high value on the confidentiality of the counseling relationship. John is aware that her personal problems are impeding her performance as a counselor. In his supervisory role, he is expected to serve not only Suzanne's interests but also those of the agency in which she is employed and of the public that she will eventually serve. When he shares his evaluations with her employer as his supervisory contract requires, and notes his reservations about her performance (without revealing the specific nature of her personal concerns), Suzanne feels hurt and betrayed. The supervisory behaviors to which she had agreed when she entered into supervision with John were in conflict with the expectations of confidentiality and acceptance that she had come to hold for John as her counselor.

Second, as the responsibilities associated with dual roles diverge, the potential for divided loyalties and loss of objectivity increases. When counselors also have personal, political, social, or business relationships with their clients, their self-interest may be involved and may compromise the client's best interest. For example, Lynn is a counselor in private practice who has entered into a counseling relationship with Paula, even though she and Paula are partners in a small, part-time mail-order business. In the counseling relationship, Paula reveals that she is considering returning to college, which means that she will have to give up her role in the business. Lynn is faced with divided loyalties because she does not want the business to fold but she does not have the time to take it over. As this example illustrates, it is difficult to put the client's needs first when counselors are also invested in meeting their own needs.

The third factor has to do with influence, power, and prestige. Clients, by virtue of their need for help, are in a dependent, less powerful, and more vulnerable position. For example, Darla is a counselor educator who is also counseling Joseph, a graduate student in the program. When a faculty committee meets to assess Joseph's progress, Joseph is given probationary status because his work is marginal. Although Darla assures Joseph that she revealed nothing about his personal problems during the committee meeting, Joseph's trust is destroyed. He is fearful of revealing his personal concerns in counseling with Darla because he knows that Darla will be involved in determining whether he will be allowed to continue his graduate studies at the end of his probationary period. He wants to switch to another counselor but is afraid of offending Darla. Counselor educators and counselors must be sensitive to the power and authority associated with their roles. They must resist using their power to manipulate students or clients. Because of the power differential, it is the professional's responsibility to ensure that the more vulnerable individual in the relationship is not harmed.

Risks in Dual or Multiple Relationships

The potential for harm can translate into risks to all parties involved in a dual relationship. These risks can even extend to others not directly involved in the relationship.

Risks to consumers. Of primary concern is the risk of harm to the consumer of counseling services. A client who believes that he or she has been exploited in a dual relationship is bound to feel confused, hurt, and betrayed. This erosion of trust may have lasting consequences. The client may be reluctant to seek help from other professionals in the future. Clients may be angry about being exploited but feel trapped in a dependence on the continuing relationship. Some clients, not clearly understanding the complex dynamics of a dual relationship, may feel guilty and wonder What did I do wrong? Suppressed anger is a potential outcome when there is a power differential. Students or supervisees, in particular, may be aware of the inappropriateness of their dual relationships yet feel that the risks are unacceptably high in confronting a professional who is also their professor or supervisor. Any of these feelings—hurt, confusion, betrayal, guilt, anger—if left unresolved could lead to depression and helplessness, the antitheses of desired counseling outcomes.

Risks to the professional. Risks to the professional who becomes involved in a dual relationship include damage to the clinical relationship and, if the relationship comes to light, loss of professional credibility, charges of violations of ethical standards, suspension or revocation of license or certification, and risk of malpractice litigation.

From a legal perspective, nonsexual dual relationships are less likely to produce sanctions than are sexual dual relationships. For instance, Neukrug, Healy, and Herlihy (1992) found that sexual dual relationships comprised 20% and other dual relationships comprised 7% of complaints made to state counselor licensure boards. However, in recent years state licensing boards seem to be addressing the issue of nonsexual dual relationships more vigorously (Pope & Vasquez, 1991). Malpractice actions against therapists are a risk when dual relationships have caused harm to the client, and the chances of such a suit being successful are increased if the therapist cannot provide a sound clinical justification and demonstrate that such practices are within an accepted standard of care.

Many dual relationships go undetected or unreported and never become the subject of an inquiry by an ethics committee, licensure board, or court. Nonetheless, these relationships do have an effect on the professionals involved, causing them to question their competence and diminishing their sense of moral selfhood. Repeated violations of any ethical standard lead professionals down a slippery slope (Bok, 1979) along which it becomes easier and easier to succumb to the temptation to commit further violations.

Effects on other consumers. Dual relationships can create a ripple effect, impacting even those who are not directly involved in the relationship. Other clients or potential clients can be affected. This is particularly true in college counseling centers, schools, hospitals, counselor education programs, or any other relatively closed system in which other clients or students have opportunities to be aware of a dual relationship. Other clients might well resent that one client has been singled out for a special relationship. Because a power differential is also built into the system, this resentment may be coupled with a reluctance to question the dual relationship openly for fear of reprisal. Even independent private practitioners can be subject to the ripple effect. Former clients are typically a major source of referrals. A client who has been involved in a dual relationship and who leaves that relationship feeling confused, hurt, or betrayed is not likely to recommend the counselor to friends, relatives, or colleagues.

Effects on other professionals. Fellow professionals who are aware of a dual relationship are placed in a difficult position. Confronting a colleague is always uncomfortable, but it is equally uncomfortable to condone the behavior through silence. This creates a distressing dilemma that can undermine the morale of any agency, center, hospital, or other system in which it occurs. Paraprofessionals or others who work in the system and who are less familiar with professional codes of ethics may be misled and develop an unfortunate impression regarding the standards of the profession.

Effects on the profession and society. The counseling profession itself is damaged by the unethical conduct of its members. As professionals, we have an obligation both to avoid causing harm in dual relationships and to act to prevent others from doing harm. If we fail to assume these responsibilities, our professional credibility is eroded, regulatory agencies will intervene, potential clients will be reluctant to seek counseling assistance, and fewer competent and ethical individuals will enter counselor training programs. Conscientious professionals need to remain aware not only of the potential harm to consumers but also of the ripple effect that extends the potential for harm.

Safeguards to Minimize Risks

Whenever we as professionals are operating in more than one role, and when there is potential for negative consequences, it is our responsibility to develop safeguards and measures to reduce (if not eliminate) the potential for harm. These include the following:

- **Set healthy boundaries from the outset.** It is a good idea for counselors to have in their professional disclosure statements or informed consent documents a description of their policy pertaining to professional versus personal, social, or business relationships. This written statement can serve as a springboard for discussion and clarification.

- **Involve the client** in setting the boundaries of the professional relationship. Although the ultimate responsibility for avoiding problematic dual relationships rests with the professional, clients can be active partners in discussing and clarifying the nature of the relationship. It is helpful to discuss with clients what you expect of them and what they might expect of you.

- **Informed consent** needs to occur at the beginning and throughout the relationship. If potential dual relationship problems arise during the counseling relationship, these should be discussed in a frank and open manner. Clients have a right to be informed about any possible risks.

- Practitioners who are involved in unavoidable dual relationships need to keep in mind that, despite informed consent and discussion of potential risks at the outset, unforeseen problems and conflicts can arise. **Discussion and clarification** may need to be an ongoing process.

- **Consultation** with fellow professionals can be useful in getting an objective perspective and identifying unanticipated difficulties. We encourage periodic consultation as a routine practice for professionals who are engaged in dual relationships. We also want to emphasize the importance of consulting with colleagues who hold divergent views, not just those who tend to support our own perspectives.

- When dual relationships are particularly problematic, or when the risk for harm is high, practitioners will be wise to work under **supervision**.

- **Counselor educators and supervisors** can talk with students and supervisees about balance of power issues, boundary concerns, appropriate limits, purposes of the relationship, potential for abusing power, and subtle ways that harm can result from engaging in different and sometimes conflicting roles.

- As more a legal than an ethical precaution, professionals will be wise to **document** any dual relationships in their clinical case notes. In particular, it is a good idea to keep a record of any actions taken to minimize the risk of harm.

- If necessary, **refer** the client to another professional.

Conclusions

In this introductory chapter, we have examined what the codes of ethics of the major professional associations advise with respect to dual or multiple relationships. We have explored a number of factors that make such relationships problematic. Factors that create a potential for harm and the risks to parties directly or not directly involved in multiple relationships have been identified. Some strategies for reducing risks were described.

What is critical is that counselors give careful thought to the potential complications before they get entangled in ethically questionable relationships. The importance of consultation in working through these issues cannot be overemphasized. As with any complex ethical issue, complete agreement may never be reached nor is it necessarily desirable. However, as conscientious professionals we need to strive to clarify our own stance and develop our own guidelines for practice, within the limits of codes of ethics and current knowledge.

2 Sexual Dual Relationships

Sexual dual relationships with clients are among the most serious of all ethical violations. According to Rutter (1989), boundaries define who we are, what is ours and what is not ours, and what is intimate and what is separate. Sexual violations of these boundaries involve an abuse of power and a betrayal of trust that can have devastating effects on clients. The consequences for counselors who engage in sexual intimacies with their clients can be severe. They may have their licensure or certification revoked, be expelled from professional associations, be restricted in or lose their insurance coverage, be fired from their jobs, be sued in civil court for malpractice, or be convicted of a felony. Because sexual relationships with clients are such serious violations, they deserve careful attention. In this chapter we focus specifically on sexual dual relationships and address these questions:

- How do professional codes of ethics address sexual intimacies with clients?

- What are the ethics of sexual relationships with former clients?

- How widespread is the practice of engaging in sex with current and/or former clients?

- Who are typically the offending therapists?

- What are the legal sanctions against these behaviors?

- What makes sexual dual relationships so particularly harmful to clients?

- How can counselors deal with sexual attraction to clients?

- What steps can our profession take to increase awareness of problems involved in sexual misconduct and prevent its occurrence?

Ethical Standards

Virtually all professional codes of ethics prohibit sexual intimacies with current clients. Many of the codes also specify that if therapists have had a prior sexual relationship with a person, they do not accept this person as a client.

- Counselors do not have any type of sexual intimacies with clients and do not counsel persons with whom they have had a sexual relationship. (ACA, 1995, A.7.a.)

- Psychologists do not engage in sexual intimacies with current patients or clients. (APA, 1992, 4.05)

- Psychologists do not accept as therapy patients or clients persons with whom they have engaged in sexual intimacies. (APA, 1992, 4.06)

- Social workers should under no circumstances engage in sexual activities or sexual contact with current clients, whether such contact is consensual or forced. (NASW, 1996, 1.09a)

- Social workers should not provide clinical services to individuals with whom they have had a prior sexual relationship. Providing clinical services to a former sexual partner has the potential to be harmful to the individual and is likely to make it difficult for the social worker and individual to maintain appropriate professional boundaries. (NASW, 1996, 1.09b)

- Sexual intimacy with clients is prohibited. (AAMFT, 1991, 1.2).

There is clear consensus among the professional associations that concurrent sexual and professional relationships are unethical, and many of the associations agree that a sexual relationship cannot later be converted into a therapeutic relationship. Is there similar consensus regarding the issue of converting a therapeutic relationship into a sexual one?

Sexual Relationships With Former Clients

In the first edition of this book we indicated that many of the codes of ethics of the professional associations were silent on the issue of whether sexual relationships with former clients are ever acceptable. In the past 5 years, this situation has changed. Now, the various associations specifically address this topic:

- Counselors do not engage in sexual intimacies with former clients within a minimum of 2 years after terminating the counseling relationship. Counselors who engage in such relationships after 2 years following termination have the responsibility to examine and document thoroughly that such relations did not have an exploitative nature, based on factors such as duration of counseling, amount of time since counseling, termination circumstances, client's personal history and mental status, adverse impact on the client, and actions by the counselor suggesting a plan to initiate a sexual relationship with the client after termination. (ACA, 1995, A.7.b.)

- Psychologists do not engage in sexual intimacies with a former therapy patient or client for at least 2 years after cessation or termination of professional services. (APA, 1992, 4.07a).

- Social workers should not engage in sexual activities or sexual contact with former clients because of the potential for harm to the client. (NASW, 1996, 1.09c)

- Sexual intimacy with former clients for 2 years following the termination of therapy is prohibited. (AAMFT, 1991, 1.12)

All the major professional associations agree that sexual contact less than 2 years after termination is unethical. The National Association of Social Workers does not specify a time period. Although we have not quoted each of the relevant standards in their entirety, all four of the organizations state that, in the exceptional circumstance of a sexual relationship with a former client even after a 2-year interval, the burden rests with the therapist to demonstrate that there has been no exploitation. Factors that need to be considered include the amount of time that has passed since the termination of therapy, the nature and duration of therapy, the circumstances surrounding the termination of the professional relationship, the client's personal history, the client's competence and mental status, the foreseeable likelihood of harm to the client or others, and any statements or actions by the therapist suggesting a romantic relationship after terminating the professional relationship. Gary Schoener, interviewed for an article in *Counseling Today* (Foster, 1996), discussed some useful questions that practitioners can ask themselves when they are considering a posttermination romantic relationship:

- What was the length and level of therapeutic involvement?

- How much transference, dependency, or power inequity remains after termination?

- Was there any deception or coercion, intentional or unintentional, by the therapist indicating that sex is generally acceptable after termination of therapy?

- Was there an actual termination? Was the decision to terminate a mutual one? Did the therapist end the professional relationship in order to make it possible to enter into a romantic or sexual relationship?

- Who initiated posttermination contact?

- What kind of consultation, if any, took place?

In contrast to the consistency shown by the professional *organizations*, there remains disagreement among *practitioners* about whether a sexual relationship initiated after termination is ever ethical. Some maintain that "once a client, always a client." They contend that the transference elements of the therapeutic relationship persist forever, and therefore, romantic relationships with former clients are always unethical. They also point out that a 2-year time limit is artificial and arbitrary, and that it is nonsensical to assume that what was unethical for 2 years becomes ethical after 2 years plus 1 day. Others contend that there are cases in which the probability for harm is not high and that each case needs to be considered individually. Generally, the majority of therapists who have been surveyed regarding this issue view posttermination sexual relationships as unethical (Borys, 1988; Lamb, 1992). However, substantial minorities ranging from 23% (Borys, 1988; Gibson & Pope, 1993) to 33% (Salisbury & Kinnier, 1996) believe they could be ethical under some circumstances. Interestingly, Salisbury and Kinnier (1996) found that counselors who believed such relationships could be acceptable also believed, on average, that the appropriate waiting time should be slightly more than 5 years, which is 2 1/2 times greater than the waiting period specified in the codes.

Those who argue that a blanket prohibition of all sexual intimacies with former clients is too extreme also argue that there is a real difference between an intense, long-term therapy relationship and a less intimate brief-term one. What should be the appropriate response, for instance, by Ellen to Craig's invitation in the following scenario?

> Ellen served her counseling internship at her university's counseling center. One of her clients was Craig, a graduate student who was a businessman returning to college for his MBA. Craig sought counseling because he was having second thoughts about committing himself to a lifelong career in the cut-throat competitive field he was in. During five counseling sessions with Ellen, he completed a series of inventories, weighed his values, and decided to switch majors. A little more than 2 years later, Craig and Ellen ran into each other at a social event. Craig asked her out on a date.

Assume that Ellen approaches you for consultation. She tells you that she does not want to be unethical, yet she also wants to accept Craig's offer for a date. Because Ellen had only five sessions with him, because the focus was on career counseling, and because the counseling took place more than 2 years ago, Ellen does not think that accepting a date with Craig is unethical. However, she wants to get your opinion and wants to know if she is overlooking some important issues. What might you say to Ellen?

If Ellen consults with us, we will first ask her to state what she sees as the pros and cons of each decision. We will explore with her the reasons she is seeking consultation. Although she does not think that accepting the date is unethical, she seems uncertain. Can she see potential problems in accepting? We will ask her if there is a pattern here. Has she dated other former clients? We will not flatly tell Ellen that accepting the date is either appropriate or inappropriate, although we will explore with her any possible consequences. We will ask her to consider carefully the factors listed by her professional association and questions such as those posed by Schoener. Our goals for the consultation are to have Ellen understand her reasons for choosing whatever course of action she may follow and be aware of and take responsibility for the possible consequences of her decision.

The counseling profession is clearer than it was 5 years ago about sexual relationships with former clients. Still, whether sexual relationships with former clients are ever acceptable, even after more than 2 years, probably will be a subject of continuing discussion. On the one hand, we need to remain aware of the harm that can result from sexual intimacies that occur after termination, of the aspects of the therapeutic process that continue after termination including residual transference, and of the continuing power differential. On the other hand, it seems reasonable to consider the wide range of circumstances that could arise, especially the differences between long-term, intense, personal counseling relationships and brief, career-oriented or other types of counseling. Under the present codes, if a counselor does consider entering into a romantic relationship with a former client after 2 years have passed, there are some safeguards that could be followed. These might include consulting with a colleague or going for a therapy session conjointly with the former client to examine mutual transferences and expectations.

Incidence

It is difficult to determine the actual incidence of sexual intimacies between therapists and clients—or between counselor educators and students or supervisors and supervisees. Various studies have shown clearly, however, that male therapists are significantly more likely to approve of and engage in sexual activities with a client than are female therapists (Gabbard, 1989; Gibson & Pope, 1993; Pope, Keith-Spiegel, & Tabachnick, 1986; Pope & Vetter, 1991). Other studies have indicated that from 9% to 13% of male therapists and 2% to 3% of female therapists report engaging in sex with current or former clients (Akamatsu, 1988; Borys, 1988; Pope & Bouhoutsos, 1986; Pope, Sonne, & Holroyd, 1993; Pope, Tabachnick, & Keith-Spiegel, 1987; Salisbury & Kinnier, 1996). One study found that a significant number of cases involve clients who are minor children (Bajt & Pope, 1989). It appears that the typical offender is a repeat offender: Holroyd and Brodsky (1977) found that 80% of psychologists who reported sexual contact had engaged in it with more than one client.

These estimates are probably conservative. Survey data may be distorted because there are compelling reasons for offending therapists to withhold information or to make false claims (Smith & Fitzpatrick, 1995). Sexual misconduct is thought to be grossly underreported (Gartrell, Herman, Olarte, Feldstein, & Localio, 1987), and Simon (1989) estimated that the real percentage of therapists who have engaged in sexual intimacies with current or former clients may be as high as 25%. Incidence rates may vary depending on the variables considered. Thoreson, Shaughnessy, Heppner, and Cook (1993) surveyed male ACA members and found that only 1.7% reported sexual contact with *current clients*. However, when the additional factors of sexual contact *after termination* and sexual contact with *students or supervisees* were considered, the prevalence rate rose to 17%. If there is any good news in all this information, it is that Anderson and Kitchener (1996) recently reviewed studies that were conducted since 1977 and concluded that the frequency of sexual intimacy between therapists and current clients is decreasing. They suggested that therapists are becoming increasingly sensitive to this issue.

The Offending Therapist

As we have seen, male therapists are far more likely to engage in sexual relationships with clients than are female therapists. Although systematic research on offending therapists is scant, the most typical profile that emerges is that of a middle-aged male therapist who is "burned out," professionally isolated, and currently experiencing some personal distress or midlife crisis (Simon, 1987; Smith & Fitzpatrick, 1995). This "lovesick therapist" often begins by sharing his own personal problems and vulnerabilities with a younger female client (Twemlow & Gabbard, 1989). This typical offender also appears to share many of the characteristics of the impaired professional who has personal problems and attempts to meet his own needs through his clients.

Of course, not all offending therapists fit this profile, and other writers have suggested that there may be a wide range of types of professionals who become involved in sexual relationships with clients. Golden, interviewed in a *Guidepost* article (Schafer, 1990), suggested that they generally fall into one of three categories: professionals who are ignorant of the standards; those who are aware of the standards but are blinded by what dual relationships can offer romantically; and sociopathic individuals who know the standards but willfully and repeatedly violate them.

Schoener and Gonsiorek (1988) have described six categories of perpetrators. *Uninformed and naive* therapists are led into sexual relationships through ignorance. They genuinely lack knowledge of ethical standards and professional boundaries and have difficulty distinguishing between personal and professional relationships. *Healthy or neurotic* counselors are aware that sexual relationships are unethical, are typically involved in limited or isolated instances, are experiencing situational stressors, and are remorseful about their behavior. They often terminate sexual intimacy on their own and may self-report and request help. *Severely neurotic* counselors have longstanding and significant emotional problems, especially depression, feelings of inadequacy, low self-esteem, and social isolation. Typically, they begin by becoming emotionally or socially involved with a client, and professional boundaries disintegrate as intimacy grows. These counselors may feel guilt and remorse, but they are less able to terminate the inappropriate behavior and may deny, distort, or rationalize their behavior.

Other counselors with *character disorders and impulse control problems* have longstanding problems and a history of legal difficulties. They are often caught due to their multiple violations and poor judgment. When consequences are pending, they show guilt and remorse, but they rarely have a true appreciation of the impact of their behavior on others. *Sociopathic or narcissistic character disordered* individuals have characteristics similar to the previous group but are more cunning and detached. They are adept at manipulating clients and colleagues into helping them avoid the consequences of their acts. Finally, *psychotic or borderline personality disordered* counselors have in common poor social judgment and impaired reality testing. It is obvious that therapists who fall into these last three categories are poor candidates for rehabilitation.

Legal Sanctions

One of the major causes of malpractice suits is sexual misconduct. Pope and Vasquez (1991) reported the following data obtained from the APA Insurance Trust: sexual impropriety accounts for 20.4% of the claims and 53.2% of the costs of malpractice cases against psychologists. Because the cost of sexual violations is high—the average lawsuit is settled for $110,000—insurance carriers typically either exclude sexual misconduct from coverage or limit the amount they will pay (Gill-Wigal & Heaton, 1996).

Austin, Moline, and Williams (1990) reviewed relevant court cases and concluded that few, if any, arguments in defense of therapists who have sex with clients are likely to succeed in court. In particular, courts have rejected claims that the client consented, determining that consent was not voluntary or informed because it was affected by transference.

Malpractice suits are tried in civil court. Increasingly, charges of sexual misconduct against mental health professionals can also be brought in criminal court. Exploitation by practitioners is so damaging to clients that it is becoming criminalized. Foster (1996) noted that state legislatures throughout the United States are working to increase the criminal sanctions for sexual misconduct. There are now 15 states that consider sexual exploitation by a therapist a felony with a maximum punishment of a fine of $150,000 and/or 20 years in prison.

Harm to Clients

As Bates and Brodsky (1989) have noted, problems in love relationships are frequently the impetus for clients to enter therapy. These authors contended that it is unforgivable for therapists to contaminate and de-objectify their roles in helping to resolve these clients' problems. Therapy is not "a mating game, or a place for lovers to meet" (p. 133).

Kenneth S. Pope, who has produced an impressive body of research into sexual dual relationships, has provided a clear and comprehensive picture of the harm that may be done to clients by sexual relationships with their therapists. In an excellent article describing a therapist-patient sex syndrome, Pope (1988) noted that clients may have reactions similar to those of victims of rape, battering, incest, child abuse, and posttraumatic stress. Ten general aspects commonly associated with the syndrome are ambivalence, guilt, emptiness and isolation, identity/boundary/role confusion, sexual confusion, impaired ability to trust, emotional liability, suppressed rage, cognitive dysfunction, and increased suicidal risk. We believe it is worth examining each of these indicators in more depth.

- **Ambivalence.** Clients who are sexually involved with their therapist may experience a sense of deep ambivalence, fearing separation or alienation from the therapist yet longing desperately to escape from the therapist's power and influence. Loyalty to the therapist may prevent clients from acting to protect themselves (resisting sexual advances or reporting the abuse) for fear that their action could destroy the therapist's personal or professional life. This ambivalence and misplaced loyalty help to explain why the behavior can go unreported completely or for a number of years.

- **Guilt.** Clients may feel guilty, as though they are somehow to blame for what has happened. Their reactions may be similar to those of incest victims. They may have a sense of guilt that they did not do more to stop the sexual activity, or that they enjoyed the relationship, or that they did something to invite such a relationship with a person they deeply trusted.

- **Emptiness and isolation.** Sexual activity between a therapist and client can seriously erode the client's sense of self-worth. Clients may feel emotionally isolated, alone, and cut off from the world of "normal" human experience.

- **Identity/boundary/role confusion.** A phenomenon often involved in a patient-therapist sexual relationship is a reversal of roles. As the therapist becomes more self-disclosing, and as meeting the therapist's needs becomes more important in the relationship, the client becomes responsible for taking care of the therapist. Clients become confused, not knowing where safe and appropriate boundaries lie, and this adds to the erosion of their sense of identity and worth.

- **Sexual confusion.** Many clients seem to manifest a profound confusion about their sexuality. Lingering outcomes can take two forms: Some clients will be threatened by any sexual activity, and others may be trapped into compulsive or self-destructive sexual encounters.

- **Impaired ability to trust.** Because therapy involves such a high degree of trust, violations can have lifelong consequences. When therapists abuse this trust, they are taking advantage of their clients in the most fundamental way. This is perhaps the core issue in sexual violations, and the consequences can extend far beyond the therapeutic relationship in question. Client victims are likely to mistrust other helping professionals, particularly therapists, and the damage may reverberate outward to other, less intense relationships.

- **Emotional liability.** This can be a long-term consequence. Clients who have been sexually involved with a therapist often feel overwhelmed by their emotions, both during the relationship and afterwards. Even with subsequent therapy, victims may reexperience traumatic emotions when they become involved with a new and appropriate sexual partner. Pope (1988) cautioned counselors who work with these victims to keep these setbacks in perspective so that clients will not lose hope.

- **Suppressed rage.** Victims may feel a justifiable, tremendous anger at the offending therapist. But this rage may be blocked from awareness or expression by feelings of ambivalence and guilt, and by manipulative behaviors of the therapist. Offending therapists may use threats and intimidation to prevent clients from reporting the behavior and can be adept at eliciting compliance, hero worship, and dependency. As is true of feelings of guilt, this anger needs to be identified, expressed, and worked through in later therapy with another therapist. If the anger is bottled up, it is likely to affect clients' relationships with significant others in their lives and with any other therapists they might later have.

- **Cognitive dysfunction.** The trauma caused by sexual involvement with a therapist can be so severe that clients may experience cognitive dysfunction. Attention and concentration may be disrupted by flashbacks, nightmares, and intrusive thoughts.

- **Increased suicidal risk.** Finally, suicide risk is increased as some clients feel hopelessly trapped in ambivalence, isolation, and confusion. These feelings, coupled with an impaired ability to trust, may prevent victims from reaching out for help.

It should be clearly understood that even if clients behave in seductive ways, it is always the therapist's responsibility to maintain a professional distance in the relationship. Therapists can help clients to understand such behavior on their part as a manifestation of transference. The therapist, not the client, has the responsibility to evaluate the therapeutic situation and to monitor the boundaries of the relationship. Therapists who have trouble keeping clear boundaries in the professional relationship are often guilty of poor judgment in other areas of their practice. Clearly, the effects on clients can be profound and violate one of our most fundamental moral principles: to do no harm.

Sexual Attraction to Clients

The existing codes are explicit with respect to sexual relationships with clients. However, they do not, and maybe they cannot, define some of the more subtle ways that sexuality may be part of professional relationships. For example, sexual attractions between counselors and clients do occur, and it is not the attraction per se that is problematic. It is acting on the attraction that is inappropriate and becomes an ethical problem.

It may be inevitable that most counselors will at some time feel a sexual attraction to a client. Barbara, a counselor in private practice, related this anecdote:

> The client was my prototype of the physically attractive man. He was tall, lean but muscular, and very good looking. As counseling progressed, it became apparent that he was sensitive to others, had a solid sense of personal integrity, and had a great sense of humor—all qualities that I admire. I realized that I found him attractive but wasn't particularly concerned about it. After all, I had it in awareness and certainly didn't intend to act on my feelings. Then, during one session he began to relate a lengthy story, and my attention wandered. I drifted off into a sexual fantasy about him, I don't know for how long, probably only a few seconds. I snapped back to reality, and as I refocused on his words I realized he was now talking about sex. I nearly panicked: Had I somehow telegraphed my thoughts? I felt my face begin to redden, and compounded my discomfort by wondering if he saw me blushing and thought I was embarrassed about the subject of sex. With real effort I directed my concern away from myself and back to him and got through the rest of the session. But I was so shaken by the incident that I immediately sought consultation.

Assume you are the person to whom Barbara turns for consultation. She wonders whether she should continue counseling this man or whether she should make a referral. Barbara tells you that she does not know how to best deal with her feelings toward him and that she worries about the effect of her attraction on the counseling process. Yet she also wonders what she might tell him if she decided to suggest a referral to another professional. What input might you offer to Barbara? If you found yourself in a situation similar to hers, what course of action might you take?

Pope, Sonne, and Holroyd (1993), in their book, *Sexual Feelings in Psychotherapy,* suggested not only that it is difficult to acknowledge sexual feelings toward a client but also that it is even more difficult to talk about these feelings with colleagues or in supervision. Despite the likelihood that sexual attraction is a common occurrence, there has been a lack of systematic research into the topic. Most practitioners report that their graduate training and internships provided no coverage whatsoever about sexual attraction and characterize their graduate training on therapists' sexual feelings as poor or virtually nonexistent (Pope et al., 1986; Pope & Tabachnick, 1993). The profession's silence on the topic has left practitioners to manage feelings of attraction by trial-and-error methods (Gill-Wigal & Heaton, 1996).

Pope et al. (1993) specified the conditions necessary for learning how to recognize and deal with feelings of attraction to a client. They believed that exploration of sexual feelings about clients is best done with the help, support, and encouragement of others. They maintained that practica, internships, and peer supervision groups are ideal places to talk about this topic. They listed some common reactions to sexual feelings in therapy, which include surprise and shock, guilt, anxiety about unresolved personal problems, fear of losing control, fear of being criticized, frustration at not being able to speak openly or at not being able to make sexual contact, anger at the client's sexuality, fear or discomfort at frustrating the client's demands, and confusion about tasks, boundaries, roles, and actions.

The tendency to treat sexual feelings as if they were taboo has made it difficult for therapists to recognize, acknowledge, and accept attractions to clients. It is not surprising that many therapists are at a loss as to how to deal with their sexual feelings in therapy. In light of these findings, we recommend that counselor education programs place more emphasis on the issue of sexual attraction. Prospective counselors need to be reassured that their feelings are a common manifestation of countertransference, that these feelings are natural, and that with awareness and preparedness they can still counsel effectively with clients to whom they feel attracted. The importance of consultation should also be emphasized, in both preservice and inservice education, to help prevent sexual attraction from crossing the boundary into an inappropriate dual relationship.

Gill-Wigal and Heaton (1996) offered some useful suggestions to therapists for managing their feelings of attraction to a client:

- Never act out feelings of attraction. Avoid actions that could foster the attraction, such as sitting close to or hugging the client, prolonging sessions, or increased self-disclosure.
- Acknowledge feelings of attraction.
- Seek to understand these feelings through conversations with supervisors, colleagues, and personal therapists.
- Take responsibility for feelings and any psychopathology. Be alert to factors such as work stress and tendencies to rationalize or make the client responsible for the attraction.
- Monitor boundaries by setting clear limits on physical contact, self-disclosure, and client requests for personal information about the therapist.
- Seek help.

Pope and Vasquez (1991) have summarized nicely the issue of sexual attraction. They stated that "To feel attraction to a client is not unethical; to acknowledge and address the attraction promptly, carefully, and adequately is an important ethical responsibility" (p. 107). In addition to improving training programs, they suggest that consulting with colleagues, obtaining supervision, and seeking our own therapy are helpful measures. An excellent resource for further understanding is *Sexual Feelings in Psychotherapy: Explorations for Therapists and Therapists-in-Training* by Pope et al. (1993).

> Consider, for a moment, how this subject applies to you. Have you had to struggle with the matter of sexual attraction in counseling relationships? If so, how did you deal with your feelings and the feelings of your clients? What would you do if you found yourself attracted to a client, or a client to you? What do you want to see included in training programs about issues of sexual attraction?

Prevention and Remediation

Sexual dual relationships are one of the most harmful types of unethical behavior. We have seen how destructive they can be for clients, counselors, and the profession as a whole. Because violations are common—and probably occur more frequently than we realize—we need to make concerted efforts toward awareness and prevention. Steps that can be taken include consumer education, support for the victims, improved counselor training, and monitoring professional practice.

Consumer education. As professionals, we seem to be communicating well with each other regarding sexual dual relationships, as is evidenced by the large number of articles in our professional journals. However, it is equally important that we communicate clearly to consumers that they have the right to services that are free from sexual exploitation. Statements of client rights should include this information and be routinely distributed. An important step in prevention is to educate the public so that they have clear expectations about the counseling process and knowledge of the boundaries of the relationship.

As Hotelling (1988) has noted, many clients do not know what avenues of redress are available to them when they have been victimized. Information about the ethical, administrative, and legal options that clients can use when they have had a sexual relationship with their counselor needs to be routinely shared with consumers. One excellent example of how this might be accomplished is the booklet entitled *Professional Therapy Never Includes Sex* (1990), published by the California Department of Consumer Affairs. This booklet was specifically designed to help victims of sexual exploitation by therapists. It describes warning signs of unprofessional behavior and presents the rights of clients. Another helpful resource for clients is a brochure, *If Sex Enters Into the Psychotherapy Relationship* (1987), published by the American Psychological Association.

Support for the victims. Many counselors may feel unprepared to help clients, students, or others who have had sexual relationships with their therapists. It is important to remember that clients who have been sexually exploited tend to be exceptionally vulnerable to revictimization when counselors fail to recognize their clinical needs (Pope & Vasquez, 1991). An abused client can be empowered by taking action against the offending therapist. As Hotelling (1988) has aptly stated, "The reality of what happened and its inappropriateness and destructiveness is affirmed; the burden of responsibility can be shifted to its rightful owner" (p. 233). Despite the potential for healing, it is extremely difficult for an abused client to pursue a complaint. In addition to the emotional toll that the process takes, it requires perseverance and some sophistication about the ethical complaint process and/or the legal system.

Counselors who work with these clients need to have a high degree of preparedness. They may need to deal with their own feelings of discomfort at being involved in a complaint against a colleague. They need to know all the possible avenues of redress and the advantages and disadvantages of each, so that these can be communicated accurately to the client. And finally, they need to keep in mind that the decisions—whether to pursue a complaint, what avenue(s) to take—rest with the client.

Women report great reluctance to file complaints that could lead to disciplinary action against their therapists or trainers (Gottlieb, 1990; Hotelling, 1988; Riger, 1991). These women often have ambivalent feelings about reporting their therapists, but they also encounter institutional barriers within the profession that contribute to their feelings of intimidation and deter them from following through with the complaint process. Gottlieb (1990) suggested that there is a need for an organizational structure within the profession that will reach out to these women and assist them in the complaint process.

Counselor education. Although we will more fully discuss issues in counselor education in chapter 4, at this point we want to note some concerns specific to sexual dual relationships. We have the impression that, generally, counselor education programs are not giving much emphasis to the topic. Whether this is due in part to erotophobia, as Vasquez (1988) has suggested, or to an assumption that there is no need to belabor the obvious, it creates a serious omission in the counselor training process. Counselor education programs have a dual responsibility: to train prospective counselors and to protect the public whom they eventually will serve. Vasquez (1988) described training strategies to prevent counselor-client sexual contact, including knowledge, self-awareness, program climate, and faculty behavior. This is an excellent resource for counselor educators who want to assess or strengthen their programs.

Bartell and Rubin (1990) contended that education can play an important role in helping trainees first to recognize sexual attraction and then to take the necessary steps to avoid acting on the attraction. They suggested that the injunctions against sexual relationships be emphasized in training programs and be well publicized as a way to eliminate dangerous liaisons.

On the matter of providing trainees with education on this subject, we think this topic is ideally introduced in a beginning class in counseling, then dealt with in more depth in an ethics course, and further addressed in seminar sessions attached to the student's field work or internship experiences. Students are bound to encounter attractions as a part of their field work, and instructors can encourage them to bring up these concerns for discussion. Students can learn to deal with their own countertransference feelings by openly discussing them in the safety of a supervision session. Some students may need to consider seeking therapy for themselves as an option, to explore their countertransferences and sexual attraction to clients.

Before attempting to educate others, instructors must gain their own clarity. Counselor educators who lack clarity will pass along their confusion to future generations of helping professionals, and counselor educators who behave in ethically questionable ways imply that those behaviors are acceptable. Counselor educators have a special obligation to be role models for what constitutes ethical behavior.

Tabachnick, Keith-Spiegel, and Pope (1991) acknowledged that numerous social and other types of activities exist for both students and faculty on and off campus, so that "little boundary blurrings" seem almost to be built into the academic system. Thoreson et al. (1993) suggested that issues of sexual contact between counselor educators and students and between supervisors and supervisees are more complex than issues of sex between client and therapist. Conflicting principles emerge, in that consenting adults have the right to establish consensual relationships, but because of the power differential involved, the notion of voluntary decision making is clouded with coercion. They recommended that education needs to address the difficult issues of conflicting ethical principles, intimacy needs, the complexities of dual relationships, power inequities between "consenting adults," and sex role stereotypes.

Monitoring professional practice. Professionals have been reluctant to report their colleagues who engage in sexual relationships with clients, students, or supervisees. Tabachnick et al. (1991) reported that 79% of psychology faculty who responded to their survey had ignored unethical behavior by colleagues. There may be a combination of explanations for this reluctance. In large measure, our sense of professional identity depends on the interpersonal bonds we form with our colleagues. We may fear being criticized or ostracized by colleagues for speaking out against "one of our own." The possibility of a defamation suit could also contribute to our hesitancy to take action. Many of us are reluctant to stand in judgment of others, particularly when we recognize our own fallibilities.

> Consider, for instance, what you might do in the following situation: You become aware that a student intern in a counseling center has dated several of his clients. You and the student intern are in the same graduate program and are serving as interns in the same center. You approach him and inform him that you have heard from one of his former clients that they were involved in a sexual relationship. He tells you that he has no problem with this because both he and his client are consenting adults, and that because he is not a licensed professional he is not bound by a set of ethical codes. In essence, he informs you that you are interfering in his personal business. Where would you go from here?

It is difficult for professionals to take action against colleagues. However, despite our reluctance, we clearly have an ethical responsibility to act when we have reason to believe that a colleague has engaged, or is engaging, in sex with clients. In fact, to fail to do so is in itself an ethical violation. It may help to keep in mind that it is not our role to investigate, judge, or punish. These responsibilities belong to ethics committees, licensing boards, and the courts.

It may also help to remember that, sometimes, sexually exploitive behavior may be a symptom of impairment (Emerson & Markos, 1996). Characteristics of counselors who have become sexually involved with their clients parallel in many ways the characteristics of the impaired professional. Some similarities are

• fragile self-esteem, possibly manifested in a narcissistic style;

• difficulty with establishing intimacy in one's personal life;

• professional isolation;

• a need to rescue clients;

• a need for reassurance about one's attractiveness or potency; and

• abuse of alcohol or other drugs.

Because one of the most common mechanisms of impairment is denial, responsibility for confronting the problem is likely to fall on the professional colleagues of an impaired counselor. One ethical course of action is to confront the counselor and to do so with sensitivity, respect, and preparedness (Herlihy, 1996). If the counselor is receptive, options such as seeking help, suspending or limiting practice, working under supervision, or self-reporting can be explored. Although the counseling profession has yet to address the rehabilitation of impaired professionals systematically, there is at least one model program for treating counselors who have sexually exploited their clients (Schoener & Gonsiorek, 1988). It is important to know whether such a program is available in the counselor's local area, and if not, to be able to provide the names of colleagues who are willing to counsel their impaired peers. However, if the impaired counselor denies, rationalizes, or justifies his or her behavior, there may be no other option than to report him or her to a supervisor, an ethics committee, or a licensing board. Although some offending therapists who are experiencing burnout or impairment can be restored to healthy functioning, there may be others who should not be allowed to practice. The high rate of recidivism and the difficulty of ensuring that an offender has been "cured" are factors that support this stance. The first and highest obligation must be to protect clients from harm.

Summary and Conclusion

Sexual relationships with clients are one of the most serious types of all ethical violations. All codes of ethics of the professional associations prohibit sexual intimacies with current clients and with former clients until a specified amount of time has passed. The effects of sexual exploitation can be profound for the client, and the consequences can be severe for the counselor and for the profession.

Sexual attraction to clients is not unethical, but acting on that attraction creates problems. This topic has not been fully addressed in counselor training programs and is deserving of more attention.

The most productive focus of future efforts will be on prevention and remediation. The counseling profession needs to make a systematic effort to address sexual exploitation among its ranks and to educate clients about what they can rightfully expect from the professionals whose help they seek.

3 The Client's Perspective

As we have seen, the beliefs and behaviors of mental health professionals regarding dual relationships have been extensively studied. By contrast, surprisingly little literature exists to describe the client's or consumer's perspective or experiences, particularly with respect to nonsexual dual relationships. As Nerison (1992) noted, this situation creates a knowledge gap: we know a great deal about how therapists behave and what they believe, but except for sexual relationships, we know very little about how these relationships have affected the other party in the dyad, the client.

We believe it is important to consider the client's perspective. In this chapter we discuss the few studies that have been conducted on consumer beliefs and attitudes toward dual relationships. We present some anecdotes in which clients speak in their own words about their experiences. We raise questions about the implications of our profession's focus on our own point of view. Our guest contributor to this chapter, Susan L. Walden, presents a rationale and offers strategies for creating a counselor-client partnership in ethical decision making. Questions that frame our discussion are

- How do clients and potential clients view dual or multiple relationships?

- How do clients describe their experiences with dual relationships, both sexual and nonsexual?

- Have the mental health professions taken a paternalistic approach to dealing with dual relationships?

Attitudes and Beliefs of Consumers

Nerison (1992) studied both the attitudes of therapy consumers and potential consumers toward dual relationships and consumers' actual experiences with sexual and nonsexual dual relationships. Over half of the 259 participants in her study were themselves professional therapists or psychologists, so that her sample was not representative of consumers in general. Her study has provided us with some information about the consumer's perspective, however. Survey participants rated sexual activity with a current client as the least acceptable type of dual relationship, with 99% rating it as never acceptable. Sexual activity with former clients was also viewed as inappropriate, with 70% rating it as never acceptable. It appears that clients' attitudes toward sexual relationships with current and former clients are very similar to therapists' attitudes as reported by researchers such as Borys (1988), Gibson and Pope (1993), and Salisbury and Kinnier (1996).

Interestingly, Nerison found a high degree of ambivalence about whether a therapist's sexual attraction toward a client is ethical. This item received the highest number of "unsure" responses, and ratings were spread evenly along all acceptability ratings. As we discussed in the previous chapter, many therapists feel unprepared to deal with their feelings of sexual attraction. It appears that this issue may be equally confusing for clients.

With respect to nonsexual dual relationships, a majority of Nerison's respondents rated the following behaviors as never acceptable: providing therapy to a current employee (78%), inviting a client to a party or social event (65%), accepting a gift worth more than $50 (60%), providing therapy to a current student (59%), going out to eat with a client after a session (56%), and offering employment to a client (55%). These results are similar to those obtained by Borys in her survey of therapist attitudes, except that client attitudes toward counseling an employee seem to be more strongly negative.

Walden (1996) studied the general public's knowledge of ethical counselor behavior, including nonsexual and sexual dual relationships. Her questionnaire was constructed from vignettes taken from the *ACA Ethical Standards Casebook* (Herlihy & Corey, 1996). Participants were uncertain about the ethicality of the behavior of a counselor in one vignette who conducted business and social relationships with clients. Only 41.5% "thought" or "strongly believed" this behavior was unethical. A second vignette described a sexual dual relationship between a counselor and a former client slightly more than a year after termination of the professional relationship. Again, respondents were uncertain, with 41.5% judging it unethical. Walden also found that there was no significant relationship between experience as a client in counseling and knowledge of counselor ethics. She recommended that counselors work to educate the public about the ethical standards of our profession, and that we take steps to include the client perspective in formulating and adjudicating our codes.

Clients' Experiences With Dual Relationships

Anecdotes in which clients describe their experiences with sexual dual relationships can be poignant and powerful. In Nerison's (1992) study, the outcomes of sexual dual relationships were universally negative for the clients. Various elements of the patient-therapist sex syndrome (Pope, 1988) can be seen in these statements by clients:

- By this time, of course, I had given up on the rest of my life. I lived the 24 hours of every day for the 5- or 10-minute phone conversations with [the therapist with whom she was sexually involved]. If it hadn't been for my appointments with him twice a week, I would never have gotten out of bed.... I had withdrawn to the point were I spent all of my time, except for when I went to see him, in the bedroom with the shades drawn. (Walker & Young, 1986, pp. 71-72)

- I think after that initial honeymoon period the power issues began to surface in a way that I was real aware of them. I believe she was also. Clearly she had more power than I did in the relationship.... By the end of the year I felt like I had lost myself.... I took the ending of the relationship much harder than she did.... I think actually that therapy was impeded.... (Nerison, 1992, p. 91)

- I felt unbearable anger that I turned toward myself, rather than toward him, and fear born of a powerless sense that it would happen again and I would not be able to stop it. I felt more lost than I had when I began therapy. And rather than acknowledge these feelings, I pushed them aside, convincing myself that he, the professional, could be trusted to help me, regardless of his methods. It was easier for me to believe in him... than it was to deal with my guilt for participating in what felt so unclean. (Bates & Brodsky, 1989, p. 36)

- I do not remember clearly planning anything. I just went straight for the medicine cabinet as soon as I got home, and I lined up all of the bottles of pills I had accumulated...and then I emptied them into my hand and swallowed them a handful at a time. After I had done it, I had the most marvelous feeling. Maybe it was the peace of mind I had originally sought through therapy. (Walker & Young, 1986, pp. 51-52)

As we noted in the previous chapter, women are often reluctant to take action against offending professionals. Even when sexual advances are unwanted and sexual feelings are unreciprocated, reporting an offender can be a painful experience. Not all instances involve a client and therapist. Other relationships involving a power differential, such as the relationship between student and professor, are potentially as harmful. Anonymous (1991) has written about her experiences with Professor X, a charismatic professor of counseling. Although Professor X singled out this student for special attention, praise, encouragement, and hugs, she trustingly failed to consider that he was "coming on to her" sexually until she learned that he had had affairs with other students. After much soul searching, she filed sexual harassment charges with the university and the ethics committees of professional associations. A lengthy process followed, filled with frustrations and disappointments for her, but in the end Professor X was found in violation and disciplined. Although this student successfully resisted the professor's attempted seduction and her complaints were successfully resolved, the experience was traumatic for her, as is evident in the following passages:

- I sat for hours, staring off into space, unable to focus. I saw Professor X as two images that refused to meld...his well-meaning, kind, and caring persona as opposed with a lustful and menacing one. I wondered if I had inadvertently given him some signal that I was approachable sexually. (p. 503)

- My anger grew as the week wore on. It emanated from deep within me—I felt consumed by it, and I felt that I would not be able to stop myself from expressing it the next time I saw Professor X. I avoided having any contact with him. (p. 505)

- I felt obsessed by the experience—it drew attention away from every area of my life. To keep myself going, I read about sexual harassment and about research regarding sexual intimacy between therapists and clients.... These activities helped me to combat the worst aspect of this problem—the loneliness. (p. 506)

It can be helpful for those who have been sexually exploited to read about experiences similar to their own. First-person accounts of sexual relationships with therapists include *Betrayal* (Freeman & Roy, 1976), *A Killing Cure* (Walker & Young, 1986), *Sex in the Therapy Hour: A Case of Professional Incest* (Bates & Brodsky, 1989), *Therapist* (Plaisel, 1985), and *You Must Be Dreaming* (Noel & Watterson, 1992).

Nerison's (1992) study reported some statements made by clients that describe their experiences with nonsexual dual relationships. Among her survey participants, 27% reported that they had become friends with their former therapists. Those who were interviewed tended to express ambivalent feelings. Despite positive outcomes, they felt a diminished sense of respect for the therapist. The following excerpt is taken from a woman who became friends with her therapist after termination:

- At first it didn't feel like a typical sort of friendship because of course she knew everything about me and I knew very little about her other than superficial details. That felt awkward.... We managed to work it out and we have a wonderful friendship.... There is a little piece of me that still feels honored that she would want to have me as a friend...but there's also a piece that fits right beside that, that kind of has lost a little respect for her.... (p. 93)

The incompatibility of roles that results when the therapist is the client's employer was particularly problematic for Nerison's participants. This can be seen in the following passages from clients who were employees of their therapists.

- I think initially I felt special.... As it progressed, I guess I felt both special and very uncomfortable.... I felt angry a lot of the time.... It was very painful, the whole thing.... There are some strengths that you gain, or some ability to cope. But that doesn't make it worth it. (p. 90)

- The impact on therapy was tremendous. I could not confide my deepest, darkest. I couldn't be there with my negativity and my hate.... It was too risky, there was too much to lose.... It is crazy making. (p. 106)

Dual relationships are sometimes unavoidable in small communities. Clients may experience discomfort and a loss of privacy, as this excerpt illustrates:

- To end up at social functions together was sort of a common event. Throughout my therapy I would often end up at the same social event or cultural event as my therapist. Several of my friends ultimately got into therapy with the same therapist.... So you'd be out to dinner with somebody and they would say, "Oh, I didn't know you were seeing so and so!" So I think one's privacy is compromised in a different way.... (p. 95).

Implications

Most counselors probably aspire to have fiduciary relationships with their clients. In a fiduciary relationship, the client's viewpoints are recognized and respected although the client's less powerful position in the relationship is acknowledged (Nerison, 1992). Counselors are likely to be uncomfortable with the notion of practicing paternalistic relationships with their clients. Nonetheless, the position taken by professionals with respect to dual relationships, as reflected in our codes of ethics and our professional literature, does seem to be paternalistic. Mental health professionals have taken the position that it is up to the *professional* to determine the boundaries of the relationship. Nerison described the assumptions underlying paternalism as (a) therapists have the power to harm clients through dual relationships, (b) therapists are in a better position than clients to know what is best for the client, and (c) they are therefore obligated to protect clients from dual relationships regardless of clients' beliefs or feelings on the matter.

We do not argue that mental health professionals should abdicate their responsibility to maintain therapeutic boundaries in the interests of avoiding paternalism. Nonetheless, we do agree with Nerison's point that loss of autonomy is the price exacted by paternalistic relationships. To us, this underscores the importance of involving the client in ongoing discussions about relationship boundaries and potential dual relationship problems. It is important that we strive to balance our responsibilities for maintaining appropriate boundaries with our commitment to making our clients active partners in the therapeutic relationship.

Susan L. Walden suggests that important therapeutic benefits can result from inclusion of the client in the ethical decision-making process. She offers some strategies for accomplishing this goal at both the organizational and individual levels.

Inclusion of the Client Perspective in Ethical Practice

Susan L. Walden

Numerous studies have investigated the knowledge, judgment, and experiences of counselors, psychologists, and social workers with respect to dual relationships and other ethical issues. We have data reflecting practitioners' opinions on appropriate ethical actions as well as their self-reported practices when faced with ethical dilemmas. Although such studies certainly contribute greatly to our understanding, they tell only part of the story. The literature is scant concerning the other party in the counseling dyad, the client. Although it is true that both the professional and the field of counseling suffer when unethical practice occurs, in many cases the party who stands to incur the greatest harm is the client. Injury to clients resulting from dual relationships, especially sexual dual relationships, has been well investigated. Pope (1994) and Nerison (1992), among others, have documented the negative effects of dual relationships on clients. Because of the potential for harm to clients, more attention must be given to the client in order to understand the client's perspective and to educate and empower clients. It must be emphasized that the inclusion of the client in ethical considerations is not an attempt to "victim blame" or to shift the responsibility for ethical practice onto the client. The professional *always* bears the onus for maintaining professionalism and ethical practice. Rather, it is suggested that the inclusion of the client can be a strong asset to the counselor in resolving ethical dilemmas and can be a source of empowerment for the client.

The question that comes to mind is Why has so little attention been accorded to the client's perspective? There are numerous possible responses to this question. First, perhaps tradition has dictated that we, as the professionals in counseling relationships, have the knowledge and training required to create and enforce the standards needed for best practice. Yet if we judge our clients as uninformed about the nature of counseling, we also deny them the potential for participation in the process of resolving ethical dilemmas. Additionally, the mental health professions have often been viewed with suspicion by others, and therapy has been seen as a venture shrouded in mystery. Perhaps our techniques and procedures have been somewhat protected from public scrutiny to preserve the mystery, to ensure that our techniques "work." If this is true, then perhaps ethics codes are a part of that mystery, and counseling might lose some impact if the client were allowed in on our secrets. Yet another potential explanation for the exclusion of the client perspective is the fear that telling a client too much about our standards of practice might intimidate a client. For example, haven't we all occasionally worried that explaining all the possible limits of confidentiality to a client might frighten the client into silence?

Another possible hesitation in involving the client in ethical considerations is that an educated consumer base might result in an increase in ethics complaints. We are charged with the responsibility of monitoring ourselves and our profession. Most of the time we do a good job, as evidenced by the fact that only a small percentage of mental health professionals are named in complaints to ethics boards. Perhaps we might do a better job, not by turning over the responsibility for monitoring practice to the consumers or by blaming the victims of unethical practice, but by enlisting the participation of the consumer. We must remember that we are not alone in the adventure of counseling.

Perhaps none of the aforementioned suggestions are accurate. It is possible that turning our focus to the client's perspective is simply a paradigm shift of sorts. We have espoused a somewhat paternalistic model of practice in the area of ethics. We, as the professionals, create a set of standards that we believe will protect the client's welfare and best interests, yet we do this without the input or presence of the consumers of our services. I suggest that involving the client represents a natural step from a therapeutic benefits stance as well as a genuine move toward the aspirational level of ethical practice.

Therapeutic benefits. At least three potential therapeutic benefits may be derived from the inclusion of the consumer perspective in ethics. First, when we make decisions about a client *for* the client rather than *with* the client, we rob the client of power in the counseling relationship. Conversely, when we create a true partnership between counselor and client, the client is empowered. The concept of a partnership emphasizes the importance and essential nature of both parties in the relationship. Although counselor and client each bring different contributions to the collaboration—the counselor's training and professional experience and the client's strengths, hard work, and life experiences—both contributions are essential for the success of the counseling endeavor.

Client empowerment through inclusion in ethical considerations is a good fit with current thinking in the mental health professions. Current therapies, particularly brief and solution-focused therapies, emphasize the collaboration between counselor and client. The aim is to work toward goals determined by the client, drawing upon the successes and strengths of the client. Why not extend this way of thinking into the arena of ethics? Bringing the client into ongoing dialogue regarding a potential dual relationship or other ethical concern should be a continuous process if we are truly to work within the client's frame of reference, respecting the client's views. We cannot pretend to understand fully the client's view of a situation or gauge the potential ramifications of certain decisions for the life and well-being of the client accurately. What we may hope to communicate is a genuine regard for the impact of a situation on the client and respect for the client's welfare in working to find the solution that best protects and respects the client. By soliciting the client's perspective, we may ultimately achieve better counseling results and the best resolution for any ethical questions that arise.

Take the case of a client who presents with complaints of social isolation. She and the counselor work for several sessions reframing her sense of isolation, highlighting her strengths, and building strategies for connecting with others in social situations. When she invites the counselor to accompany her to a party, the counselor is concerned about the dual relationship implications but fears hurting the client. Rather than just turning down the client's offer or making excuses of previous plans, the counselor might engage the client in a discussion of the ramifications of such a venture, eliciting the client's thoughts and feelings about potential situations that might occur, including the impact on the client and the counseling relationship. It is true that many clients may be unable to see the potential risks involved in the situation, and the ultimate decision will still rest with the counselor. However, in many cases, the counselor and client working together may arrive at a solution that allows the counselor to preserve the counseling relationship and helps the client feel a part of the decision-making process.

A second therapeutic benefit derived from the inclusion of the client perspective may be more culturally appropriate practice. The counseling profession is growing in its understanding of the demands of counseling in a culturally pluralistic society. Our codes of ethics may reflect primarily western values and certain cultural biases, but they do not have to be applied in a culturally encapsulated manner. Further, the 1995 ACA Code of Ethics does address culturally appropriate practice, such as in the provisions made for bartering, although other issues that might arise are not directly addressed by the code, such as the giving of gifts, which is an important aspect of the culture of some clients. When the counselor has strict beliefs or policies regarding accepting gifts, misunderstandings may occur; however, if counselors are willing to understand the client's perspective and share their own perspectives, a solution may be reached by working together. Without such an exchange of views, the client may be offended by the counselor's behavior. With an exchange, client empowerment and the selection of a solution more in keeping with the client's cultural values are possible. We can be culturally inclusive in the application of ethical standards, and the inclusion of the client perspective may be an important step toward this goal.

A third potential therapeutic benefit resulting from the inclusion of the client perspective involves the resolution of transference or countertransference issues. When personal feelings emerge in the counseling relationship, often they may be manifestations of feelings related to other persons in the lives of the client or counselor. When these feelings are of a romantic or sexual nature, they may be expressed inappropriately if not acknowledged and worked through. Therapeutic gains may result for the client if feelings of transference are acknowledged and the accompanying issues addressed. If romantic feelings toward the counselor are not addressed, however, a vulnerable or impaired counselor may misinterpret the client's expressions of attraction or attachment and possibly act inappropriately toward the client. By the same token, the counselor's feelings of countertransference should be acknowledged by the counselor and perhaps supervision or personal therapy sought if the feelings persist and are unresolved. Serious harm may be avoided and therapeutic gains may be realized through the resolution of transference and countertransference issues. Open discussion between counselor and client and a willingness to get at the origins of these issues may make the difference between a successful counseling relationship that produces the desired gains for the client and a relationship that could become unhealthy and result in harm to the client.

Aspirational level of ethical practice. Not only are there potential therapeutic benefits to be gained by including the client's perspective in ethics, but such practices also speak to the attainment of the aspirational level of ethical practice. At the aspirational level, the practitioner is concerned with the spirit of the rules, the intent of the standards, and the impact of counseling on the client rather than on simply complying with "the rules" and avoiding complaints of impropriety (Corey, Corey, & Callanan, 1993; Herlihy & Corey, 1996). Functioning at the aspirational level of ethics means that the counselor's concern is for the welfare of the client. The inclusion of the client's voice in ethical concerns speaks to this higher level of ethical functioning.

When a practitioner has decisions to make or ethical dilemmas to resolve, certainly the responsible professional consults the appropriate standards, and hopefully, this individual will also be mindful of the impact of potential decisions on the welfare of the client. However, even the most well-meaning practitioner cannot fully understand the client's perspective or investment in the situation without the input of that client. Although we may see a situation as being relatively low risk for a client, the client may view the situation differently. I also question whether it is truly possible to attain the aspirational level of ethical functioning *without* including the client in the decision-making process. In order fully to prize and value a client and best represent what is in the client's best interests, should we not involve the client in the process? Only by asking the client can we really know what a situation looks like through the client's eyes.

The potential benefits of including the client perspective in ethics are many. Numerous therapeutic advantages may be gained, and a practitioner has moved closer to the aspirational level of ethical practice. Ultimately, such genuine regard for the client's welfare may bring about benefits for the counselor, for the profession, and, most importantly, for the client.

Operationalized client inclusion. With the rationale in place for the inclusion of the client perspective in ethics, the question becomes how to put this process into practice. Infusion of the client perspective begins on two major levels: the organizational level and the individual level. At the organizational level, our professional organizations can utilize several strategies to promote the client perspective. First, we must continue and strengthen our efforts at educating members of the public in general and our clients in particular regarding ethical practice. Frequent reference has been made in the literature to the benefits of educating consumers of counseling services regarding ethical considerations (Allen, 1986; Herlihy & Corey, 1994; Shimberg, 1986; Vinson, 1987). Additionally, numerous state licensure boards and other ethics bodies have begun to require that practitioners provide professional disclosure statements and post their toll-free numbers for client use. These developments are much needed and provide a useful source of information for our clients. Professional organizations such as the American Counseling Association should include in public relations efforts attention to appropriate professional conduct. Our efforts at public education often center around making ourselves and our services known to consumers. Why not include information about the nature of counseling and ethical practice?

A second strategy for client inclusion at the organizational level involves client participation in the creation and adjudication of ethics codes. We must move away from the paternalistic model currently in place in which we (the professionals) create and adjudicate our codes of ethics without the voice of the consumers. There is precedent for consumer participation in an ethics committee of a professional organization. In 1987, the Ethics Committee of the American Psychological Association added a nonpsychologist member of the general public to its committee (APA Ethics Committee, 1987). No report was found to indicate how this public member was selected or to document the success or implications of this endeavor. Given the vast human resources we have in ACA, it does seem that the logistical aspects of appointing a consumer member to the ACA Ethics Committee could be managed if the membership and leadership of the organization supported such a move. By adding the voice and unique perspective offered by a consumer, we might be better able to formulate standards that protect our clients, better understand the implications of ethical and unethical practice for the client, and also indicate to the public that we as a profession are interested in protecting the rights and welfare of those who utilize our services.

A third component of client inclusion at the organizational level is to develop models that involve the client in the resolution of ethical dilemmas. The ethical decision-making model published by the ACA Ethics Committee—in *A Practitioner's Guide to Ethical Decision Making* (1995)—is a useful tool for the resolution of ethical dilemmas; however, the model does not call for consultation with the client as a part of the decision-making process. Hillerbrand and Stone (1986) suggested that the client is an integral part of the "ethical community of the counseling relationship," capable of participating in determining appropriate actions in ethical dilemmas. The Feminist Model for ethical decision making (Hill, Glaser, & Harden, 1995) calls for consultation with the client at every stage of the decision-making process. In cases involving dual or multiple relationships, client risk may be great, and inclusion of the client seems especially important. A comparison of the two models is as follows:

ACA Ethics Committee Model (1995)	*Feminist Model (1995)*
1. Identify the problem	1. Recognizing a problem
2. Apply ACA Code of Ethics	2. Defining the problem (collaboration with client termed essential at this stage)
3. Determine nature and dimensions of dilemma	3. Developing solutions (with client)
4. Generate potential courses of action	4. Choosing a solution
5. Consider consequences of all options and choose	5. Reviewing process (with client)/rechoosing
6. Evaluate course of action	6. Implementing and evaluating (with client)
7. Implement action	7. Continued reflection

The models are similar in steps involved, but the ACA Ethics Committee model makes no mention of client involvement. In the fifth step, which calls for the consideration of the consequences of all options, readers are reminded to "ponder the implications of each course of action for the client" (p. 13). The authors of the Feminist Model specifically stated that consultation with the client "as fully as is possible and appropriate" is an essential step in ethical decision making (p. 27). The inclusion of the client in the decision-making process is a stated component of four steps of the Feminist Model, and the authors suggested that the client may and should be included throughout the process whenever possible. The decision-making model presented in the final chapter of this book provides an excellent model for the resolution of ethical dilemmas involving dual relationships, and the model includes consultation with the client.

The two models just compared could be easily blended. The actual steps are not that different. What is important is that the ACA Ethics Committee model should reflect the importance of collaboration with the client in ethical matters that are often of great consequence to the client. Such a step at the organizational level certainly would both instruct practitioners about the importance of including the client perspective and give them concrete strategies to use. The support of such practices from the professional organization would surely impress upon the membership the importance of the client perspective and should ultimately lead to fewer misunderstandings and healthier relationships between counselors and their clients.

At the individual level there are also numerous strategies that may be employed to involve the client in ethical matters. Informed consent is probably the process that most commonly includes the client in discussions of ethics, and practitioners can discuss potential dual relationship and other boundary issues at the outset. Whether or not your state licensure board requires the provision of a professional disclosure statement, it is a sound practice that provides information and resources for your clients. A good practitioner will revisit areas of informed consent periodically and especially as ethical concerns arise. Because informed consent by nature necessarily involves the client, perhaps just reframing it as a process rather than an event will help counselors be more inclusive of the client as the counseling relationship progresses. Another strategy for the individual practitioner involves utilizing a professional decision-making model when ethical dilemmas arise. This model should include consultation with the client at any and all possible stages during the process.

One final suggestion for infusing the client perspective involves the counselor educator. As counselor educators, we teach ethical principles to our students through our courses and through our deeds. If we teach students the process of informed consent and how to include the client in ethical decision making, we are equipping them from the beginning with a client-oriented philosophy and strategies. In addition, we can model these practices for them through our dealings with them in the teacher-student relationship.

Conclusions. I will be the first to admit that the inclusion of the client in ethical matters may not be appropriate in all situations and that not all clients may be able to participate fully or objectively in the resolution of ethical dilemmas. Nonetheless, I do believe that the client perspective is an essential component of sound ethical practice. There are therapeutic benefits to be gained in terms of client empowerment, culturally appropriate practice, and the resolution of transference and countertransference issues. We reach higher toward the aspirational level of ethical practice when we value the client's perspective. There are few risks involved in bring the client into ethical matters and the benefits are many, not only for the professionals and for the profession but also primarily for the client. In sum, when we value our clients, we do all that is possible to understand the world through their eyes. When we listen to our clients, we teach them that their voice is important and is heard. When we make our clients partners in ethical decision making, we empower them. When we include our client's perspective, we decrease the likelihood of harm to clients and increase the opportunities for positive results in counseling.

This chapter on the client's perspective concludes our introduction to dual or multiple relationships. In chapter 1, we attempted to lay a foundation by defining dual relationships and discussing relationship boundary issues. We looked at risks and the potential for harm, and offered some safeguards to minimize risk. In chapter 2, we explored sexual dual relationship issues. In this third chapter, we focused on the client's perspective and suggested a rationale and strategies for including clients in ethical decision making. In the next three chapters, we turn to boundary issues in counselor education and training.

4 Issues in Counselor Education

Numerous dual relationship issues present themselves in the counselor training process. Some of these issues involve subtle and complex questions about where boundaries should be drawn when counselor educators play multiple roles and have multiple responsibilities with their students. In this chapter we explore relationship boundary issues that commonly arise in counselor education programs and present the thoughts of two guest contributors. Holly A. Stadler presents a faculty perspective. She identifies potential areas of conflict in the various roles taken by counselor educators and students and suggests that prudence and ethical reasoning are essential in creating an ethically congruent training environment. Michelle C. Muratori presents a student perspective on dual relationships between faculty and students, reflecting on her experiences in two very different training programs.

The focus questions that guide us through our discussion include

- What are the implications for counselor educators and students of the 1995 revisions to the ACA Code of Ethics?

- What kinds of conflicts do counselor educators face in the multiple roles they fulfill in their work?

- Can some forms of role blending in the professor-student relationship be beneficial?

- What are the responsibilities of counselor educators in teaching students about dual relationships? How can the issues best be raised and explored, and how can students be prepared to deal with dual relationship dilemmas?

The 1995 ACA Code of Ethics addresses the issue of relationship boundaries between student and professor, and between student and student, much more extensively than did the previous (1988) code. The primary standard that speaks to the dual relationship issue is as follows:

- Counselors clearly define and maintain ethical, professional, and social relationship boundaries with their students and supervisees. They are aware of the differential in power that exists and the student's or supervisee's possible incomprehension of that power differential. Counselors explain to students and supervisees the potential for the relationship to become exploitive. (F.1.b.)

Clearly, there are parallels between the counselor-client and professor-student relationship. In each relationship, it is the responsibility of the person in the more powerful position to define and maintain appropriate boundaries, and to engage the person who is in the less powerful, more dependent position in ongoing discussion and explanation to prevent problems when possible and to resolve them when they do arise.

Sexual Dual Relationships

The 1995 ACA Code of Ethics explicitly forbids counselor educators from engaging in sexual relationships with students or subjecting them to sexual harassment of any kind (Standard F.1.c.). It may surprise you to learn that the previous code did not contain such a standard. The previous code prohibited sexual dual relationships between counselors and clients, and the intent was to include educators and their students under the umbrella of this general standard. However, the language was not clear, and the ACA Ethics Committee found that some educators used this lack of clarity as a means of justifying sexual contact with students (Glosoff & Herlihy, 1995). The codes of ethics of other professional associations have had more long-standing prohibitions against sexual dual relationships between students and educators: the APA code has included such a provision since 1992, and the AAMFT since 1988.

Despite the clear statements in codes of ethics of professional associations, faculty-student sexual relationships do occur, although it is difficult to estimate the incidence rate. Over a decade ago, Glaser and Thorpe (1986) found that 17% of their sample of female psychologists reported having had sexual contact with faculty members or clinical supervisors during their graduate training. More recent studies have found that 5 to 6% of female counselors and about 4% of male counselors experienced sexual contact with their professors or supervisors while they were students (Miller & Larrabee, 1995; Thoreson, Shaughnessy, & Frazier, 1995; Thoreson, Shaughnessy, Heppner, et al., 1995). It may be that the incidence of faculty-student sexual relationships has actually decreased, or it may be that doctoral-level mental health professionals are more likely to have engaged in sexual contact with their own teachers or supervisors. It does seem clear that male counselors are more likely to have engaged in sexual contact while in the high-power role (professor or supervisor) and female counselors are more likely to have had these experiences while they were in the low-power role as students (Thoreson, Shaughnessy, & Frazier, 1995). Several studies (Glaser & Thorpe, 1986; Hammel, Olkin, & Taube, 1996; Miller & Larrabee, 1995) have indicated that women's attitudes toward their experiences change over time: in retrospect, they believe their sexual contacts with professors were more coercive, more of a hindrance to the working relationship, and more damaging to their professional careers than they believed at the time. These studies raise questions about students' ability to consent freely to such relationships and about how prepared they were to deal with the ethics of such intimacies at the time. Moreover, it seems clear that educators and supervisors tend to have professional power and authority long after direct training ends.

Both Miller and Larrabee (1995) and Hammel and his colleagues (1996) have taken the position that engaging in sexual behavior with students is highly inappropriate and contrary to the spirit of the codes of ethics of most professional organizations. Additionally, Hammel et al. have made a strong recommendation that the APA take a clearer and more encompassing stand against sexual relationships during training, suggesting that the association forbid them outright. Miller and Larrabee emphasized that educators and supervisors function as role models for the profession and occupy positions of power. They added that, because of the detrimental impact of sexual involvements during training, educators and supervisors ought to refrain from any sexual involvements with students or supervisees.

Concern about the harm caused by sexual relationships between students and professors is not limited to faculty in counseling or psychology programs in university communities. The University of Iowa, California State University, the University of Virginia, and the University of Oregon have implemented policies that forbid all professors and administrators from dating students they teach, mentor, or supervise (James, 1996; Leatherman, 1993). The president of the University of Oregon described the policy at that institution as "an essential ethical statement we must make...to counter anyone's capacity for the illusion that the exploitation of others in a power relationship is acceptable" (James, p. 1).

Role Conflicts for Counselor Educators

Counselor educators confront some nonsexual relationship boundary issues that are inherent in the very nature of counselor training. It is a well-accepted assumption in the profession that the counselor's personal characteristics influence therapeutic outcomes. This assumption makes it incumbent on counselor training programs to focus on counselors-in-training as persons as well as on their academic performance. Students need to develop a strong sense of self-awareness along with an understanding of interpersonal dynamics if they are to become effective counselors (Glosoff & Herlihy, 1995). Thus counselor training programs blend academic study and experiential or personal learnings, and according to the ACA Code of Ethics, counselor educators must use their professional judgment when they conduct training experiences that require student self-growth or self-disclosure. They must provide safeguards so that students are aware of the ramifications their self-disclosure may have on professors who play multiple roles as teacher, trainer, and supervisor. One of these safeguards is that "evaluative components of experiential training experiences explicitly delineate predetermined academic standards that are separate and not dependent on the student's level of self-disclosure" (Standard F.3.b.).

Role conflicts can occur because we not only encourage personal growth but also serve as gatekeepers to the profession. According to Standard F.3.a., counselor educators are responsible for ongoing evaluation of students and are aware of any personal limitations of students that might impede performance. When students are unable to provide competent service due to these limitations, we must refer them for assistance. If remediation efforts are unsuccessful, we must dismiss students from the program or refuse to endorse them for completion of the program (Standard F.1.h.).

Certainly, if we do not attempt to help students become aware of personal factors that could impede their functioning as counselors, we are neither doing them a service nor helping their future clients. As personal problems or limitations of students become evident, we have an ethical duty to encourage and even challenge students to face and deal with these issues lest these issues impede their performance as helpers. If students who have unresolved personal issues or who hold rigid and dogmatic attitudes, values, or prejudices are allowed to graduate from our programs, we cannot say that we have kept the welfare of the consumer in mind. We think that programs should provide, as part of the curriculum, opportunities for students to examine their personal lives, with special emphasis on their needs, motivations, and life experiences that may impact their abilities to function effectively as practitioners.

Ethical quandaries sometimes arise when it is through a nongraded experiential component of a course that we become aware of personal problems or limitations of students. It might be a dyadic practice session between two students in which one is serving as the counselor and the other as the counselee; it might occur in an experiential portion of a group counseling class; or it might emerge in exploring the student's difficulties in working with a certain client in practicum. If we raise our concerns with these students in a way that leads to a negative evaluation or an administrative action, students may feel that we have betrayed their trust no matter how carefully we have explained in advance any possible repercussions. If we fail to raise the concerns, we violate our responsibility to monitor the profession.

The revised ACA Code of Ethics provides more specific guidance to counselor educators than was previously available. Some subtle questions remain, however, that are more difficult to answer and require professional judgment (Glosoff & Herlihy, 1995). Even when we consciously adhere to our pledge to keep self-growth experiences nongraded, how can we avoid unintentionally incorporating knowledge gained through students' self-disclosures into our evaluation of their performance? When student limitations are personal or interpersonal rather than academic, how can we address those limitations while still respecting the student's right to privacy? Can we require students to seek personal counseling when their personal problems are interfering with their ability to provide services?

The preceding discussion underscores the importance of providing informed consent for students in counselor training programs. The personal growth aspects of a program need to be made known to prospective students prior to their entrance into a program. Because many of us challenge students to think about their personal lives and their values and invite them to explore a range of feelings, students have a right to know where there may be potential problems. We ought to tell our students what we are doing to ensure that we are keeping their interest and welfare in mind, and we should talk about the procedures and practices we use to minimize the potential negative consequences of any role blending.

Relationship Boundaries Between Students and Professors

In the first edition of this book, we raised the question of whether a counselor educator should ever counsel a student. At that time, we noted that this was one of the most controversial questions pertaining to dual role relationships of counselor educators, and two guest contributors presented contrasting points of view. Today, with the 1995 revised Code of Ethics in effect, we have a clear answer to this question:

  • If students or supervisees request counseling, supervisors or counselor educators provide them with acceptable referrals. Supervisors or counselor educators do not serve as counselor to students or supervisees over whom they hold administrative, teaching, or evaluative roles unless this is a brief role associated with a training experience. (F.3.c.)

Although counselor educators should not enter into formal therapeutic relationships with students, this does not mean that we must remain aloof and distant from our students as persons. In the first edition of this book, Lloyd (1992) raised a concern that counselor educators might be developing a "dual relationship phobia." He cautioned that no constituency (institution, student, or profession) is well served when counselor educators avoid the struggles of making responsible decisions by hiding behind a prohibition against multidimensional relationships. His concern was that opportunities for live demonstrations of individual and group counseling, and for supervision with a personal focus, might be lost if counselor educators approach dual relationship issues too conservatively.

We agree that it is as possible to err on the side of caution as it is to err on the side of carelessness about relationship boundaries. Hopefully, the 1995 ACA Code of Ethics has provided guidelines that will be helpful to counselor educators and students who are searching for an appropriate middle ground. Mentoring relationships, as we noted in the introductory chapter, are not dual relationships of the type that the code is intended to discourage. A mentor serves as adviser, confidant, friend, teacher, and supervisor—and there are possibilities that the mentee can benefit a great deal from this special relationship. Mentoring often involves collaborative research efforts, and conflicts can arise around such issues as giving credit for publication of research findings. Unfortunately, most of us know of students who have felt pressured to have their work presented under the first authorship of their major professors. Two standards in the Code of Ethics provide safeguards to ensure that counselor educators do not take unfair advantage of their more powerful positions. First, Standard F.1.d. requires that students be given adequate credit for their contributions to research. Second, Standard G.4.c. mandates that students be credited as principal authors of articles based on their dissertations or theses. For mentoring relationships to work as they are intended, it is essential that the professor and student talk candidly before engaging in them to establish clear working guidelines and that an open dialogue be maintained.

Other types of role blending occur in the counselor training process. Live demonstrations of counseling that occur in classes can enhance student learning and can fall within the ethically permissible bounds of "a brief role associated with a training experience." Counselor educators can certainly remain ethical and relate to students on an unstructured and personal level, making themselves available to students beyond class time and office hours. Issues raised during a class session are often continued over a cup of coffee after class, major professors attend graduation parties of their doctoral students to extend their congratulations, and graduate student associations sponsor social events as well as lectures and other educational opportunities. None of these or other, similar situations need be problematic. A key factor, as guest contributor Michelle Muratori comments later, is the counselor educator's level of comfort and aptitude in moving among formal and informal roles.

Bowman, Hatley, and Bowman (1995) assessed both faculty and student perceptions of dual relationships in mentoring, friendships, monetary transactions, informal social interactions, and romantic/sexual relationships. They admitted that certain dual relationships are unavoidable in most training programs and suggested that dual relationships may be more accurately evaluated when viewed from the perspective of how the faculty member and student *behave* within the relationship, rather than concluding that the mere existence of a dual role is necessarily unethical.

To conclude our discussion of the topic of relationship boundaries between students and professors, we want to note that counselor educators "do not accept close relatives as students" (Standard F.1.e.). This restriction might be problematic for professors who teach in universities in isolated, rural communities and who have a close relative who wants to pursue a degree in counseling. These situations might require careful planning (to ensure that the student takes courses with other instructors) or personal sacrifice (such as commuting a significant distance to pursue graduate studies at another university). Nonetheless, the dual relationship problems that are inherent in teaching and evaluating a spouse, or son or daughter, necessitate making these alternative arrangements.

Dual Relationships Between Students

In doctoral programs, advanced students are often involved in the supervision of students who are seeking their master's degrees. The supervision of students by students raises a potential for problematic dual relationships. Miller, in the most recent edition of the *ACA Ethical Standards Casebook* (1996), presented an interesting case study that demonstrates problems that can occur when students are put in the position of supervising other students. When students are involved in leading counseling groups or providing clinical supervision for their peers, counselor educators are required to take steps to ensure that students "placed in these roles do not have personal or adverse relationships with peers" and that they fully understand their ethical obligations (Standard F.2.e.). Careful supervision and monitoring are needed to ensure that dual relationship problems between students are avoided whenever possible, and that they are resolved when they do occur.

———◆———

Holly A. Stadler provides a thoughtful discussion of the various roles played by counselor educators and students. She discusses the importance of prudence in ethical decision making and offers suggestions for managing ethical dilemmas in the training environment.

Dual Relationships in Counselor Education

Holly A. Stadler

Educators and students in counseling programs engage in a wide variety of roles and relationships as a function of their program-related activities as well as their participation as members of the larger society. For the most part, these roles and relationships do not converge in ways that elicit ethical concerns. Occasions do arise, however, in which such convergences could be seen as ethically problematic. Over the years, professional groups such as the American Counseling Association have recognized the need to offer increasingly explicit guidance with regard to dual role relationships. For example, a counselor educator might be asked to join the board of directors of an agency employing one of her current students. Or a practicum student could find out that one of his clients at the university counseling center plans to attend a self-help group of which the student is a member. Herlihy and Corey have noted earlier in this chapter that there is sufficient evidence of ineffective management of these relationships. If the counseling profession is to enjoy the public trust, counselor educators, supervisors, and counselors-in-training must manage dual relationships prudently and reasonably.

I have been asked to address dual relationships in counselor education, leaving to others the topic of such relationships in supervision. To underscore the theme of Brown and Prager (1985) that "developmental growth can occur optimally in an ethically congruent environment" (p. 403), I focus here on the training environment as a necessary locus of instruction, supervision, and modeling of prudence and reason in dual relationships. To do this, I begin with a review of the 1995 ACA Code of Ethics with special attention to dual relationships in counselor education. Then I identify a number of types of multiple roles and relationships and associated concerns that occur in counselor education, and conclude with a call for sound ethical reasoning and the exercise of prudence in dual role situations.

Dual relationships and the 1995 ACA Code of Ethics. Along with evidence of failure on the part of some professionals successfully to negotiate dual relationships has come increased specificity in codes of ethics about the boundaries of such relationships. With respect to counselor education, the 1995 Code of Ethics takes special note of these issues by highlighting them in specific sections and goes beyond the general statements characteristic of previous codes to articulate positions on dual relationships that directly and indirectly relate to counselor education. Where previous codes were silent, the 1995 Code of Ethics takes on potential dual role concerns in counselor education such as close relatives of faculty as students in counselor education programs, peer relationships among students, counselor educators leading student self-growth experiences, and exploitive employment relationships.

These standards in the 1995 Code of Ethics also draw attention to two of the most frequent and troubling dual relationships between faculty and students: counseling relationships and sexual relationships. I have written elsewhere (Stadler, 1986a, 1992) about ethical perspectives on counseling relationships between educators and students. It is not necessary to revisit that issue here other than to note "the inherent inadvisability of pursuing options that involve conflicting obligations" (Stadler, 1992, p. 56).

In addition, numerous others (Glaser & Thorpe, 1986; Miller & Larabee, 1995; Pope, Levenson, & Schover, 1979; Robinson & Reid, 1985) have engaged the topic of sexual relationships between educators and students, and I encourage you to pursue those sources. In both areas—boundaries regarding counseling relationships and sexual relationships—Kitchener's (1988) guideline that these relationships should be considered a priory unethical because the "conflict of interests is great, the power differential large, and the role expectations incompatible" (p. 220) can be applied.

Multiple roles and relationships. Rest (1982) has noted that one of the chief attributes of effective ethical decision making is the ability to recognize the existence of an ethical dilemma. Thus it is useful to anticipate some of the possible role and relationship conflicts (excluding the already discussed sexual or counseling relationships) that could develop as counselor educators fulfill their academic responsibilities in multiple roles that include educator, researcher, colleague, administrator, and consultant.

Consider that the objectivity of the selection and evaluative aspects of the educator role (such as admission decisions or assignment of grades) can be compromised by noneducational roles that involve, for example, business, social, or familial relationships. These noneducational dual relationships can be cause for concern. The 1995 Code of Ethics is specific about prohibiting close family members from being students or supervisees of a counselor educator (Standard F.1.e.). The standard governing employment relationships can also offer guidance in interactions with teaching and research assistants: "Counselors do not engage in exploitive relationships with individuals over whom they have supervisory, evaluative, or instructional control or authority" (Standard D.1.k.).

To recognize a common dual relationship for faculty in the *researcher* role, reflect on the faculty member conducting research on counselor education who directly solicits students in counselor education classes to participate in a study. This scenario frequently comes to the attention of institutional review boards at universities. For our purposes, however, it is important to note that students in this situation might either feel that they could gain some advantage over other students or feel coerced to participate in a faculty study. A similar situation can occur with clients whose therapist requests their participation in dissertation or other research. Strategies for soliciting research participants should incorporate procedures that avoid placing potential participants in dual role conflicts.

Dual roles in *collegial* and *administrative* relationships are also potential sources of conflicting interests and obligations. For example, consider colleagues who are in a business partnership or who are intimate partners. Serving together as members of a curriculum committee might not produce any inordinate conflicts beyond those that already take place in such a committee. But if one of the partners is in a position to evaluate the other for tenure or merit pay, there could be serious ethical implications. Concerns about the objectivity of the evaluator and the interests being served in the evaluation could overshadow the actual record of the person under review. Conflicting interests may deter candor and cloud judgment when untenured faculty members are in selection or evaluation roles regarding an applicant, student, or colleague who has a dual relationship with a tenured faculty member.

With respect to the *consulting* role, many universities expect that faculty members will offer their expertise to the community. Here questions of selection and evaluation are likely to cause the most difficulty. For example, personnel in a consultee agency might be enrolled or be seeking enrollment in the program with which the faculty member is associated.

Counselor education students may also face role and relationship conflicts because of their multiple roles, including student, teacher, researcher, and peer. Several of these roles entail concerns similar to those discussed previously. The 1995 ACA Code of Ethics makes it clear that students are responsible for their own ethical conduct. With respect to the *student* role, this includes not initiating dual relationship entanglements with faculty members, supervisors, or clients.

With regard to *teaching* and *research* roles, the concerns and potential conflicts for students are also similar to those of faculty members. Issues of objectivity in student evaluation and selection and of noncoercive solicitation of research participants apply equally to students who teach and serve as research assistants.

Students also must take responsibility for not creating dual relationships with clients and for avoiding turning peer or friend relationships into therapeutic relationships. The Code of Ethics makes reference to one aspect of *peer* role relationships: "Counselors make every effort to ensure that the rights of peers are not compromised when students or supervisees are assigned to lead counseling groups or provide clinical supervision" (Standard F.2.e.). Counselors-in-training must guard against engaging in therapeutic relationships with peers, friends, and family. Counselor educators are familiar with the counseling student who, unable to set boundaries on relationships, is exhausted by the multiple demands of one-sided, quasi-therapeutic friendships with others seeking "professional advice."

Managing ethical quandaries in the training environment. My observation, based on having participated on and chaired state and national counseling ethics committees, is that many complaints that come before those bodies are due to imprudence and lack of sound ethical reasoning. As mentioned earlier, the training environment is a necessary locus of instruction, supervision, and modeling of prudence and reason in dual relationship situations. Ethical sensitivity in professional life requires both the intellectual tools to formulate justifications for conduct and the disposition to do good. Counselors-in-training can learn to make informed ethical choices based on a reasoned account of the nature of the circumstance, the application of ethical principles as action guides, and the development of a course of action (Kitchener, 1984; Stadler, 1986b). Ethics coursework and practicum/internship supervision are typical opportunities for instruction and modeling in ethical decision making. These opportunities also prepare students to anticipate common ethical concerns such as child abuse reporting (Stadler, 1989) and to use ethical reasoning strategies to articulate justifications for possible courses of action. Infusion of topics of ethical concern in all aspects of the curriculum and in research projects further alerts students to the various manifestations of ethical dilemmas and the operation of ethical principles while modeling ethical sensitivity.

Ethical decisions based on application of moral principles help to answer the question, What should I do? Virtue ethics help in reflection on the question, What kind of person should I be? "A moral virtue is a fixed disposition, habit, or trait to do what is morally commendable" (Beauchamp, 1982, p. 150). Prudence is one of a group of virtues or traits of character that augment principle-based decision making. Pellegrino and Thomasma (1993) have described prudence as the "indispensable connection between cognition of the good and the disposition to seek it in particular acts" (p. 84). Prudence moves us from thought to action in the moral domain. Some (Meara, Schmidt, & Day, 1996; Pellegrino & Thomasma, 1993) believe that prudence is the defining virtue of professional moral life. Meara et al. have described prudence as "...appropriate restraint or action, deliberate reflection upon which moral action to take, an understanding of the long-range consequences of choices made, acting with due regard for one's vision of what is morally good, and a knowledge of how present circumstances relate to that good or goal" (p. 39).

Students usually enter counselor education programs with their character traits well formed. Careful selection procedures have been used to identify applicants who are best suited for the profession. If the profession is concerned about monitoring ethically troublesome dual relationships, then the virtue of prudence might be one character trait to look for in the candidate selection process. During the course of training, faculty can support, model, and habituate (Wilson, 1993) this character trait through reinforcement and demonstration of the general practice of prudence (for example, clinical prudence), not merely prudence in ethical matters. Discussions of situations that might test a student's prudence (such as crisis intervention) can augment general reflections on Who do I want to be as a counselor?

Conclusion. In an ethically congruent training environment, counselor educators and counselors-in-training are guided by a sense of mutual respect and respect for the counseling profession and for those served by the profession. We acknowledge the conflicts and complexities of dual relationships. Through the exercise of prudence and ethical reasoning, the boundaries of multiple roles and multiple relationships can be managed effectively so as to respect all those engaged in and served by the counseling profession.

Teaching Students About Boundary Issues

We agree with Stadler's contentions and believe that multiple roles will come into play in counselor education. Apart from sexual relationships with students, which are clearly unethical, a wide range of dual and multiple relationships exist that are part and parcel of the training process. Rather than lumping all these nonsexual multiple relationships with unethical sexual relationships, professional training ought to focus on teaching students how to manage situations involving multiple roles and relationships. We conclude our portion of this chapter with a look at these questions: What is the responsibility of counselor educators in teaching students about dual relationships and boundary issues? How can the issues best be raised and explored, and how can students be prepared to deal with dual relationship dilemmas?

In the ethics courses we teach, we spend considerable time discussing dual and multiple relationships. Our students show a great deal of interest in discussing the issues. Many of them have never really considered the potential risks of dual relationships, so the discussions serve to increase their awareness of potential ethical dilemmas. We examine dual and multiple relationship standards contained in the codes of ethics of the various professional organizations. We use case vignettes to introduce ethical dilemmas, frequently roleplaying a vignette and then discussing possible courses of action. Students are encouraged to think about their values as these pertain to a host of dual relationship issues. The combination of reading codes and articles, enacting case situations, participating in debates, and being challenged to defend a position typically results in an increased awareness of the pervasiveness of dual relationships. Students begin to develop a sensitivity to the subtlety and complexity of the topic.

Through careful attention to program planning and evaluation, students can be helped to increase their sensitivity to dual relationships that are unethical and harmful. Recommendations for training programs include the following:

- Programs should present literature in which the nature, causes, and consequences of dual relationships are explored.

- The ethical and clinical implications of both sexual and nonsexual dual relationships need to be reflected in virtually all clinical course-work and supervision. Real-life dilemmas that surface during students' practica and internships should be addressed in the individual and group supervision sessions that accompany them.

- When programs include a separate ethics course, ample time should be devoted to examination of dual relationship issues.

- The issue of sexual attraction should be addressed, initially in didactic course work and then in supervision throughout students' field experiences.

- In coursework containing experiential components, the relevant dual relationship issues should be specified at the outset and carefully worked through as they occur on a case-by-case basis.

- Institutions and programs within institutions need to develop clear and explicit standards regarding potential dual relationships between students and educators.

- Written, operationally defined procedures need to be developed for avoiding conflicts of interest in monitoring and enforcing institutional standards regarding dual relationships.

———————————◆———————————

Michelle Muratori presents a student perspective on boundaries in the relationship between faculty and students. She reflects on her experiences in an undergraduate human services program at one institution and in a master's program at another university, and identifies important variables in managing dual relationship questions.

Dual Relationships in Counselor Education Programs: One Student's Perspective

Michelle C. Muratori

After I graduated from an innovative undergraduate human services program that had a strong experiential focus, I traveled half way across the country to begin my graduate work in a counseling psychology program that is acclaimed for its strong clinical emphasis and comprehensive training program. Although both programs share a deep respect for clients and a reverence for the process of psychotherapy, the philosophies undergirding their approaches to training counselors are quite dissimilar. After having been exposed to both programs with their respective views on how most effectively to prepare professional counselors, I have a compelling need to reconcile some of these ideological differences so that I am able to integrate these two experiences in a way that feels coherent and meaningful. In this contribution, I limit my focus to views on dual relationships in counselor education programs.

This topic might be approached from two different angles. I could compare and contrast how the two programs approach the issue didactically and inform their students about inherent dangers and possible advantages of dual relationships. Or I could discuss how the programs have structured their courses to include or exclude components that might increase or decrease the likelihood that dual relationships will develop. Actually, these two approaches are not mutually exclusive. I have discovered that my undergraduate program, which has incorporated experiential components into its structure, also places great emphasis on examining the ethical implications of the dual relationships that may be encountered in the program. Of course, such dual relationships may be inevitable byproducts of a structure that requires students to examine facets of their personal lives and histories in order to augment their professional growth and enhance the development of their clinical skills.

For example, one of the most challenging yet rewarding courses was a group leadership course. It was comprised of an intensive weekend training workshop that often stirred up powerful personal issues, an academically oriented class that examined the theoretical and clinical aspects of leading groups, a more experiential class in which the group leaders facilitated a process-oriented self-exploration group once a week, and weekly supervision that might focus on a combination of personal and clinical material. Needless to say, with this structure, dual relationships could hardly be avoided. Although the professor did not evaluate the students on the basis of personal material they disclosed at the training workshop, and instead graded the students solely on the quality of their papers and scores on objective tests, critics may argue that it is impossible for a professor to be completely objective once he or she is aware of the personal details of a student's life. That is, a professor's perception of a student's performance on a subjective task such as a term paper could be colored by prior knowledge of the student's personal background. Although this view is plausible, it does not match my experience. The professor was adept and genuinely able to wear different hats, skilled in roles both as teacher/evaluator and as supervisor/therapeutic agent. Perhaps more importantly, he was able to make the transition between these roles. In retrospect, that seems to have been the critical factor.

It should be noted that this group course was designed so that the supervisors were not in a position to grade the students for their performance as group leaders or for their levels of self-disclosure in the experiential exercises. Thus without pressure to perform for a grade as group leaders or members, the students felt free to be "imperfect" and "real" and direct their focus toward honing their clinical skills. This group leadership experience was powerful and instrumental in my growth as a clinician.

My impression is that this program did an outstanding job of creating a safe climate in which students could freely explore the gray areas associated with the dual relationships that were inherent in the program as well as the range of dual relationships that could conceivably develop between therapists and clients. Students who are encouraged to explore these nebulous areas and who are taught to struggle with ambiguity are substantially better prepared to deal with dual relationships in an appropriate manner. I argue that encouraging the beginning student to consider all sides of the issue will lead to the development of a strong ethical sense and may even preclude ethical violations. I think beginning students need to be given credit for having the capacity to comprehend the complexities of this multifaceted issue.

The graduate program I currently attend endorses a more conservative view about dual relationships in counselor education programs. Rather than incorporate experiential exercises into the structure of the program, the program administrators seem to feel that the potential dangers in dual relationships warrant a more cautious approach to training counselors. For example, faculty members would certainly encourage trainees to seek professional help from a therapist in the community if their work with clients was triggering some unresolved personal issues. However, unlike faculty in my undergraduate program, they might deem it inappropriate to provide an experiential growth-oriented course for students. Their rationale might be that there are abundant resources in the community to facilitate students' growth and resolution of personal issues, and that an academic setting is not the most suitable environment in which to address such issues due to the hazards of dual relationships. Although I do not believe that all dual relationships have to be avoided, I do respect this program's commitment to maintaining solid boundaries. Because I sense that the program's faculty members might consider it problematic or unprofessional to adopt a format for the program that includes experiential groups or similar types of experiences in the curriculum, I think they are wise to avoid such a format. Once again, I stress the importance of counselor educators being aware of their capacity and degree of willingness to wear several hats at once. If faculty are not oriented in this way, then I believe they are behaving ethically by refusing to engage in such practices. If a program is deeply anchored in the belief that students should not disclose personal information to faculty members and that faculty members should not be privy to such material, then it will be a mistake to introduce a more experiential component without the structure to support it. It seems that such an experience will be doomed to failure, and for students, participation will only reinforce the message that self-disclosure is dangerous and should be avoided. Students would surely lose faith in a program that offered a course that proved to be destructive to them, and these negative feelings could reverberate outward to the profession at large.

Counselor educators, like therapists, need to be mindful of the facts that their roles are inherently powerful and that they are in a position to abuse that power. Just as clients tend to imbue their therapists with omnipotence, a parallel process occurs between counselor trainees and their professors. With this in mind, it is important that counselor educators consider the ramifications of entering into dual relationships with students. I believe there are instances in which dual relationships in counselor education programs can be productive without being harmful. However, the potential pitfalls should not be glossed over. In the final analysis, counselor educators must feel comfortable with the choices they make regarding this issue. Because faculty members typically have more than one function, role blending does seem inevitable. However, it is crucial that no dual relationship be developed at the student's expense.

Conclusion

In concluding this chapter, we are reminded that actions speak louder than words, and that counselor trainees learn by observing the conduct of their professional role models. Therefore, it behooves counselor educators to model ethical *behavior*, including maintaining clear boundaries and being open to discussing any potential problems that might arise. One key to fostering ethical management of dual relationships also lies in the *awareness* of counselor educators. If we are unaware of the potential problems, we are likely to find ourselves involved in relationships that are harmful both to student and to professor. Another key lies in carefully and systematically teaching our students about the dual relationships and potential dual relationships that they may encounter while they are our students and later as practitioners. If we—and our students—are clearly aware of the potential for conflicts of interest, for exploitation, or for misusing power, then these situations are much less likely to occur.

5

Issues in Supervision and Consultation

In previous chapters we have seen how some subtle and complex boundary issues can emerge in the dyadic relationships between counselor and client and between faculty member and student. These issues can be even more complicated when a relationship is tripartite, as in the relationship among supervisor, supervisee, and client, or among consultant, consultee, and client or client system. In this chapter, we first explore multiple roles and relationships in supervision, and guest contributor L. DiAnne Borders adds a thoughtful perspective. We then look at issues in consultation, with input from guest contributor A. Michael Dougherty.

SUPERVISION

Supervisors play a critical role in helping counselors-in-training and novice counselors to understand and manage dual relationships. Students may learn about dual relationships during their academic course work, but it is during their internships and other field experiences that they come face to face with the issues. Slimp and Burian (1994) believed it is vital that the professionals responsible for supervising counselors-in-training take the initiative in examining dual relationship concerns, so that novice practitioners are prepared to respond appropriately when such relationships begin to develop not only during internship but throughout their professional lives.

There is an inherent duality in the supervisory relationship, and the complexity of the supervisory role can create some unique boundary issues. In this section of the chapter, we review some of the literature on these issues, share our own views, and present the guest contribution of L. DiAnne Borders. Questions that guide our discussion include

- What guidance do codes of ethics and specialty guidelines offer supervisors?

- How prevalent is sexual contact in the supervisory relationship and what are its effects?

- What are the ethical issues in social and business relationships between supervisors and supervisees?

- How can supervision include exploration of the supervisee's personal issues as well as cases and remain within ethical boundaries? What is the appropriate balance for supervisors between attending to the professional development and the personal development of the supervisee?

- How can informed consent procedures help to prevent problematic dual relationships?

- How can supervisor countertransference best be dealt with in supervision?

- What are the ethical and legal ramifications when the supervisee does not perform competently? How can this create role conflicts for the supervisor?

Ethics Codes and Guidelines

Most of the standards in the ACA Code of Ethics that address faculty-student relationship boundaries apply equally to the supervisor-supervisee relationship. These standards are found in the section on teaching, training, and supervision, and have been discussed in the previous chapter. Here we briefly review them as they apply to the supervisory relationship. We also highlight standards in the ACES *Ethical Guidelines for Counseling Supervisors* (1993) that clarify and give more specific guidance regarding multiple relationships and relationship boundaries in supervision.

According to the ACA Code of Ethics, it is the responsibility of the supervisor to define and maintain professional and social relationship boundaries clearly with supervisees. Supervisors are aware of the power differential in the relationship, and explain to supervisees how this differential creates a potential for exploitation. The ACES Ethical Guidelines state that

- Supervisors should not engage in any form of social contact or interaction which would compromise the supervisor-supervisee relationship. Dual relationships with supervisees that might impair the supervisor's objectivity and professional judgment should be avoided and/or the supervisory relationship terminated. (2.10)

- Supervisors who have multiple roles with supervisees should minimize potential conflicts. When supervisors function in more than one role (such as teacher, clinical supervisor, and administrative supervisor), the roles should be divided among several supervisors when possible.

When this is not possible, it is important carefully to explain to the supervisee the expectations and responsibilities associated with each supervisory role. (2.09)

The ACA Code of Ethics notes that, although supervisors have the responsibility to help supervisees understand how their personal issues may interfere with working effectively with clients, it is not appropriate for supervisors to change the supervisory relationship into a counseling relationship. If supervisees request personal counseling, the supervisor provides them with appropriate referrals. The ACES Ethical Guidelines are in agreement and clarify the extent to which personal issues should be addressed in supervision:

• Supervisors should not establish a psychotherapeutic relationship as a substitute for supervision. Personal issues should be addressed in supervision only in terms of the impact of these issues on clients and on professional functioning. (2.11)

The ACA Code of Ethics and the ACES Ethical Guidelines both acknowledge that supervisors, through ongoing evaluation and appraisal, are aware of limitations or impairment of supervisees that might interfere with their performance. They assist supervisees to improve, but when supervisees are unable to provide competent services, supervisors do not endorse them for completion of a training program or for certification, licensure, or employment.

According to the ACA Code of Ethics, when supervisors conduct training experiences that require supervisee self-growth or self-disclosure, they provide safeguards so that supervisees are aware of the ramifications their self-disclosures may have on supervisors who also have ethical obligations to the profession. The ACES Ethical Guidelines recommend that supervisors should take care to eliminate or minimize potential role conflicts. The ACES document also states that when a supervisor recommends that a supervisee participate in remedial activities involving personal growth or self-disclosure, the supervisor should not be the direct provider of these activities.

The ACA Code of Ethics prohibits supervisors from accepting close relatives as their supervisees. Also prohibited are performing the roles of both site supervisor and training program supervisor for a student or supervisee, and the acceptance of any form of remuneration from a site for placing a supervisee at that site (Standard F.2.h.).

Two additional standards found in the ACA Code of Ethics address the supervision of supervision and highlight its multilayered nature. Standard F.1.f. requires that doctoral students who supervise the practicum or internship experiences of master's students are themselves adequately supervised as they learn these new skills. Standard F.2.e. addresses the need to ensure that the rights of peers are not compromised when supervisees provide clinical supervision for their peers—again requiring that the novice supervisor be carefully supervised.

The counselor licensure movement has produced another group of supervisors: those who work with licensure applicants (Borders, Cashwell, & Rotter, 1995). Although only a few states (e.g., Louisiana, South Carolina, Texas) now require that individuals be licensed or qualified as supervisors in addition to their licensure as counselors, we expect that the number of states with such requirements will grow. Training in supervision for master's level counselors who are already in practice will most likely involve course work that involves the participants in conducting practice sessions to develop their supervisory skills. This practice will in turn need to be supervised by the course instructor. The complexity of managing boundary issues can be challenging when the relationship is tripartite, involving a client, supervisee, and supervisor. When relationships involve clients, a supervisee, a novice supervisor, and the supervisor of the supervisor, sorting out the roles and responsibilities can be a daunting task.

Sexual Dual Relationships in Supervision

Of course, if a sexual relationship becomes a part of the supervisory relationship, this confounds the entire process. Both the ACA Code of Ethics and the ACES Ethical Guidelines state clearly that sexual contact between supervisors and supervisees is forbidden. There seems to be a clear consensus of beliefs about sexual relationships between supervisors and supervisees. Bowman et al. (1995) presented to faculty and graduate students in CACREP-accredited programs a series of scenarios, one of which depicted a romantic relationship while the professor was supervising the student's practicum. All faculty and 99% of the students believed this was unethical.

As we have noted in previous chapters, actual prevalence of sexual misconduct is difficult to determine. Miller and Larrabee (1995) surveyed female ACES members, 6% of whom reported sexual experiences with educators or supervisors during their graduate training. Over half of the sexual contacts were with course instructors, and only 28% were with clinical supervisors. A similar ratio was found for sexual advances. Miller and Larrabee cautioned that findings on perceptions of coercion imply that sexual involvements with supervisees are detrimental.

The Boundary Between Counseling and Supervision

Supervisors play multiple roles in the supervision process, performing their functions in the role of teacher, counselor, or consultant as appropriate. Although they have a responsibility to clarify their roles, the boundaries are not always clear.

Several of the focus questions that we asked at the beginning of this chapter are so interrelated that they cannot be discussed separately. Is it ever appropriate to integrate both counseling and supervision in the same relationship? What are the problems involved in blending the two roles? How can supervision include exploration of the supervisee's personal issues as well as cases? The following vignette illustrates how some of these issues may arise:

Andrew is a counselor educator and supervisor who regularly teaches an internship seminar. Andrew makes it clear to students at the initial class meeting that he conducts his seminar using a group supervision format that focuses on the counselor as a person. He informs his students that "The main emphasis will be on your own dynamics and reactions to your clients—not on an analysis of your clients, counseling skills and techniques, or case management strategies. Of course, you will learn various alternatives for working with your clients, but our primary concern will be on how your attitudes and behaviors may be influencing your clients. Thus you will be expected to examine your needs, motivations, and most of all your potential sources of countertransference in these group supervision sessions."

Andrew's chairperson questions the appropriateness of his style of teaching the seminar. Other instructors focus on teaching specific skills and interventions and do a great deal of case management work. The chairperson thinks that Andrew is opening himself to the possibility of blurring his role as an educator by focusing on the personal dimensions of his supervisees. She suggests that he recommend to his students that they seek personal counseling apart from the program and that he focus his course more on skill development.

In his defense, Andrew claims that he is not conducting group therapy, but rather that he is asking his students to look at how their own dynamics influence their interventions with their clients. He deals with personal problems of his supervisees only to the extent that these problems appear to be influencing their work. He sees it as his job to help them become aware of the ways that they are impacting their clients.

Do you think that Andrew's chairperson has legitimate reasons for her concern that he is getting involved as both educator and therapist with his supervisees? What do you think of Andrew's approach to group supervision? What do you see as the appropriate balance between teaching supervisees about their own dynamics and the dynamics of their clients? What is the balance between focusing on supervisee self-awareness and teaching skills? What are some potential benefits and risks to Andrew's supervisees? Would you want to be a student in the class?

Although a dual relationship occurs when a supervisor becomes the supervisee's counselor, the distinction between the therapeutic aspect of the supervisor's role and the role of the counselor is not well defined (Whiston & Emerson, 1989). It can be difficult to determine when a supervisory relationship has become a counseling relationship. When supervisees have personal problems, supervisors may be tempted to counsel them. However, because the primary goal of supervision is to protect the welfare of the client, the personal growth of the supervisee cannot become the primary focus of supervision. When supervisors agree to counsel their supervisees, these dual relationships model dangerously inappropriate behavior for supervisees, who may later perpetuate the behavior when they become supervisors themselves (Tyler & Tyler, 1994). If supervisors overextend the boundaries of supervision into a therapeutic relationship, there is the potential that the supervisor's objectivity will be impaired and that the supervisee will be inhibited from making full use of the supervision process. It has been argued that, because of the power differential and evaluative components in the relationship, supervisees cannot give true informed consent to a therapeutic relationship with their supervisor (Miller & Larrabee, 1995; Sherry, 1991). Any therapy is likely to be compromised because supervisees will be concerned that their self-disclosures will negatively impact their evaluations. Instead of entering into a counseling relationship with a supervisee, the supervisor should make a referral to another professional.

When a supervisor recommends personal counseling for a supervisee, this may infuse an emotionally charged issue into the relationship. The supervisee may feel threatened and believe he or she has been judged to be incompetent. The supervisory relationship could become strained, and the supervisee might be less open about his or her own experiencing in discussing cases with the supervisor. Wise, Lowery, and Silverglade (1989) have noted that whether the student receives the suggestion of personal counseling as a criticism or as a helpful aspect of supervision depends on the supervisor's tact, attitude, and timing in making the recommendation.

> If you are a supervisor and were faced with the need to recommend counseling for a supervisee, how might you go about it? What factors might you consider in making your recommendation, and what might you tell the supervisee?
>
> If you are a supervisee, how do you think you would react if your supervisor made such a recommendation to you? Might this change the nature of the supervisory relationship, from your perspective?

From our perspective, effective supervision includes a focus on the impact of the counselor on the counseling process. When supervision focuses exclusively on client cases or problem-solving strategies for working with clients, some opportunities for positive experiences are lost. The results of a study by Sumerel and Borders (1996) seem to indicate that a supervisor who is open to discussing personal issues with supervisees in an appropriate manner does not necessarily affect the supervisor-supervisee relationship negatively. Ladany and Friedlander (1995) found that the stronger the emotional bond between supervisor and supervisee, the less role conflict experienced by the supervisee. Usher and Borders (1993) found that counselors preferred a supervisor who is collegial and relationship oriented over one who is task oriented.

Supervision can be useful in helping students become aware of personal limitations or unresolved problems that intrude into effective helping. However, there is a difference between helping students identify and clarify those concerns they need to explore versus converting supervision into an in-depth personal therapy session. For instance, if a student becomes aware of an unresolved issue with his mother that is being played out in his counseling sessions with "motherly" women, it is appropriate to focus on how his personal limitations are blocking effective counseling, but it is not appropriate to abandon the supervisory focus for a therapy experience. In such cases, students will hopefully be encouraged to find a resource where they can get the therapy they need for themselves personally and professionally.

> Distinguishing where the appropriate boundary lies between supervision and counseling can be difficult. If you are a counseling supervisor, where do you stand on these issues? Do you believe that the supervisory and counseling roles are separable? Or do you think that some role blending is inevitable? How might you defend your position if a colleague challenged your views?
>
> If you are a graduate student working under supervision, or a counselor working under supervision toward your licensure or certification, what do you think about these issues? Where do you want your supervisor to draw the line in dealing with any personal concerns you may be facing?

Social and Business Relationships With Supervisees

Another boundary issue concerns social relationships. Stoltenberg and Delworth (1987) have suggested that friendships and social relationships between supervisors and supervisees should be avoided when possible. They have recommended that if such relationships are entered into, possible ramifications should be openly explored. Hararr, VandeCreek, and Knapp (1990) have admitted that it is inevitable that supervisors will encounter trainees in social settings and community activities. They advised that a supervisor need not avoid supervisees on such occasions, unless the supervisor believes the professional relationship will be compromised. However, they did caution against attempting to supervise relatives, spouses, friends, former clients, or others with whom they might find it difficult to be candid about performance.

It can be tempting to relax the boundaries as supervisees near completion of their training programs or their postmaster's supervision. As supervisees near the end of their training, interactions with their supervisors often take on a collegial tone, and the social relationships that might develop out of a sense of collegiality and common interests may help to mark the supervisee's transition to becoming a professional peer. Nonetheless, Slimp and Burian (1994) noted that the supervisor is still in a position to evaluate supervisees and to recommend them for future employment, and that a social relationship could compromise the supervisor's ability to make an objective evaluation.

Some relaxing of boundaries may be both inevitable and appropriate, however. There is a difference between client-counselor and supervisee-supervisor relationships in considering postprofessional relationships. Some have argued that "once a client, always a client," but that claim is not made about supervisees. Our supervisees evolve into our professional colleagues. It is important to remember, though, that the perception of change in role relationships does not necessarily accompany the fact of the change. The end of formal supervision does not automatically mean that a supervisee perceives that he or she is now on equal footing with the former supervisor.

Regarding business relationships with supervisees, Slimp and Burian (1994) believed it is not uncommon for interns in field placements to be hired as staff members' employees. They cited examples ranging from baby sitting to assisting staff members in research or consulting activities, and noted that it could be quite difficult for an intern to resist staff members' requests for paid services. Such situations place the supervisee in double jeopardy, and if the baby sitting, research, or consulting activities do not go well, the negative consequences are compounded. Trust, respect, and a sense of safety are damaged; the reputations of both individuals may be diminished if the problems come to light; the quality of training is likely to be affected; and the staff member's evaluation of the supervisee will almost certainly be influenced. Additionally, others within the training agency are affected because fellow interns may feel left out of what they perceive to be preferential treatment, and staff members may become fractionalized as they develop opinions about the relationship. Such dual relationships have implications for the profession, as well, because supervisees who learn that such relationships are acceptable may engage in them with their clients. For all these reasons, Slimp and Burian recommended that these types of relationships be avoided.

It seems evident, from our discussion to this point, that some boundaries in the super-
visory relationship are clearly demarcated. Supervisors should not enter into sexual or
romantic relationships with their supervisees, supervision should not be converted into
therapy, and business relationships with supervisees should be avoided. There are, howev-
er, some much more subtle boundary issues in supervision. L. DiAnne Borders offers a
thoughtful personal perspective on these issues.

Subtle Boundary Issues in Supervision

L. DiAnne Borders

Supervisors should not provide counseling for their supervisees, nor should they have intimate and/or sexual relationships with them. There seems to be widespread consensus on these two "rules" in ethical standards (e.g., ACA Code of Ethics, 1995; ACES Ethical Guidelines, 1995), in the supervision literature, and in the practical common knowledge of practitioners. These same resources, however, indicate that supervisors should avoid other roles and interactions with supervisees that could inhibit their ability to provide adequate supervision. Although most professionals probably will not argue with this statement per se, its interpretation and application in everyday supervision sessions leave many of us questioning and wondering, particularly because dual if not multiple roles are inherent in the supervisory position.

My primary dilemmas come in my interactions with doctoral students. In my role as a counselor educator, I am required to teach and advise all of the doctoral students I supervise. Many serve as graduate assistants in some capacity under my direction. As doctoral chair, I also directly oversee the program and dissertation work of a number of them, and am able to serve in other mentoring roles for some (e.g., coauthor, copresenter). Many of these other responsibilities and roles are much longer term than the one or two semesters that I supervise the students' counseling or supervision work. We get to know each others' work styles, prefer- ences, and goals, and see each other's highs and lows over time. We discover our particular relationship dynamics and figure out how we best work together.

As a result, my supervision of doctoral students is colored by my other knowl- edge of them and my responsibilities for them. On the positive side, I some- times can predict those situations in which the student will need extra help, and often I already have some sense of how feedback is most easily heard. In addi- tion, the context of the supervisory relationship frequently provides the needed vehicle for bringing to light issues that I need to address with a student. There are negative consequences also, however. Recently, for example, I did not push an observation as far as I could (or should) have because I thought it would be too much on top of the student's anxiety and deadlines related to her disserta- tion. She graduated without the assumed benefit of this particular feedback.

My broader knowledge of and interactions with these students also often brings to light how our personal and interpersonal dynamics can or do affect our supervisory work together. There is the session in which I realized this was the third time in 1 week that I had urged a supervisee to urge his client to break free of constraints, act outside the norm, and/or explore an untapped aspect of self. Was this perhaps a theme of my own, I realized I must ask, rather than some coincidence of supervisee (or client) issues? And there are those times that I realize I am allowing too much supervision time to be spent in philosophical discussions that the supervisee and I enjoy, or when I am aware of how much I rely on a supervisee's sense of humor (being overly prone to seriousness myself), both in and outside of our supervision sessions. With other supervisees, I must refuse to stand on the pedestal, even though they need me (or any other supervisor) to be there, but wonder if I might so quickly recognize the dynamics and respond the same way if it was one of those times in my life when I needed to be appreciated or admired. Such dynamics challenge the boundaries of the supervisory relationship, even though they also may enrich it at times. Nevertheless, I struggle with how to be human without being overly familiar or inappropriately self-revealing.

It could be easy to become good friends with many of my supervisees. We have similar interests, they are often good cooks, and we have some understanding of each other's professional pressures and goals. Over the years, however, I have learned to be cautious. Social relationships and friendships tend to interfere with two priorities: to be consistent and fair with all supervisees, and to feel free to say whatever I need to say in supervision. The more relaxed atmospheres created by sharing a good meal or other social event seem to blur the boundaries for both supervisor and supervisee. I find it somewhat uncomfortable to confront a supervisee shortly after we have been in each other's homes, and I have seen confusion on a supervisee's face when I did confront. I have heard supervisees, my own and others, wonder what academic benefits a peer might be getting because of his or her social relationship with a supervisor. In addition, certainly my experiences on the ACA Ethics Committee have made me more sensitive to the potential problems in even well-intentioned acts of friendship. As co-chair of the Ethics Committee, I learned details of clear abuses of power, often rationalized as a "natural" outgrowth of the multiple roles a counselor educator and supervisor plays with students, and I tried to sort out what seemed to be supervisees' unfortunate misunderstandings of a supervisor's benign overtures of friendship and support.

As a result, I more and more have limited my social encounters with students to officially sanctioned events (such as departmental picnics) and more frequently address these issues up front with supervisees (and students in similar roles). As the ethical guidelines make clear, it is always *my* responsibility to maintain appropriate boundaries and monitor dual or multiple roles with supervisees and students. Given the power differential, which exists in whatever relationships we have with students, supervisees are at a great disadvantage in terms of bringing to my attention that they feel uncomfortable or unsure about such issues.

Clearly, such issues need to be addressed in supervisor training programs. In fact, doctoral students often encounter boundary and multiple role issues *before* they graduate. "I just realized," a recent note from one student indicated, "that I'm in the same class with one of my supervisees. Do we need to do something about this?" Recognition of potential problems is a critical first step, to be followed by discussions of how to handle the situation, thus providing an important learning opportunity for supervisees and their peers. I can have hope that they will recognize similar dilemmas in the future.

The many gray areas and potential hazards also suggest to me that supervisors always have need of supervision and/or consultation regarding their work with supervisees. The need will vary not only by supervisee but also by the relevant circumstances in a supervisor's life. We are more vulnerable in terms of our own needs and motivations at various points in time. Just as we seek additional monitoring of our work with clients during these times, we also must consider how our circumstances and personalities may impact the supervision process.

Interestingly, there is very little research on the gray areas and more subtle issues regarding boundaries and multiple roles presented in this chapter. Even less attention has been given to the *supervisor's* dynamics alluded to here. This may be because typically the supervisors are conducting the research and/or because the relevant variables are difficult to identify, let alone operationalize. We should not continue to pretend, however, that we become objective, neutral supervisors simply via having earned a diploma.

Although I have written primarily about my boundary and role confusion with doctoral students, I have experienced similar issues with master's level students. I would be surprised if similar issues were not found in supervisory relationships in employment settings, and for private practitioners working with counselor licensure applicants. Guidelines for assessing these situations and determining how to respond would be helpful for all, so that we can avoid problematic boundary violations and, when necessary, appropriately negotiate how to handle such situations.

Decision-Making Models for Supervisors

Several writers have offered models to assist supervisors in working though the supervision process with their boundaries intact. Wise et al. (1989) have suggested a stage-oriented approach. In the *self-focus* stage, supervisees begin to see clients but lack knowledge and experience. Supervision is most helpful when it concentrates on skill development, clarifying concerns and providing structure. In the *client focus* stage, supervisees have increased interaction with clients, and they typically increase their initiative and become less dependent on their supervisors. The supervisor continues to concentrate on skill development and case conceptualization. Personal counseling might be recommended only if the supervisee remains too dependent on the supervisor or is not making adequate progress due to personal issues. In the *interpersonal focus* stage, supervisees become more comfortable with their skills and shift their focus from issues of competence to issues of self-awareness. This may be the most appropriate time to recommend personal counseling to promote supervisee openness and awareness. In the final *professional focus* stage, supervisees have begun to develop a therapeutic personality and a sense of professional identity. A consultation model of supervision is most appropriate, and personal counseling should be recommended only to deal with "blind spots" in specific areas or life stressors that are impeding performance.

Whiston and Emerson (1989) have taken a somewhat different approach. They suggested that Egan's (1994) three-stage model can provide a practical method for distinguishing between supervising and counseling. They believed that supervisors should limit their work to Egan's first stage of exploring and clarifying a supervisee's personal problems when those problems are impeding his or her work. After the supervisor has identified the personal issues, the supervisee then has the responsibility for resolving them. If the supervision process moves into Egan's second and third stages—establishing goals and taking action regarding the personal problem—supervision then becomes counseling and should be provided by an independent counselor rather than the supervisor.

Informed Consent in Supervision

One way to clarify the multiple roles of supervisors is to provide a written informed consent document that can be given to all supervisees at the outset of the relationship. If there is a frank discussion at the beginning about the mutual responsibilities of supervisors and supervisees, conflicts are less likely to develop at a later time. As a part of the informed consent discussion, supervisors can explain that supervision is a complex process and that supervisors are required to function in multiple roles. They can take this opportunity to be clear from the outset that personal issues might be activated in supervision, and that if these issues affect performance, the supervisee will be asked to work them through with another professional (Bernard & Goodyear, 1992). The risks and safeguards of multiple relationships can be explored. This not only can lead to more effective supervision sessions, but it can also model the importance of informed consent in therapy. Supervisees can learn firsthand how to convey information to their clients that will enable them to become active partners in the therapeutic process.

The ACES Ethical Guidelines mandate that informed consent should be a basic part of the supervisory relationship. Ladany and Friedlander (1995) found that supervisees experienced less role ambiguity when their supervisors made expectations clear. McCarthy et al. (1995) contended that informed consent should be clearly articulated through written documents and a discussion between the supervisor and supervisee. Accountability can be increased by having a written contractual agreement for supervision. When expectations are discussed and clarified from the beginning of a supervisory relationship, the relationship is likely to be enhanced and quality client care will be promoted. McCarthy and her colleagues recommended that the contract include statements concerning ethical and legal parameters of the supervisor-supervisee relationship. Topics should include dual relationship issues, structuring of the supervisory relationship, limits to confidentiality, and professional guidelines for ethical treatment of clients.

Countertransference Issues

Supervisor countertransference is a phenomenon that is bound to occur in some supervisory relationships, when supervisors have intense reactions to certain supervisees. We hope that supervisors monitor their countertransference, and that when these issues arise they seek their own supervision, or at least consult regularly with colleagues. To help ensure that evaluation remains fair, Bernard and Goodyear (1992) have recommended getting a second opinion about a supervisee's abilities.

Countertransference does not have to be viewed negatively. Indeed, by monitoring our countertransference in the supervisory process, we can learn some important lessons about supervisees. Our reactions to supervisees can tell us something about them as well as ourselves. We suggest that supervisor countertransference be dealt with in a manner similar to therapist countertransference. First, it is important to be aware of our countertransference reactions. It is crucial that we understand our needs and how they may be triggered by certain supervisee behaviors. This is especially true when a supervisor finds himself or herself sexually attracted to a certain type of supervisee. What is crucial is that supervisors do not exploit supervisees for the purpose of satisfying their needs and that they do not misuse their power over supervisees. When a supervisor has unmet needs that interfere with effective supervision, the supervisee is placed in a difficult position. As supervisors, it is important that we recognize our countertransference issues and seek consultation. We also have an obligation to take further measures to protect our supervisees when we are unable to successfully resolve our issues. These might include seeking personal therapy, referring the supervisee to another supervisor, or inviting a colleague to cosupervise sessions if the supervisee agrees to this.

Supervisee Incompetence: Ethical and Legal Considerations

Supervisors are both ethically and legally responsible for the actions of those they are supervising. For example, if a client of a supervisee commits suicide, the supervisor is likely to be more vulnerable than the supervisee from a legal standpoint. The reality of the fact that supervisors are responsible for all of the cases of their supervisees does place special pressures on the supervisor that could create a conflict. If the supervisor becomes aware that the supervisee lacks basic relationship skills or lacks personal maturity, what is he or she to do? Is it appropriate to bring this to the attention of the faculty? A determination must be made regarding whether the supervisee is personally qualified to remain in the training program. The legal ramifications of the supervisor's responsibilities when the supervisee is not functioning competently underscore the importance of clearly defining the nature of the supervisory relationship from the outset. Students should know about the consequences of not competently fulfilling their contracts. To be sure, supervisors have a duty to do what is in the best interest of the supervisee, yet they also have a responsibility to the welfare of the clients who are being seen by the supervisee. This matter deserves full discussion at the outset of the supervisory relationship.

CONSULTATION

Consultation, like supervision, is a complex, tripartite process. It involves at least three parties: a consultant, a consultee, and a client system. The client system can consist of an individual, a group, an organization, or a community. Consultation has been defined as "a process in which a human services professional assists a consultee with a work-related problem with a client system, with the goal of helping both the consultee and the client system in some specified way" (Dougherty, 1995, p. 9).

Although counselors are often the service providers for consultation, consultation is not the same as counseling. In fact, consultation deals exclusively with the consultee's work-related problems, and thus by definition does not deal with the personal concerns of the consultee. Nevertheless, in actual practice it can be difficult to determine where to draw the line between consultation and counseling. When this line is crossed, a dual relationship is created. Dual role conflicts also occur when a consultant functions as a supervisor to a consultee. Some of the questions that consultants encounter in their work are

- What conflicts occur when a consultant maintains two professional roles in the consultation relationship, such as counselor and consultant, or supervisor and consultant?

- How can consultants set clear boundaries to distinguish between work-related and personal concerns of their consultees?

- How can consultants best avoid potential role conflicts?

Role conflicts often occur when a consultant blurs the boundaries between the professional and personal concerns of the consultee. The following example illustrates how this can occur.

> Willene contracts with a community mental health agency to provide consultation for volunteers who work with people who are dying and their family members. Willene has been hired as a consultant by the agency director to teach people basic helping skills (listening, attending, and some crisis intervention strategies). Willene is working with these volunteers as a group, and many of the participants express a need to talk about how they are affected personally by working with those who are dying. Their work is opening up feelings of helplessness, fears of dying, and unfinished business with grieving their own losses. Willene decides that it seems more important to attend to the needs being expressed by the volunteers than to focus on teaching them helping skills. Her interactions with the volunteers focus more and more on helping them explore their personal issues, and only secondarily on teaching skills.

To what extent to you think that Willene's shift in focus can be supported? On what basis? What potential dual relationship issues do you see in this situation?

Conflicts can occur when a consultant maintains two professional roles in the consultation relationship, such as serving as both counselor and consultant or both supervisor and consultant. A. Michael Dougherty presents a rationale for avoiding these types of dual relationships.

Dual Role Conflicts in Consultation

A. Michael Dougherty

Do the conflicts that might occur when a consultant maintains two profession-al roles in the consultation relationship outweigh the benefits that serving in the two roles may create? I believe that counselors should be extremely cautious before they engage in two professional roles in the consultation relationship. As a rule of thumb, counselors should take a conservative stance and avoid main-taining multiple professional roles with their consultees. My rationale for this stance includes seven considerations.

First, the complexity of the consultation process has contributed to disagree-ment among authorities in the field as to the boundaries of the consultant's role. This disagreement makes it difficult to ascertain what is ethical or unethi-cal in many situations surrounding consultation, including dual relationships. Because of its tripartite nature, the consultation relationship is more complex than the counseling relationship, and an additional professional role only increases the complexity of an already intricate process. For example, when does the feedback of consultation become the evaluation of supervision? When does acknowledgement of the negative emotions of a consultee cross the boundary into counseling concerning those emotions?

Second, there is disagreement in the field concerning the definition of con-sultation, which makes it difficult to define the appropriate roles the consultant can assume during the consultation relationship. An additional professional role only complicates these difficulties. For example, how does a consultant dif-ferentiate a work-related from a personal concern of a consultee and then go about contracting to consult regarding the work-related concern and counsel regarding a personal concern? Because work-related and personal concerns are typically intricately intertwined and consultation is so difficult to define, it is best to limit contact with the consultee to one professional role.

Third, counselors, when they consult, should be wary of multiple roles that might create conflicts of interest that could in turn reduce the efficacy of the consultant role. Consultants should not allow themselves to be drawn into any roles that are incompatible with their stated purposes and contract. Consultants should decline to take on additional roles when these roles reduce freedom of expression or objectivity, or limit the consultant's commitment to the consultee organization. By engaging in dual relationships when consulting, counselors may easily jeopardize their commitment to the consultee organization. For example, when a consultant takes on the additional role of supervisor, the con-sultant may be placed in the position of being expected to share information with parties-at-interest about a supervisee and yet maintain the confidentiality of the consulting relationship because the supervisee is also a consultee. Consider the following situation:

As a consultant, you agree to supervise John, who is also your consultee. In a meeting, John's immediate superior asks you for some information to be used in his annual evaluation. As both a consultant and supervisor you have noticed some professional skill deficits in John and have been working with him to upgrade his skills.

What kind of information could you share as a supervisor without breaking your obligation to maintain the confidentiality of the consulting relationship? The level of difficulty in answering this question suggests that professional dual relationships involve significant risk in terms of conflicts of interest.

Fourth, consultants need to guard against putting the consultee in interrole conflict in which two roles cause contradictory expectations about a given behavior. For example, consultation focuses on work-related concerns, and counseling focuses on personal concerns. Because it is difficult to differentiate these two foci, it is best to keep the expectations as simple as possible so that the consultee will not confuse the two relationships and bring up personal issues during consultation and work-related ones during counseling.

Fifth, the training of counselors conditions them to move naturally toward affective concerns and personal problems, and it is hard to turn off this tendency in other types of relationships such as consultation. This tendency can be particularly dangerous if the counselor, when consulting, determines that the locus of the work-related concern lies more in the personal issues of the consultee than in the client system itself. Further, it is easy to move toward counseling consultees when they talk about the anxiety they are experiencing in a work-related problem. Counselors might, therefore, have a tendency to want to offer counseling services to a consultee based on the perception that the consultee will benefit both personally and professionally from such an additional relationship. Focusing on the emotional needs and concerns of consultees, however, breaks the peer relationship inherent in consultation and should therefore be avoided. Consultants should remember that referring the consultee for counseling is typically an option.

Sixth, the consultee may have an obligation to his or her organization not to use consultation for personal purposes because the organization has provided consultation services for professional, not personal, growth. Further, if the consultant agrees to provide counseling and this is kept private, the consultee might wonder later what other kinds of "cheating" the consultant might do (e.g., breaking confidentiality). Consequently, dual relationships, if not approved by the consultee organization, may well raise some issues regarding the professional behavior of the consultant and consultee alike.

Seventh, if the consultant simultaneously engages in consulting and counseling roles with a consultee, word may get out that the consultant is "a great counselor." Many prospective consultees who have work-related concerns may avoid seeking consultation because they are concerned that the consultant will try to counsel them on a personal level.

In summary, professional dual relationships are best avoided whenever possible when consulting. They make a complex process and relationship even more complex. The additional weight of another relationship makes it more difficult for the consultant and consultee to conduct their business of assisting the client system in being more effective.

CONCLUSIONS

In this chapter, we have highlighted the implicit duality that exists in the supervisor- supervisee relationship and have noted the difficulties in determining where the boundary lies between supervision and counseling. Because supervision involves a tripartite relationship among supervisor, supervisee, and clients of the supervisee, supervisors have multiple loyalties. They have obligations not only to the supervisee but also to the clients of the supervisee, the supervisee's employer, and ultimately to the profession. When these loyalties conflict, supervisors are confronted with difficult decisions. Supervisors play a vital role as gatekeepers to the profession.

Although it is not appropriate for supervisors to function as therapists for their supervisees, we contend that good supervision is therapeutic in the sense that the supervisory process involves dealing with the supervisee's personal limitations, blind spots, and impairments so that clients are not harmed. Informed consent is crucial in supervision. Supervisees are owed the same kinds of explanations as are clients about the potential problems involved in dual relationships.

We have also explored the conflicts that can occur when a consultant attempts to function in the dual role of consultant and counselor or consultant and supervisor. The dual role of consultant/supervisor should be avoided because supervision involves evaluation and thus violates the peer nature of the consultation relationship. Serving as both consultant and counselor is also to be avoided because "counseling contaminates the consultation relationship" (Dougherty, 1995, p. 256), which should focus on work-related concerns. When a consultant determines that a problem resides more in the personal concerns of a consultee than in the client or client system, the consultant should refer the consultee.

6 Preparation of Group Counselors

This chapter focuses specifically on the training of group counselors. We have devoted a separate chapter to this topic because there is controversy regarding how group counseling courses should be taught. At the heart of the controversy is the question of how to manage dual relationships that may occur in experiential training.

Most group work educators agree that there is a need for an experiential component in a group counseling course to assist students in acquiring the skills they need to function as effective group leaders. It is common practice to combine the didactic and experiential aspects of learning in a single course. Yet there does not appear to be clear agreement about the goals for these experiences or how students should be evaluated. Faculty who teach group courses often function in multiple roles. This raises the issue of potential dual relationships because these instructors often include an experiential dimension that focuses on self-awareness and self-exploration.

Questions addressed in this chapter include

- What guidelines are provided by the ACA Code of Ethics regarding dual relationships with respect to training group leaders?

- How can students' rights to privacy be protected in experiential course work involving self-disclosure?

- What are the best methods for teaching group counseling courses?

- How can group counseling skills best be evaluated?

- How can faculty model the management of dual relationships in the training of group leaders?

There are diverse viewpoints on the most ethical and effective ways to train group counselors. Two guest contributors present their views. Holly Forester-Miller takes the position that counselor educators have an ethical obligation to require students to participate in a group counseling experience. Rod Merta summarizes research that he and his colleagues have conducted on approaches to teaching group counseling courses and suggests that counselor educators should model the management of dual relationships by providing safeguards in the training process.

Combining Experiential and Didactic Approaches

A controversial ethical issue in the preparation of group workers involves the common practice of combining experiential and didactic methods in training group leaders. Merta, Wolfgang, and McNeil (1993) found that a large majority of counselor educators continue to use the experiential group in preparing group counselors. There is considerable diversity in the training models and safeguards that can be employed. We agree with writers who assert that an experiential component is essential in the teaching of group counseling courses. Although there are certain problems in teaching students how groups function by involving them on an experiential level, we think that such difficulties can be resolved. Clear guidelines need to be established so students understand their rights and responsibilities, and the multiple roles and responsibilities of instructors need to be clarified. This type of arrangement calls for honesty, maturity, and professionalism from both the instructor and the students.

Those who teach group courses often function in multiple roles. Although the blending of the roles of group facilitator, instructor, evaluator, and supervisor does present potential problems, the literature has revealed that there are a number of different strategies being employed in the preparation of group counselors. Merta et al. (1993) acknowledged that no single training model or combination of safeguards is apt to solve the dilemma of protecting students from adverse dual relationships and at the same time provide them with the best possible training. It is challenging for those who teach group courses to differentiate between experiential training workshops and counseling groups. The group process involves elements common to both training and counseling groups. Group courses can be vehicles for personal growth as well as teach students about how groups function. As Holly Forester-Miller indicates in her contribution later in this chapter, it is essential that faculty who teach group courses or conduct training workshops for group workers monitor their practices.

The Ethical Use of Experiential Approaches to Training

Pierce and Baldwin (1990) have addressed the ethical issues involved in protecting student privacy when personal growth experiences are required as part of the training of group counselors. They contended that student participation in a personal growth experience is essential in the training of group counselors. They developed guidelines for instructors to address the ethical dilemma that group trainers and supervisors face as they evaluate their students' use of appropriate and facilitative group leadership skills. Some of their recommendations are

- Students should be given information about what to expect before they enter a program. Providing a written statement that explains the rationale for participation in personal growth activities is likely to improve student participation.

- Students can be made aware that personal involvement in group participation is a basic part of the group course. Information can be offered about both the benefits and the difficulties of self-disclosure.

- Trainers need to demonstrate sensitivity to the privacy needs of the students in their group courses. They can avoid asking probing questions that are likely to elicit highly personal material.

- Students can be involved in selecting topics or themes that they are willing to explore in a group context.

Merta, Johnson, and McNeil (1995) conducted a national survey of 262 counselor education programs. A large majority (91%) of the programs reported that they have a required course in group work. Many group counselor educators identified the required group course as being introductory rather than as serving to prepare students to be group counselors. Only a minority of them require participation in adjunct training or therapy groups or in a supervised practicum, and only a minority use guest lectures or demonstrations. The most popular experiential component is in-class role-playing, and the most popular personal growth experience is the adjunct experiential (personal growth) group. Less than half of those who teach group courses lead the experiential component themselves.

One way that many educators attempt to minimize the conflicts involved in combining didactic and experiential components in a course is to avoid grading students on their participation in the experiential activities. This practice is consistent with the ACA Code of Ethics. We believe it is wise to avoid grading students in a group class on their actual participation in the group, either as members or as leaders. If group participation were graded, this could encourage "performances" by those striving to be "good group members" or "ideal group leaders." Ethical practice requires that instructors spell out clearly the criteria for grading and evaluating student learning. The criteria may include written reports, oral reports and presentations, essay tests, and objective examinations. Although students' performance in the experiential group should not be graded, students *can* be expected to attend regularly.

Perhaps a crucial factor that makes multiple relationships problematic in teaching group courses is the competency of the person who teaches them. We have concerns about faculty who teach group courses who have never experienced a group themselves as a member, or who are inadequately prepared to teach group process. There is the potential for exploiting students if those who teach group courses are using the group as a way of meeting their own needs at the expense of students. There are issues of power and control, the undue use of pressure, and bias that clouds the instructor's objectivity and judgment. It is essential to be aware of the potential pitfalls that grow out of dual relationships and to develop strategies to reduce chances of exploiting or harming students. Although there is no way to eliminate the potential for negative outcomes, students who are informed of the rights and responsibilities involved in participating in a group course are less vulnerable to being exploited. If students are denied opportunities to experience a group from a personal perspective, it seems to us that they are being deprived in their education and that their group class will have limited value.

In examining the ethics of requiring participation in an experiential group for students in a group counseling class, the question that should be asked is Is it ethical for group leaders to consider themselves qualified to lead groups if they have never been group members themselves? We endorse participation in a group as part of a leader's training. Learning from books and lectures is important but has its limitations; certain skills can best be learned by direct experiencing. Struggling with trusting a group of strangers, recognizing and working through conflict, challenging one's resistances, risking vulnerability, receiving genuine support from others, feeling and expressing closeness, and being confronted are all vital learning experiences for future group leaders. We think that group experience for leaders is indispensable, if for no reason other than that it provides a deep understanding of what clients face in groups.

<hr/>

Similar views are presented by Holly Forester-Miller in her contribution. She summarizes some of the various perspectives and takes the position that experiential groups are a vital part of training effective group leaders. She argues that counselor educators have an ethical obligation to require students to participate in group counseling experiences, and that the benefits of including an experiential aspect outweigh the potential risks to students, especially if safeguards are designed and implemented.

Dual Relationships in Training Group Workers

Holly Forester-Miller

In the past, counselor educators have debated whether it was ethical and/or appropriate to require students to participate in an experiential group as part of their training in group counseling. The current literature indicates that a group experience is an essential component of training group counselors (Corey & Corey, 1997; Forester-Miller & Duncan, 1990; Merta et al., 1993; Yalom, 1995). The Association for Specialists in Group Work concurs. Its revised *Professional Standards for the Training of Group Workers* (ASGW, 1991) state that "The practice domain should include observations and participation in a group experience, which could occur in a classroom group" (p. 5). Because a group experience is such a necessary component of training, it is apparent that it will be unethical and inappropriate to send group counselors out into the field without this very important aspect of training.

In teaching individual counseling skills, we demonstrate and role-play counseling situations for our students. They also practice their skills on each other, for several reasons. First, it gives them a "safe" place to practice. Second, they can give each other valuable feedback based on their counseling knowledge. Third, it gives them the opportunity to experience the counseling process from the client's perspective. These same reasons are relevant to the practice of group counseling skills. In group counseling the process and dynamics are very different from individual counseling, and skills are of no value if the counselor does not understand the process and dynamics that are occurring. Students can read about group process, but until they experience it, I do not believe they can fully understand it. Students have told me time and again that they thought they understood what the book was saying about the stages of a group but that it was so different actually to watch the process occur in our personal growth group. This is especially true of the dynamics that occur during the stage we refer to as the *transition or storming stage*. For example, it is extremely helpful for students to see the leadership being challenged, to observe the nondefensive response of an experienced leader, and to be able to discuss that experience with the leader as a part of a class discussion.

It seems to me that it is our ethical obligation to require students to participate in a group counseling experience. It is no longer a matter of *whether* it is appropriate. The question now is *how* this group experience can be offered in an ethical and appropriate way.

The ACA *Code of Ethics and Standards of Practice* (1995) deals with this issue:

- Counselors use professional judgment when designing training experiences conducted by the counselors themselves that require student and supervisee self-growth or self-disclosure. Safeguards are provided so that students and supervisees are aware of the ramifications their self-disclosure may have on counselors whose primary role as teacher, trainer, or supervisor requires acting on ethical obligations to the profession. Evaluative components of experiential training experiences explicitly delineate predetermined academic standards that are separate and not dependent on the student's level of self-disclosure. (F.3.b.)

The idea of conducting self-growth experiences as being ethical is reinforced, and the counselor educator's attention is directed to the method of delivering and grading such experiences in the standards of practice:

- Counselors who conduct experiences for students or supervisees that include self-growth or self-disclosure must inform participants of counselors' ethical obligations to the profession and must not grade participants based on their nonacademic performance. (SP-42)

The personal growth group and/or training group experience built into group counseling courses is very different from a therapy group. The main differences lie in the intensity of the experience and the depth of sharing on the members' parts. Yet the stages of the group and the leadership issues at each stage remain the same, thus offering a wonderful learning opportunity while minimizing the risks to the students. As long as counselor educators do the proper planning for the group experience and, as with any group, design the experience always keeping in mind the purpose and objective of the group, the risks of the dual relationship will be low.

Forester-Miller and Duncan (1990) recommended several guidelines and conditions under which the risks to students are minimized. Several that apply here and have not already been mentioned are that the personal growth experience not be related to the process of program screening, whether for admission or for continuing in the program; that students be evaluated only on their level of group skill acquisition; and that students not be allowed to lead a group of their peers without the professional responsible for the group being present.

In addition to offering guidelines, Forester-Miller and Duncan (1990) also provided four alternatives for providing a group experience to students that meet the conditions suggested:

1. having the master's level group experience led by postmaster's students under faculty supervision;

2. having the instructor lead or colead the group, but utilizing a blind grading system for assessing the students' learning and skill acquisition;

3. requiring that the students participate in a counseling group that is external to the academic setting; and

4. having the instructor lead the group with the students utilizing the role-play technique.

These are all viable options open to the counselor educator who teaches group counseling. The one I prefer is to lead the group and utilize a blind grading system. This approach offers several benefits to the students. They are able to experience the "real" thing firsthand, to see the group process at work, and at the same time experience it from the perspective of the client. The students have the opportunity to try on the leadership role in an ongoing group with the faculty member present to offer assistance and feedback. The students are provided with an effective leader role model in which the faculty member can feel confident of the skill level being demonstrated and the types of techniques being modeled. This approach also provides a common experience for the students and instructor to utilize in discussing group process and giving examples. Further, it affords students the unique experience of seeing the faculty member utilizing the skill and applying the strategies that have been discussed, and being able to discuss the effectiveness of the interventions in the various situations.

Forester-Miller and Remley (unpublished manuscript) surveyed members of the Association for Specialists in Group Work regarding their perceptions of the effectiveness of the group training in their master's degree counseling programs. The study was based on comparing the perceived effectiveness of the five training methods delineated by Merta et al. (1993). The training methods included no experiential group, no-feedback experiential group, feedback experiential group, instructor-observed experiential group, and instructor-led experiential group. Respondents who were taught utilizing the instructor-led experiential group model indicated that they gained a higher level of competency in processing interactions and in managing groups as the leader than did the other respondents.

The benefits of such an experience certainly outweigh the risks, especially if the faculty member has planned the experience to minimize these risks. It seems to me that we owe it to our students and to their future clients to provide the best training possible, utilizing the most effective teaching methods available. Therefore, not offering a group counseling experience as part of group counselor training would be neglectful and unethical. Some dual relationships are not only ethical but beneficial.

In his contribution, Rod Merta summarizes research that he and his colleagues have conducted on approaches to teaching group counseling courses and the role of experiential groups in these courses. He shares his latest thinking on ethical ways to include an experiential component in group counseling. He takes the position that it is best for group counselor educators to model the management of dual relationships by providing safeguards when experiential and didactic aspects of training are combined.

The Experiential Group: Avoid or Manage?

Rod Merta

In the fall of 1989, I was a novice counselor educator assigned to teach the introductory course in group work for master's level students. Not having specialized in group work, I began to reflect back on how I had been introduced to group counseling. My instruction had consisted of both didactic and experiential training components, and my instructor had initiated us into group dynamics by plunging us into a group session the very first day of class. Now, 10 years later as I was preparing my course, a senior colleague dropped by my office to caution me against leading any form of experiential or growth group myself. The colleague expressed concern that the dual relationship that would result if I led such a group could adversely affect my students. I was perplexed by the assumption that such dual relationships were necessarily adverse. If this were true, how had I managed to survive adversity as an experiential group member 10 years ago?

Committed to the dual maxims that "the show must go on" and "tenure is everything," I chose to retain the experiential group for my course but to use advanced graduate students to lead the group. Feeling less than comfortable with this arrangement, I asked my graduate assistant, John Sisson, to review the literature on dual relationships and the experiential group. Although there was ample literature, it was largely confined to position statements by counselor educators for and against the continued use of the experiential group. John and I found ourselves troubled by several related issues. First, what was being described in the literature as an ethical issue appeared to us to be more of an ethical dilemma. If counselor educators eliminated or altered the experiential group to protect students from potentially adverse effects of inherent dual relationships, were not students, counselor educators, and the profession being denied an effective training experience? Second, we found no research on how graduate students in counseling viewed the experiential group. The literature review had uncovered two student accounts of adverse consequences resulting from participation in an experiential group, but there was no evidence that systematic research had been conducted on larger samples of students, assessing both the advantages and disadvantages of experiential group participation. Although these two accounts certainly warranted the concern of counselor educators, did they warrant the revision of teaching practices? Third, there was no evidence of systematic research on how counselor educators were employing or discontinuing the use of the experiential group.

In keeping with recommendations made by Merta and Sisson (1991), we conducted a telephone survey of counselor educators in the Rocky Mountain states on their use of the experiential group and surveyed the students in this initial group course. The results of both surveys strongly suggested that participation in an experiential group was highly valued. Later, Merta et al.(1993) conducted a national survey of counselor educators to determine their use of the experiential group. I continued annually to survey students enrolled in the introductory course in group work regarding their experiences as participants.

The national survey of counselor educators resulted in three conclusions: a large majority of counselor educators continue to use the experiential group; significant diversity exists in ways that counselor educators are employing traditional alternative models to the experiential group and in the ways they are providing safeguards; and the diversity of models and safeguards translates into considerable variation in the degree to which students are at risk for experiencing adverse dual relationships and for receiving poor training. A substantial majority (88%) of counselor educators continue to employ the experiential group in their introductory group course. They employ five models along a continuum as follows: 12% utilize no experiential group; 8% have someone outside of the department lead the experiential group, and no feedback on student participation in group is required; 19% refer the group out but require feedback (e.g., attendance, skill proficiency); 22% have the instructor observe the group by means of mirror, tape, or in person, and model; and 39% have the instructor actually lead the experiential group. Safeguards include making participation in the experiential group voluntary (39%), providing participants with informed consent prior to admission to the counseling program and thereafter (28%), training students in limiting their self-disclosures (38%), and not evaluating students on their participation in the group (16%).

This diversity of models and safeguards strongly suggests that counselor educators are grappling with the ethical dilemma and are attempting to manage it by protecting students while ensuring quality in their training and gatekeeping functions. In examining the continuum of models, the model using no experiential group seems to be most effective in protecting students and the most at risk for foregoing training and gatekeeping responsibilities. The model with the instructor leading the group appears to be most effective in fulfilling training and gatekeeping responsibilities and least effective in protecting students. Counselor educators employing the more intrusive models must adopt adequate safeguards to ensure the protection of their students. Counselor educators employing the less intrusive models need to ensure that they are providing their students with adequate experiential exercises in which student interpersonal and intrapersonal effectiveness in group work can be enhanced and evaluated.

The annual process of conducting anonymous surveys of participants in our instructor-observed experiential groups for the past 7 years has produced several findings. The vast majority of students (a) highly value their participation in the experiential group, (b) prefer not to be graded on their participation, (c) prefer a doctoral-student-led, instructor-observed (videotaped) experiential group to other models of leadership and observation, (d) worry more about member breaches of confidentiality than leader breaches, and (e) are inhibited in disclosing more by the anticipated reactions of other members than by concern about grading or promotion through the program. This ongoing survey research and group leader feedback have helped to shape the experiential group to maximize student protection, training, and gatekeeping. This process is helping me to manage my dual relationships with students as well as those between master's level group members and doctoral student group leaders. The outcome is not as important as the process because the experiential group has changed and will continue to change from year to year as new student feedback is solicited. Consequently, I do not recommend that other counselor educators imitate our model. Instead, I encourage them to model the managing of dual relationships by enlisting their students' support in the process of evaluating and possibly altering their current mode.

Not all dual relationships in counselor training and practice need to result in adverse consequences for students or clients. Rather than stripping our programs of key training components or setting unrealistic standards for ourselves and our students, is not it a more realistic and beneficial goal to manage rather than avoid dual relationships? The experiential group has inherent dual relationships with the potential for adverse consequences for our students. However, we are professionals trained to evaluate our teaching methods and capable of sharing with our students the responsibility of managing dual relationships. Do we not better prepare our students for handling the dual relationship issues they will encounter in the future by modeling the managing of dual relationships?

After reading the views of Forester-Miller and Merta, what are your views regarding the experiential group? How do you think you might respond in the following situation?

As a part of a master's degree training program for group counselors, students are engaged in supervised work that involves facilitating an experiential group for the introductory course in counseling taken by all students in the counseling program. Some of these beginning students, who are also required to enroll in a section of a self-exploration group as part of the introductory course, are wondering about the ethics of having other students in the role of facilitator. A few oppose the idea of being expected to self-disclose in a group setting with student leaders, even though these leaders are under the supervision of a faculty member. The complaining students think that this is a dual relationship issue because their student leaders are enrolled in the same program.

What do you think about the practice of using students to facilitate self-awareness groups for other students, assuming they are given adequate supervision? What safeguards can you suggest to protect both the student facilitator and the students who are members of the group? If this group were conducted by a faculty member who teaches the group course (and who is likely to have the students in a future class), what issues need to be addressed?

If you are a counselor educator who teaches group counseling courses, where do you stand on the issues raised in this chapter? What safeguards do you think are necessary to protect both your students and the public they eventually will serve?

If you are a student in a counselor education program, what are your reactions to this controversy? What kinds of learning experiences do you think you need in order to become an effective group leader?

Conclusions

The controversy about dual relationships in the preparation of group counselors is likely to continue for some time. As the issue has been framed in some of the literature, conscientious counselor educators are caught in a "no win" ethical dilemma. On the one hand, if we remove ourselves from what many consider to be problematic dual roles (such as combining didactic and experiential learnings by performing multiple functions that may include any combination of instructor, supervisor, group leader, and consultant) we are vulnerable to charges that we have abdicated our responsibility to the profession and the public to assure competent service. On the other hand, if we do teach by combining roles, we are vulnerable to charges that we have abdicated our responsibilities to respect the privacy of our students.

It seems to us that, regardless of the model that instructors use, the key elements are the qualifications of instructors and the way the model is presented. Thus a given model may not itself be the problem, but rather how specific instructors implement it. What is crucial is the openness of the instructor and his or her ability to treat students with respect and to make the expectations for the course clear from the outset. It is essential to keep in mind the primary purpose of a group counseling course, which is to teach students leadership skills and provide an understanding of how group process works. Although the main aim of a group course is not to provide personal therapy for students, participating in such a group can and ought to be therapeutic. Students can make choices about what personal concerns they are willing to share, and they can also determine the depth of their personal disclosures. A group course is not designed to be a substitute for an intensive self-exploration experience, but learning about how groups function can be enhanced through active and personal participation in the group process.

It seems obvious to us that counselor educators need to continue to work to clarify the question of how group counseling courses can best be taught. We do believe that if counselor educators choose to keep group experiences free from evaluation, then other procedures need to exist within the program to screen out unsuitable candidates. At this point, there is a wide range of choices that counselor educators can make in preparing students to be group counselors. We each must choose according to our own stance on the issues, balancing our responsibilities to our students, the profession, and consumers of counseling services.

7 The Counselor in the Community

In this part of the book we turn to multiple relationship issues that confront counseling practitioners in their work. In later chapters (8, 9, and 10) we focus on various specialty areas in mental health practice and explore some of the unique boundary issues that are inherent in these specializations. In this chapter, we address a number of questions that may be relevant to all counselors who work in the community, regardless of their particular specialty area of practice. These questions include

- Is it ethical to barter with clients for goods or services?
- Should a counselor ever counsel a friend or social acquaintance?
- What unique issues do rural practitioners face?
- Should a counselor ever accept a gift from a client?
- What are the appropriate limits of self-disclosure, and how could overextending these limits create a dual relationship problem?
- Should counselors ever socialize with clients? What about former clients?
- What alternative roles do counselors need to assume in order to serve a culturally and ethnically diverse clientele effectively?

A basic theme that runs through this chapter is that there is a cultural context to the determination of what are considered to be appropriate therapeutic boundaries. As Brown (1994) noted, a boundary that facilitates therapeutic movement for one person may block growth for another due to factors of race, ethnicity, class, work setting, and the unique relational matrix between the human beings in the therapy room. Three guest contributors add their voices to this chapter: Holly Forester-Miller discusses boundary issues that arise for rural practitioners, Derald Wing Sue presents multicultural perspectives on relationship boundaries and multiple roles, and Thomas A. Parham examines dual relationship issues from an African worldview.

Bartering for Goods or Services

In the most recent revisions of the ethics codes of mental health professionals, the standards pertaining to bartering have been refined and expanded. Although bartering practices are not encouraged, the codes do recognize that there are circumstances in which bartering may be acceptable and that it is important to take into consideration cultural factors and community standards. For example, the ACA Code of Ethics states

- Counselors ordinarily refrain from accepting goods or services from clients in return for counseling services because such arrangements create inherent potential for conflicts, exploitation, and distortion of the professional relationship. Counselors may participate in bartering only if the relationship is not exploitive, if the client requests it, if a clear written contract is established, and if such arrangements are an accepted practice among professionals in the community. (A.10.c.)

It needs to be acknowledged that there are potential problems in bartering, even though the practice may be motivated by an altruistic concern for the welfare of clients with limited financial resources. Kitchener and Harding (1990) pointed out that the services a client can offer are usually not as monetarily valuable as counseling. Thus, over time, clients could become trapped in a sort of indentured servitude as they fall further and further behind in the amount owed. Another potential problem concerns what criteria should be used to determine what goods or services are worth an hour of the therapist's professional time.

Generally, we are inclined to think that the practice of bartering opens up more problems than it is worth. As an example, consider a client who pays for therapy by working on the counselor's car. If the mechanical service is less than desirable, the chances are good that the counselor will begin to resent the client on several grounds: for having been taken advantage of, for being the recipient of inferior service, and for not being appreciated. The client, too, can begin to feel exploited and resentful if it takes many hours of work to pay for a 50-minute therapy session, or if the client believes the therapy is of poor quality. Feelings of resentment, whether they build up in the counselor or in the client, are bound to interfere with the therapeutic relationship.

Although we can see potential problems in bartering, we think it is a mistake to condemn this practice too quickly. In some cultures or in some communities, bartering is a standard practice, and the problems just mentioned may not be as evident. For instance, rural environments may lend themselves more to barter arrangements. We know a practitioner who worked with farmers in rural Alabama who paid with a bushel of corn or apples. Within their cultural group, this was a normal way (and in some cases, the only possible way) of doing business. There are many different kinds of barter arrangement that could be agreed upon between counselor and client, as Holly Forester-Miller illustrates in her contribution later in the chapter. There are also alternatives to bartering, such as using a sliding scale or doing pro bono work.

> What is your own stance toward bartering? Do you see it as unacceptable for yourself in your own practice, or can you foresee instances when you might consider working out a barter arrangement that meets your professional code's criteria for ethical practice? What alternatives to bartering might you consider with your clients who are unable to pay your fee?

Counseling a Friend or Acquaintance

The ACA Code of Ethics and many writers have cautioned against counseling a friend. Kitchener and Harding (1990) pointed out that counseling relationships and friendships differ in function and purpose. We agree that the roles of counselor and friend are incompatible. Friends do not pay their friends a fee for listening and caring. It will be difficult for a counselor who is also a friend to avoid crossing the line between empathy and sympathy. It hurts to see a friend in pain. Because a dual relationship will be created, there is always the possibility that one of the relationships—professional or personal— will be compromised. It may be difficult for the counselor to confront the client in therapy for fear of damaging the friendship. It will also be problematic for clients, who may hesitate to talk about deeper struggles for fear that their counselor/friend will lose respect for them. Counselors who are tempted to enter into a counseling relationship with a friend might do well to ask themselves whether they are willing to risk losing the friendship.

A question remains, however, as to where to draw the line. Is it ethical to counsel a mere acquaintance? A friend of a friend? A relative of a friend? We think it is going to absurd lengths to insist that counselors should have *no* other relationship, prior or simultaneous, with their clients. Often clients seek us out for the very reason that we are not complete strangers. A client may have been referred by a mutual friend, or might have attended a seminar given by the counselor. A number of factors may enter into the decision as to whether to counsel someone we know only slightly or indirectly. Borys (1988) found that male therapists, therapists who lived and worked in small towns, and therapists with 30 or more years of experience all rated remote dual professional roles (as in counseling a client's friend, relative, or lover) as significantly more ethical than did their comparison group. Borys speculated that men and women receive different socialization regarding the appropriateness of intruding on or altering boundaries with the opposite sex: men are given greater permission to take the initiative or otherwise become more socially intimate. In a rural environment or a small town, it is difficult to avoid other relationships with clients, who are likely to be one's banker, beautician, store clerk, or plumber. Perhaps more experienced therapists believe they have the professional maturity to handle dualities, or it could be that they received their training at a time when dual relationships were not the focus of much attention in counselor education programs. At any rate, whatever one's gender, work setting, or experience level, these boundary questions will arise for counselors who both counsel and conduct their business and social lives in the same community.

A good question to ask ourselves is whether the nonprofessional relationship is likely to interfere, at some point, with the professional relationship. Sound professional judgment is needed to assess whether objectivity can be maintained and role conflicts avoided. Yet we need to be careful not to place too much value on "objectivity." In our view, being objective does not imply a lack of personal caring or of subjective involvement. Although it is true that we do not want to get lost in the client's world, we think that we do need to enter this world in order to be effective.

A special kind of dual relationship dilemma can arise when a counselor needs counseling. As therapists, we are people too, with our problems. Many of us will want to go to our friends, who might be therapists, to hear us out and help us sort out our problems. Our friends can be present for us in times of need and provide compassion and caring, yet not in a formal therapeutic way. We will not expect to obtain long-term therapy with a friend, nor should we put our friends in a difficult position by requesting such therapy.

Issues in Rural Practice

In rural communities, counselors may have to play several roles. In comparison to their colleagues who practice in urban or suburban areas, they often find it more difficult to maintain clear boundaries. Sleek (1994) pointed out that ethical issues plague rural practice and that therapists in sparsely populated areas confront a range of unique ethical dilemmas. For example, a therapist who shops for a new tractor encounters a potential dual relationship issue if the only person in town who sells tractors happens to be a client. However, if the therapist were to buy a tractor elsewhere, this could cause strain in the relationship with the client because of the value that rural communities place on loyalty to local merchants. As another example, consider the matter of clients who want to barter goods or services for counseling. Some communities operate substantially on a swap basis rather than a cash economy. As we have suggested, this does not necessarily have to be problematic, but there is potential for conflicts in the therapeutic relationship if the bartering agreements do not work well.

Holly Forester-Miller explores how practicing in a rural community might make a difference in the appropriateness of dual relationships and how they can best be managed.

Rural Communities: Can Dual Relationships Be Avoided?

Holly Forester-Miller

If you were raised in an urban environment and have practiced exclusively in urban or suburban settings, the dual relationship issues experienced in rural communities may never even have occurred to you. Life in rural communities can be quite different from life in cities and can raise some complex issues for mental health providers. I was raised on Long Island, New York, and then lived and worked in several rural communities in various states, so these differences have become all too evident to me. Initially, though, I was caught off guard.

Living in an urban area gives one a sense of anonymity that does not exist in rural communities. As Gainsley (1996) so aptly stated, "Remember, we all shop at the same Walmart." In most rural communities, it is impossible to avoid dual relationships. Everyone functions in the community, and paths are bound to cross at some point. In a small town, the issue of counseling acquaintances is a moot point because nearly everyone is an acquaintance. Counselors need to distinguish among levels of acquaintanceship and friendship and set clear demarcations in deciding who will be appropriate to accept as clients.

Values and beliefs may vary significantly between urban dwellers and their rural counterparts. As counselors we need to work to ensure that we are not imposing values that come from a cultural perspective different from that of our clients. Not all white, middle-class Americans have the same culture. For example, the values and beliefs surrounding issues such as marriage and the role of females in the family are often dramatically different in rural communities than they are in urban areas.

Bartering is a common practice in some regions and offers an opportunity for some individuals to receive counseling services. In the Appalachian culture, for example, it is a matter of pride to be able to provide for yourself and your loved ones. When I practiced in Appalachia, I once counseled a suicidal teenage girl. I had discussed fees with her single-parent mother, who was insistent that she not receive free services. We set a significantly reduced fee. After a short time, it became apparent to me that even this small amount was a drain on this family's resources. So I broached the issue with the mother again, and offered to see her daughter for free. This was not acceptable to her. She stated that she could make it and take care of her family. She then asked if I might like her to make a quilt for me, instead of paying in money. Not wanting to get involved in designing and planning a quilt with her, I asked her if she had one already made that she was willing to sell. She said that she did, brought in the quilt, and told me the amount she wanted for it. We arranged for that amount to be on account for her daughter's counseling. This was a good solution because it allowed her daughter to receive needed counseling services and afforded the mother an opportunity to maintain her sense of pride that she could pay her own way.

The ACA Code of Ethics recognizes the realities of bartering as both a helpful payment method and as a potentially exploitive arrangement. The inclusion of the phrase in Standard A.10.c. that bartering may be acceptable "if such arrangements are an accepted practice among professionals in the community" is an important acknowledgement of cultural differences and rural traditions.

Group counseling also poses some interesting dilemmas in rural communities. We typically assume group members do not know each other and have no outside relationships. This is an assumption that cannot be made in a rural community. The group members are very likely to know each other and to have relationships with each other, which adds new dimensions to the process of trust building in group work.

Is it possible to avoid dual relationships in rural communities? I seriously doubt it. Counselors in rural communities need to be aware of the issues and challenges of dual relationships so that they are prepared to handle them appropriately and to minimize the risks to their clients.

Accepting Gifts From Clients

Borys (1988) surveyed counselors about a number of dual relationship questions, including accepting gifts from clients. Only 16% of her respondents believed that it was never or only rarely ethical to accept a gift worth less than $10, but the percentage of those who disapproved rose to 82% when the gift was worth more than $50. Apparently, the monetary value of gifts is a major factor for counselors in determining whether it is ethical to accept them. There are other factors, however, that need to be examined as well. First, counselors need to be sensitive to cultural differences. As Derald Wing Sue points out later in the chapter, gift giving has different meanings in different cultures. The motivation of the client also needs to be considered. If the offering of a gift is an attempt to win the favor of the counselor or is some other form of manipulation, it is best not to accept the gift. In addition to the motivation of the client, the relationship that has developed between the counselor and the client should be considered. Offering a gift might be the client's way of expressing appreciation, and if the therapist were to simply say, "I cannot accept your gift," the client might feel hurt and rejected. An example might be a client who brings a potted plant to a termination session as a way of saying "thank you" for the work that the counselor and client have accomplished together. By contrast, the acceptance of other gifts might be improper. For example, a client who is a corporate executive might offer her counselor a stock tip based on her insider's knowledge. The counselor needs to explain to the client why it is improper to profit financially from information gained through a counseling relationship, and this could lead to a productive discussion about why the client felt a need to make such an offer. As is true of so many ethical dilemmas, one possibility is for the therapist to discuss his or her reactions with the client about accepting a gift.

One way to avoid being put in the awkward position of having to refuse a gift is to include a mention of policy in your professional disclosure statement. The statement could include the information that, although counseling sessions may be intimate and personal, the relationship is a professional one and does not allow you to accept gifts. Although being clear with clients at the outset of the relationship does prevent some later problems, there will be instances when small gifts are offered and might be received in the spirit in which they were offered.

Thus we believe that a number of factors need to be considered in the decision of whether or not to accept a gift from a client. These include the worth of the gift, the stage of the counseling relationship, the motivations of the client in offering it, and the motivations of the counselor in accepting or refusing it. Rather than using a price tag or some other arbitrary criterion to determine the ethics of accepting gifts, the counselor might choose to have a full and open discussion with the client about the matter.

> In your own practice, have you ever accepted a gift from a client? Have you ever had to refuse the offer of a gift? What criteria did you use in making the judgment as to whether to accept or refuse the gifts

Limits of Self-Disclosure

Borys (1988) found that 65% of her respondents believed it was never or only rarely ethical to disclose details of current personal stressors to a client. The wording of this item may have led to a higher percentage of negative responses than might otherwise have been found: going into detail about one's own stressors is certainly less appropriate than other forms of self-disclosure. Certainly, it is often relevant for a counselor to disclose his or her reactions to a client in the here-and-now of the therapy session, and this is more likely to have a therapeutic effect than disclosing details of one's personal life to a client. The *purpose* of self-disclosure is what needs to be kept in mind. As with other counseling interventions, self-disclosure must be a thought-out process. We must determine whether our self-disclosures are clinically sound therapeutic interventions or are subtle boundary violations. When counselors disclose personal facts or experiences about their lives, the disclosures should be appropriate, timely, and done for the benefit of the client. If we find ourselves going into detail about our personal lives with our clients, we need to ask ourselves about our intentions and whose needs we are meeting. Clients are seeking our help for their problems, and they are not there to listen to our stories about our past or present struggles. Self-disclosure is a means to an end, not a goal in itself. If we lose sight of the appropriate professional boundaries with our clients, the focus of therapy might well shift from the therapist attending to the client to the client becoming concerned about taking care of the therapist.

A key ingredient in maintaining appropriate boundaries of self-disclosure is the mental health of the counselor. If we are not being listened to by our significant others, there is a danger that we might use our clients to satisfy our needs for attention. Our clients might become substitute parents, children, or friends, and this kind of reverse relationship is certainly not what our clients need. Instead, when we have conflicts or unresolved personal concerns, we need to address them with a colleague, supervisor, or therapist.

Social Relationships With Clients

Among Borys' (1988) findings were that 92% of respondents believed that it was never or only rarely ethical to invite clients to a personal party or social event; 81% gave these negative ratings to going out to eat with a client after a session. Respondents felt less strongly about inviting clients to an office or clinic open house (51% viewed this as never or rarely ethical) and accepting a client's invitation to a special occasion (33%).

One important factor in determining how therapists perceive social relationships with clients may be their theoretical orientation. Borys found psychodynamically oriented practitioners to be the most concerned about maintaining professional boundaries. One reason given for these practitioners' opposition to dual role behaviors was that their training promotes greater awareness of the importance of clear, nonexploitive, and therapeutically oriented roles and boundaries. In the psychodynamic view, transference phenomena give additional meaning to alterations in boundaries for both client and therapist. A further explanation is that psychodynamic theory and supervision stress an informed and scrupulous awareness of the role the therapist plays in the psychological life of the client—namely, the importance of "maintaining the frame of therapy."

A counselor's stance toward the issue of socializing with clients appears to depend on several factors. One is the nature of the social function. It may be more acceptable to attend a client's special event such as a wedding than to invite a client to a party at the counselor's home. The orientation of the practitioner is also a factor to consider. Some relationship-oriented therapists might be willing to attend a client's graduation party, for instance, but a psychoanalytic practitioner might feel uncomfortable accepting an invitation for any out-of-the-office social function. This illustrates how difficult it is to come up with blanket policies to cover all situations.

> What are your views about socializing with current clients? Do you think your theoretical orientation influences your views? Under what circumstances might you have contact with a client out of the office?

Former Clients

Having considered the matter of socializing with current clients, we now look at posttermination social relationships between counselors and clients. In the first edition of this book, Kitchener (1992) noted that the nature of the relationship once the therapeutic contract has been terminated is one of the most confusing issues for counselors and their clients. Clients may fantasize that their counselors will somehow remain a significant part of their lives as surrogate parents or friends. Counselors are sometimes ambivalent about the possibility of continuing a relationship because they are aware of real attributes of clients that under other circumstances might make them desirable friends, colleagues, or peers.

Nonetheless, there are real risks that need to be considered. Studies have suggested that memories of the therapeutic relationship remain important to clients for extended periods after termination and that many clients consider reentering therapy with their former therapists (Vasquez, 1991). This reentry option is closed if other relationships have ensued. Kitchener (1992) maintained that the welfare of the former client and the gains that have been made in counseling are put at risk when new relationships are added to the former therapeutic one. She stated that

> Once someone has terminated his or her counseling relationship with us, our contract to help them ends. No one would suggest that because we have once seen a person in therapy we have a lifelong obligation to help them. But it is equally implausible to suggest that just because our contract has ended we ought willfully to engage in activities that will undo the benefits that have accrued from our ser-

vices. If counselors were generally to engage in such activities, they would be promoting for themselves an endless supply of clients. Fix someone, hurt them, fix them again and so on. Both our obligations to avoid hurting and to help our clients would be violated. (pp. 146–147)

Kitchener suggested that many of the same dynamics may be operating in nonsexual posttherapy relationships as in sexual ones, although not at the same level of emotional intensity. Her conclusion was that counselors should approach the question of posttherapy relationships with care, and with awareness of their strong ethical responsibility to avoid undoing what they and their clients have worked so hard to accomplish.

Two recent studies have indicated that there is little consensus among therapists regarding whether nonromantic posttherapy relationships between therapists and former clients are ethical. The majority of the participants in a study by Anderson and Kitchener (1996) did not hold to the concept of "once a client, always a client" with respect to nonsexual posttherapy relationships. Some participants suggested that posttherapy relationships were ethical if a certain time period had elapsed. Others proposed that such relationships were ethical if the former client decided not to return to therapy with the former therapist and if the posttherapy relationship did not seem to hinder later therapy with different therapists.

Another recent study by Salisbury and Kinnier (1996) found similar results regarding counselors' behaviors and attitudes regarding friendships with former clients. The major finding was that many counselors are engaged in posttermination friendships and believe that under certain circumstances such relationships are acceptable. Seventy percent of the counselors believed that posttermination friendships were ethical approximately 2 years after termination of the professional relationship. Although most codes of ethics now specify a minimum 2-year waiting period for sexual relationships with former clients, the codes do not address the issue of friendships with former clients.

> What are your thoughts about social relationships with former clients? Do you think that codes of ethics should specifically address nonromantic and nonsexual posttherapy relationships? Under what circumstances might such relationships be unethical? When might you consider them as ethical?

Alternative Counselor Roles in Working with Diverse Clients

Counselors who work in the community are likely to encounter challenges in meeting the needs of diverse client populations. Working effectively with culturally and ethnically diverse clients may entail a willingness to assume nontraditional roles and to adopt various roles at different stages in the helping process. Some of this role shifting may look like multiple relating and crossing of boundaries that are traditionally marked, yet some combining of roles may be necessary in order to counsel effectively in a multicultural community.

Counselors who work with ethnically diverse clients may need to make a shift in their thinking. Sticking with a singular role may have limitations in reaching certain clients. According to Atkinson, Thompson, and Grant (1993), practitioners are generally best trained to play the role of psychotherapist, yet this is also the role most frequently misapplied in working with racial/ethnic minority clients. Atkinson and his colleagues believed that the conventional role of psychotherapist is appropriate only for clients who are highly acculturated and want relief from an existing problem that has an internal etiology.

Some writers have criticized conventional approaches to therapy that focus on a client's intrapsychic conflicts and tend to place undue responsibility on clients for their plight. At the extreme, some interventions can be perceived as blaming client problems on the client rather than as examining real factors in the environment that may be contributing to the client's problem. Many of the writers in the field of multicultural counseling and those with a community orientation have emphasized the necessity of recognizing and dealing with environmental conditions that often create problems for ethnically diverse client groups, rather than merely working to change an individual client's behavior. In selecting roles and strategies to use with diverse clients, Atkinson, Thompson, et al. (1993) believed it is useful to take into account the client's level of acculturation, the locus of problem etiology, and the goal of counseling. These writers and Atkinson, Morten, and Sue (1993) have suggested that several alternative roles—advocate, change agent, consultant, adviser, and facilitator of indigenous support systems—are appropriate for counselors who work in the community.

Because ethnic minority clients are often oppressed to some degree by the dominant society, counselors can function as *advocates*, speaking on behalf of clients who are low in acculturation and who need help with problems that result from discrimination and oppression. In the role of *change agent*, counselors can make use of political power to confront and bring about change within the system that creates or contributes to many of the problems that clients face. In this role, counselors assist clients to recognize oppressive forces in the community as a source of their problems and teach clients strategies for dealing with these environmental problems. By operating as *consultants*, counselors can encourage ethnic minority clients to learn skills they can use to interact successfully with various forces within their community. The client and the counselor work together collegially to address unhealthy forces within the system and to design prevention programs to reduce the negative impact of racism and oppression. The counselor as *adviser* discusses with clients ways to deal with environmental problems that are contributing to their personal problems. For example, recent immigrants may need advice on coping with problems they will face in the job market or that their children may encounter at school.

For many ethnically diverse clients, seeking help in the form of traditional counseling is foreign. Often they are more willing to turn to social support systems within their own community. By acting as *facilitators of indigenous support systems*, counselors can encourage clients to make full use of resources in their communities including community centers, extended families, neighborhood social networks, churches, and ethnic advocacy groups. Counselors need to learn what kinds of healing resources exist within a client's culture. In many cultures, professional counselors have little hope of reaching individuals with problems because these people are likely to put their trust in the healers who are a part of their culture such as folk healers, acupuncturists, and spiritual healers. At times, it may be difficult for counselors to adopt the worldview of their clients, and in such instances it could be helpful to *make a referral to an indigenous healer*. Counselors can then structure their activities to complement or augment healing resources that are available to the client.

For counselors who hope to reach a diverse range of client populations, it is essential to be able to employ therapeutic strategies in flexible ways and to assume various roles in helping clients. Combining roles will be necessary to help many clients effectively. Thus community counseling calls for practitioners who are familiar with community resources, know the cultural backgrounds of their clients, have skills that can be used as needed by clients, and have the ability to balance various roles.

***

Derald Wing Sue expands on these ideas and eloquently presents an ethical framework for viewing dual or multiple relationships from a multicultural perspective.

Multicultural Perspectives on Multiple Relationships

Derald Wing Sue

Increasingly, mental health professionals are being confronted with situations that challenge the standards of practice and codes of ethics developed by their professional associations (Herlihy & Corey, 1996; Sue, 1996). Such is the case with dual or multiple relationships. Once counselors have entered into a therapeutic relationship with a client, the role they play becomes relatively prescribed. Traditionally, that role has been defined as working for the "therapeutic good" of clients, avoiding undue influence, allowing clients to make decisions on their own, setting clear boundaries, and maintaining objectivity by preventing personal bias from entering counseling decisions. It is believed that such a therapeutic relationship is sacrosanct, and indeed ethical codes have arisen around it to protect clients from being "taken advantage of" or "harmed."

Codes of ethics have clear guidelines that warn against multiple relationships because such relationships potentially compromise the therapeutic role. There is good reason for the existence of these standards. Yet some mental health professionals have begun to raise questions and issues regarding the universal applications of such standards to all situations, problems, and populations (Sue, Ivey, & Pedersen, 1996). First, concepts of mental health, the therapeutic process, and the roles helping professionals play are grounded in modern European American culture. Some cultural groups may value multiple relationships with the helping professional. Second, some dual relationships may be unavoidable. This is especially true when therapists live in smaller or rural communities where the possibility of other contacts is high. Last, some mental health professionals believe that multiple relationships based on non-traditional helping roles may be more beneficial than harmful. Let us briefly explore several of these particular arrangements.

The multicultural counseling and therapy movement has sensitized many to the fact that standards of normality and abnormality, the counseling role, and what is considered therapy are culture-bound (Carter, 1995; Ridley, 1995; Sue & Sue, 1990). In Asian culture, for example, it is believed that intimate matters (self-disclosure) are most appropriately discussed with an intimate acquaintance (relative or friend). Self-disclosing to a stranger (counselor) is considered a taboo and a violation of familial and cultural values. Thus certain Asian cultures may encourage a "dual" or "multiple" relationship in which the helper is also a relative or close personal friend. An Asian client's desire to have the traditional counseling role evolve into a more personal one is often perceived by a European-American-trained counselor as inappropriate and manipulative. Additionally, gift giving is a common practice in many Asian communities to show gratitude, respect, and the sealing of a relationship (Sue & Zane, 1987). Such actions are culturally appropriate, yet counselors unfamiliar with such practices may feel that it is inappropriate to accept a gift because it blurs boundaries, changes the relationship, and creates a conflict of interest. They may politely refuse the gift, not realizing the great insult and cultural meaning of their refusal for the giver.

The multicultural counseling movement has also challenged the traditional roles played by counselors. Most counselors are taught that therapy is conducted in an office environment, is directed toward remediation, and is a one-to-one process. They are taught that the counselor is relatively inactive and that clients must make the decisions and take responsibility for their own actions. Yet many cultural groups like African Americans, Hispanic/Latino(a) Americans, and

Asian Americans prefer to receive advice and suggestions because they perceive the counselor to be an expert, with higher status, possessing special knowledge and expertise. The roles they find helpful may not be the traditional counseling role, but other, more active roles. As discussed earlier in this chapter, Atkinson, Thompson, and Grant (1993) and Atkinson, Morten, and Sue (1993) have identified different helping roles that the professional needs to develop in order to become multicuturally competent. These roles are associated with client needs and characteristics: internal versus external locus of the problem, level of acculturation/knowledge of the home culture, and whether the overall goal is one of remediation or prevention. Playing more than one of these roles implies the establishment of a dual or multiple relationship.

In smaller communities and in our historical past, it was not unusual for citizens to play multiple roles such as storekeeper, neighbor, teacher, and friend. With increasing urbanization, such cross-mixing of relationships has become rare in the cities. As Forester-Miller discussed earlier, a counselor or therapist in a smaller community may find it exceedingly difficult not to have other relationships with her or his clients.

Our codes of ethics now recognize that multiple relationships may be unavoidable, that not all such relationships are harmful, and that under certain conditions they may even be therapeutically beneficial. In general, the guidelines discouraging dual relationships are well intentioned and basically sound. However, they must not be rigidly applied to all situations. As we have seen, community characteristics (rural versus urban, small versus large, and community acceptance of certain practices such as bartering), multicultural redefinitions of counseling roles, and cultural perceptions of helping practices must be considered. Given the fact that counselors may unavoidably find themselves in a dual relationship or faced with a potential one, what guidelines can be used to minimize potential harm?

- **Personal and professional integrity must be the guiding force** behind a decision to enter a dual relationship or maintain one. Such a statement implies that the counselor considers the good of the client first and does not allow personal or professional agendas to interfere with the therapeutic relationship. The decision must be based not solely on "good intentions" but on whether the relationship actually impairs or harms the therapeutic goals or whether the risks for harm are too great.

- **Counselors must be thoroughly knowledgeable about their profession's code of ethics** and the spirit in which it was developed. Written statements cannot cover all situations. Many, like the examples given earlier, are not covered by clear guidelines, and to stick to "the letter of the law" may actually harm clients.

- Besides understanding the driving force of the codes, **counselors must educate themselves about cultural and community standards of practice.** For example, if a counselor decides to accept a gift from a client or to accept barter as a means of exchange, the actions must be judged according to the client's cultural context and by the community's normative standards.

- **If a counselor does not feel comfortable with a dual relationship or if it contains too many potential risks, it is the responsibility of the counselor not only to make this clear to the client, but also to offer alternative means** by which services can be obtained (other community resources or helpers).

- It is unrealistic to expect any single helping professional to rely solely on self-monitoring as a means for avoiding problematic dual relationships. **In all situations when a counselor considers entering or is unavoidably involved in a dual relationship, it is recommended that consultation with colleagues be sought.** Indeed, continual consultation and monitoring of the situation must be the cornerstone of any continuing dual relationship.

Sue has made it clear that as counselors working in the community, we need to rethink and revise our traditional definitions of therapeutic boundaries if we are to reach and serve a multicultural clientele effectively. Thomas A. Parham agrees and further discusses multiple relationship issues from an African -centered worldview.

An African-Centered View of Dual Relationships

Thomas A. Parham

"Culture provides a general design for living and a pattern for interpreting reality." (Nobles, 1986)

Over the last decade or more, taboos against dual relationships have been discussed extensively in the psychological and counseling literature, and several writers have presented convincing arguments against mental health professionals developing or maintaining dual relationships with their clients or students. In developing their positions, these writers have anchored their objections to dual relationships in several primary themes. First, dual relationships are discouraged because they potentially compromise the clinician's objectivity and professional judgment. Apparently, it is believed that secondary and tertiary relationships increase the probability that professionals will develop strong emotional ties that will compromise their ability to make objective decisions.

Second, dual relationships are discouraged in order to prevent the helpee (either client or student) from projecting inappropriate dependency needs onto the helper. A third rationale centers around the power differential between helper and helpee and the degree to which those dynamics contribute to or invite helpee exploitation by the professional.

Dual relationships not withstanding, I find it interesting to note that most ethical codes and standards are infused with particular cultural values and assumptions (primarily Eurocentric). If one accepts this observation, then perhaps we may invite ourselves to question whether certain ethical principles and standards for providers of service are sensitive to different cultural groups whose values and worldview (i.e., designs for living and patterns for interpreting reality) are markedly different from those of European American psychologists and counselors. I believe such is the case with the principles of dual relationships when applied to African American people and their community.

African-centered ethical codes begin and develop in a concern for the quality of human relations. A fundamental African principle states that human beings realize themselves only in moral relations to others. Unlike Eurocentric ethical standards, which appear to be designed to control people's behavior, African-centered ethics invite people to aspire to "right ways of being." The African worldview fundamentally believes in the ontological principle of consubstantiation, that is, elements of the universe are of the same substance. Thus there is an innerconnectedness between the helper and the helpee, such that developing and maintaining emotional and spiritual connections is considered facilitative.

The African worldview recognizes the holistic nature of the self. The emotional and spiritual dimensions of a person's life (including decision making) are just as valuable as the rational and behavioral ones. The African-centered worldview also recognizes that the group or collective is the most salient element of existence, rather than the individual. As such, what is advantageous for the client or student *as a part of a community* is a guiding principle for role definition of the professional.

Consequently, application of an African-centered worldview will cause one to question the need for *objectivity* absent *emotions*, the need for *distance* rather than *connectedness*, and the need for *dichotomous relationships* rather than *multiple roles*. Karenga (1984) discussed this idea further in his analysis of the *Book of Declarations of Virtues*. Using Maat (law and righteousness) as its guiding principles, this text served as the cornerstone for the standards of moral and ethical behavior in the African tradition. In the first declaration, an individual should be able to say of his or her efforts (i.e., professional practices) that they "have done what the people love and God praises." Furthermore, each of the declarations stresses the multiple roles people are expected to play in helping and assisting others (e.g., strong support for the needy, a helpful adviser an effective guide, a protector of the weak, a knowledgeable instructor). In essence, proper conduct and decisions whether or not to engage in a helping role are not based on "potential for exploitation" but rather on right intent of the helper. Therefore, a mental health professional could be expected to engage in multiple roles (in potentially a dual relationship), particularly if this were deemed by the client and the counselor to be in the client's best interest.

To illustrate the complexity of the situation and the dissonance many African American psychologists and counselors feel in adhering to the codes' cautions against dual relationships, consider the situation of Counselor X, who is on staff in a mental health center where he or she is the only African American clinician. Due to Counselor X's ethnicity, visibility in the community, cultural competence, and commitment to serve the community, he or she is called upon and agrees to teach a multicultural course, run a therapy or support group, serve as a mentor to African American students, and carry a case load of a dozen clients, 20% of whom are African American. In the course of the counselor's responsibilities, it is highly probable (and fairly typical) that there will be an African American student in the class who may also want to be seen by an African American in therapy and who also desires some advice and direction on a range of life issues from an African American mentor.

To deny a student the opportunity to be served in any of these ways because of the potential for a dual relationship adheres to the ethical standards of professional associations but violates a cultural mandate to "do what the people love and God praises." And although ethical standards regarding dual relationships may make provision for "exceptional circumstances" due to unavailability or acute distress, it could and should be argued that the scenario just described is commonplace in most communities and academic institutions across this nation where African Americans are concerned and that the concern over dual relationships may not be widely shared in the African American community, which may emphasize moral behavior and personal character over laws and rules to control professional conduct.

In summary, dual relationships standards are important to consider when we provide services to clients or students in our professional roles. However, it is also important to consider that cultural traditions and value systems that differ markedly from those underlying the standards embraced by professional associations should also be taken into account as we develop appropriate roles and responsibilities for a profession that is becoming increasingly multicultural.

Conclusions

It seems to us that this chapter has underscored the point that managing multiple roles and relationships is not a matter driven by fixed rules. Decisions will depend on the needs of clients, what is customary in a community, the integrity of the counselor, the structuring of the counseling relationship, the client population, and many other factors. Counselors who work in the community will be challenged to manage a variety of roles if they are to be effective helpers. As each of our guest contributors has persuasively argued, it is crucial that we focus on what is best for our clients and how we best can reach them.

8 Focus on Specialty Areas:
Private Practice
Group and Family Counseling

This is the first of three chapters that focus on various specializations practiced by mental health professionals. We begin this chapter with an exploration of boundary issues unique to private practitioners. Because these specialists practice in the community, many of the same themes seen in the previous chapter reemerge, yet as Harriet L. Glosoff so aptly demonstrates, they take on their own twists when applied to the specific context of private practice. Later in the chapter, we look at dual or multiple relationship issues that arise when working with multiple clients in groups or families.

PRIVATE PRACTICE

For some therapists in private practice, circumstances can make it particularly difficult to maintain boundaries between their professional and personal or social lives. Private practitioners who work and live in small communities will probably find it impossible to avoid interacting with their clients outside the office. Those who share the same political affiliations, sexual orientations, or cultural backgrounds as their clients may also experience considerable overlap between the professional and nonprofessional aspects of their lives.

Private practitioners who use their personal residences for their offices may need to exercise particular care in keeping their personal and professional lives separate. Although having a private practice in one's home is not an ethical issue in itself, this practice does open up some potential dual relationship issues. Richards (1990) has made the point that the needs and rights of the therapist's family should receive equal consideration to those given the client in a home office situation. It is not fair to children to banish them from the house, yet it is certainly not fair to clients to subject them to interruptions and household noises. If we do use a home office to see clients, we must design a private space for our work with them. They should not have to contend with interference during the therapy hour. Another consideration is that therapists, by using their home as an office, are revealing a good deal of information about themselves and their lifestyles. Finally, it is important to assess what clientele are appropriate and inappropriate for a home office practice. For example, clients who are potentially dangerous or who have serious problems with recognizing and respecting boundaries should not be seen in such a setting.

Harriet Glosoff raises additional points for private practitioners to consider.

Multiple Relationship Issues in Private Practice

Harriet L. Glosoff

Many issues surrounding nonsexual multiple relationships are not clear cut. For private practitioners, the difficulty of dealing with these issues can be compounded by isolation, geographical and cultural factors, and the financial exigencies involved in being self-employed.

Isolation. Work is traditionally one way in which individuals gratify a variety of psychological as well as financial needs. People often look to work settings as one place to meet people with whom they can form friendships or romantic relationships. In some ways, choosing to become a therapist, especially in a private practice setting, limits these opportunities. Hill (1990) contended that therapy itself is lonely work for therapists. The relationships formed between therapists and clients are intimate ones, but this intimacy is one way with therapists in the role of "givers." Therefore, therapists must look to other personal and work relationships for the chance to be "takers." Private practitioners, even those in group practice, cannot typically rely on work to meet this need. Their days are filled primarily with seeing clients, often individuals they like and admire, and this may leave them feeling more lonely than practitioners in community settings who have greater opportunities to interact with people who are not clients.

One characteristic of most types of multiple relationships is that therapists put their needs above those of their clients (Brown, 1994). This essentially involves clinicians looking for reciprocity in a relationship that is not, by its nature, reciprocal (Hill, 1990). The very human needs for intimacy, feeling admired or valued, and for some sense of control or power do not vanish as therapists walk into sessions with their clients. These needs naturally play out in nontherapeutic relationships in which different players get the chance to have their needs take precedence over those of their friends, family members, or partners (Biaggo & Greene, 1995; Brown, 1994). However, in psychotherapeutic relationships, a sense of mutual responsibility for needs cannot occur. Brown, referring to "the dance of relationships," noted that "...therapy is always a pas de deux in which we [therapists] are the supporting partner" (p. 36).

Private practice affords certain freedoms not found in many other settings (such as setting one's own hours and having greater choice over length of sessions). Yet freedom and choices are accompanied by responsibility and problems not always encountered in more restricted settings. One such problem for private practitioners is that they must often grapple with their responsibilities and choices without a structure for support and feedback from other colleagues (Greenburg, Lewis, & Johnson, 1985). Herlihy (in Herlihy & Corey, 1992), in fact, asserted that the Achilles heel of private practice is most probably isolation. This isolation presents private practitioners with an increased potential for emotional stress and burnout (Greenburg et al., 1995). When practitioners feel lonely, experience burnout, or are emotionally stressed, they are also more likely to engage in behaviors that could be considered violations of appropriate therapist-client boundaries. These behaviors may range from seeking affirmation for being a good therapist to seeking a friendship or a sexual relationship (Hill, 1990).

Pope and Vasquez (1991) contended that mental health professionals use their own unique rationalizations when faced with making ethical decisions. A sense of loneliness or isolation can easily lead to decisions based on rationalizations instead of on clinical rationales. Depending on one's theoretical orientation, mental health, and client circumstances, it may be easier or more difficult to blur this line between rationalization and rationale.

Although some theoretical approaches place injunctions on therapists self-disclosing or revealing personal information, self-disclosure is considered one way of strengthening therapeutic alliances and equalizing relationships. Yet therapists' self-disclosures may be part of an unconscious agenda to have their own needs met rather than a way to empower clients (Greenspan, 1986). Practitioners in independent private settings may fall prey unintentionally to using self-disclosures in sessions to counter feelings of isolation. This may sometimes be harmless, but with many clients it can be seen as an invitation to developing a personal relationship. In fact, inappropriate self-disclosure is often a precursor to other inappropriate boundary violations including initiation of friendships or sexual relationships (Biaggo & Greene, 1995; Simon, 1991). Inappropriate self-disclosure may be especially problematic if there are no colleagues with whom to "bounce off" ideas and share reactions to clients. Practitioners in other community settings have more opportunity to receive feedback from their colleagues in both formal and, equally important, informal ways.

Geographical and cultural factors. Professionals who choose to enter private practice do not cease to be members of their communities. They do not become nonsocial, nonpolitical beings. Because of this, it is unlikely that practitioners can totally avoid nonprofessional contacts with their clients. This is especially true for those who live and work in certain cultural and political communities that are close knit.

Clients often seek clinicians who share similar values or characteristics. Therefore, therapists' political affiliations, sexual orientations, and racial or ethnic backgrounds may lead to dual relationships (Smith & Fitzpatrick, 1995). Private practitioners must remain vigilant against any temptation to use political affiliations as a way to solicit business. For example, a therapist who serves on a political committee should not use the meetings as a forum for marketing therapy services.

Therapists in small communities often find themselves in situations that lead to seeing clients outside their sessions. Brown (1994) noted that clients may befriend therapists' partners or friends in small communities before knowing about their relationships. This leads to an unintentional connection to a therapist's social life. This may be particularly problematic for some clinicians such as feminist and lesbian therapists whether they live and work in a small town or large city (Biaggo & Greene, 1995; Brown, 1994) "because lesbian partners, both being women, tend to have less separate social spheres than do heterosexual partners" (Brown, p. 327). In addition, feminist therapists, therapists who are from racial or ethnic minority groups, therapists who are politically active, and therapists who are recovering substance abusers may all be part of small communities (regardless of the actual size of their town) and participate in community events and activities that bring them into contact with clients. This creates dilemmas for private practitioners, including how much they can be themselves out in public (such as dancing in the park at a concert or expressing unpopular beliefs at a political meeting). Does this mean that practitioners should not attend community events where clients may be present? Adhering to this as a hard-and-fast rule is overly cautious, in my mind. Clients seeing their therapists as real people may not be negative (Biaggo & Greene, 1995). Further, it is unreasonable to ask therapists never to attend a concert simply because a client may have the same taste in music. It is reasonable, in fact essential, for practitioners to discuss with their clients how seeing them outside the office affects them and how these encounters should be handled.

Financial issues. Finances are another factor that can create ethical quandaries for private practitioners. Berman (1985) raised the point that all therapy involving a fee for services inherently involves a form of multiple relationship—by blending business arrangements with therapy. Private practice exacerbates the problems in this duality. Clinicians in private practice more directly experience the financial impact of clients canceling their sessions or not showing up, insurers not reimbursing for services or limiting the number of sessions, and other fluctuations in income (Herlihy & Corey, 1992). Obviously, finances may influence how private practitioners conduct business. They may be more tempted to engage in behaviors that keep clients in therapy for longer than necessary. They may unconsciously (or consciously) increase clients' dependence or choose not to challenge clients when it might be therapeutically appropriate to do so for fear that clients may not come back and that they will lose income (Berman, 1985). It is essential for private practitioners to learn how to meet their need for income without seeing their clients primarily as objects of this income.

Of course the temptation to increase clients' dependence will be less problematic with the increased move toward managed mental health care. However, at the same time that managed care policies may decrease the problem of prolonging therapy unnecessarily, they create another problem. Regardless of decisions made by third-party payers, practitioners are responsible for making appropriate arrangements for continuation of care as considered clinically necessary. Because of this, counselors may find themselves providing services for little or no fee in order to implement clinically sound and ethical treatment plans.

Even though the ACA Code of Ethics directs counselors to engage in pro bono services or activities that yield little or no financial reward (Standard A.10.d.), I wonder if managed care will lead to an increased temptation to engage in bartering rather than an increase in the delivery of services at a reduced fee or as pro bono services. As has been discussed elsewhere, professional codes of ethics do not prohibit bartering, although they discourage it because it creates a potential to distort therapeutic relationships, exploit clients, and present conflicts.

Conclusions and suggestions. Hill (1990) noted that she is surprised that boundary violations do not happen more frequently. Given the intimate nature of therapy and the stressors involved with private practice, I share her surprise. However, I wonder how many multiple relationships exist that go unreported because clients are unaware of the harm, or potential harm, to them. How often have therapists hugged clients to appease their own need to nurture even though such behavior might interfere with clients' growth? Codes of ethics provide guidance in sorting out generally acceptable and unacceptable behaviors. They cannot, however, answer the question of whether it is appropriate to hug a specific client in a specific situation. More important than looking to codes of ethics for strict rules on what behaviors are and are not considered boundary violations, I agree with Biaggo and Greene (1995) who contended that therapists must develop for themselves a core set of standards that guide their ethical decisions. I further believe that therapists must base their actions on theoretically sound principles. Although many believe that common sense can help us see the potential dangers involved with multiple relationships, as Alfred Adler said, "If common sense were so common, everyone would have it" (in Gottlieb, 1994, p. 287). When we get caught up in our own issues, our common sense often leaves us. I offer the following suggestions as food for thought for practitioners, especially for those in private practice.

- **Recognize the complexity of therapeutic relationships.** First and foremost, I believe therapists must recognize that overlapping relationships do exist. I have seen too many professionals hide their heads in the sand and deny the complex nature of balancing the demands of being a therapist and remaining a human being. Refusing to acknowledge the nature of power differentials in therapeutic relationships is similar to refusing to acknowledge that we have personal biases that come into our sessions with us; but denial does not make the potential problems disappear and precludes developing strategies to prevent them. As noted in the Feminist Therapy Code of Ethics, acknowledging the potential for conflicting interests is essential if therapists are to monitor their actions and prevent potential harm to clients (Rave & Larsen, 1995).

- **Attend to self-care.** Most codes of ethics speak to the need for counselors to recognize their own needs and values. It is important for therapists to go beyond acknowledging needs and attend to taking care of themselves. It is essential to have friends and colleagues who are not clients, and to find ways to meet social and emotional needs other than those that involve a community shared with clients (Berman, 1985; Biaggo & Greene, 1995; Greenburg et al., 1985). Further, practitioners need to examine what possible harm can come to them, as well as their clients, if they enter into a multiple relationship. For example, they may come to resent watching out for their clients who are also friends, or they may actually end up minimizing their own personal needs to a degree that is unhealthy (Biaggo & Greene, 1995). This can lead to further erosion of appropriate boundaries with their clients, thus setting a dangerous cycle into motion. Seeking therapy to prevent or break such cycles is appropriate.

- **Engage in peer consultation.** As noted previously, peer consultation can counter the feelings of isolation experienced by many private practitioners, including those in group practice (Greenburg et al., 1985). I strongly recommend that private practitioners formalize some type of regular peer consultation rather than seeking assistance only in emergency situations or when faced with an ethical dilemma.

- **Engage in ongoing self-evaluation.** As Gerald Corey noted (Herlihy & Corey, 1992), peer consultation that focuses on issues of countertransference allows clinicians time and support to examine their own reactions, needs, and motivations. However, activities such as critiquing tapes of therapy sessions (with client permission, of course) and keeping a journal of reactions, feelings, and concerns (being careful to protect clients' identity) can be done on one's own. These may be ways to examine if certain behaviors come up more frequently with some clients than with others and to examine the extent to which interventions are well thought out. Biaggo and Greene (1995) suggested that clinicians check on their tendencies toward acting impulsively with some clients. They noted that this may be a sign that there is tension in the therapeutic relationship that calls for discussion between therapist and client.

- **Acknowledge potential for multiple relationships and possible harm to clients.** Informed consent applies to helping clients understand that their therapists also live in a community. It is important to discuss with clients how meetings outside of the office are to be handled along with the potential for the development of multiple relationships and how this may harm clients. It is the therapist's responsibility to educate clients about therapeutic boundaries and ways that clients can identify behaviors that are indicative of inappropriate boundaries. In addition, clients must be informed about avenues for recourse if they believe their therapist has engaged in improper behavior (e.g., reporting them to licensing boards and professional associations).

- **Use sound clinical judgment.** In examining potential for harm to clients, it is essential to examine not only the behavior in question (such as self-disclosure, serving on a committee with a client, or attending religious services in the same setting) but also the individual client(s) involved. For example, one will expect clients who are diagnosed as having a personality disorder to interpret therapist behaviors differently from clients who may not have as many boundary issues. Therapists should also remember that even individuals who are basically healthy will react in a variety of ways. For example, a therapist's self-disclosure about his or her own experience with adolescent depression may empower one client to think of depression in ways other than a pathological condition (Greenspan, 1986). This same disclosure may be seen by another client as intrusive, a shift in focus away from the client's needs, a message minimizing the client's experience, or advice in disguise. Berman (1985) suggested that therapists consider clients' ego strength and ability to self-differentiate before engaging in behaviors that may confuse clients about healthy therapeutic boundaries.

- **Remember the bottom line.** Regardless of theoretical orientation, personal philosophies, or financial situations, therapists are responsible for meeting their clients' therapeutic needs, not the other way around. Clinicians do not have to give up attending social or community events simply because clients may be present. They are not required to ignore the realities of the business aspects of their practice. However, they must think through possible consequences of their behaviors and take responsibility for preventing harm to their clients.

GROUP AND FAMILY COUNSELING

Counselors in all settings work both with individual clients and with groups and families. Boundary issues can be particularly complex when counselors are dealing not only with multiple roles and relationships but also with multiple clients. Questions that provide a framework for our discussion here include

- How can group leaders determine what kinds of personal and social relationships with group members are appropriate or inappropriate?
- Are there potential conflicts in admitting a former client into a counseling group? How about a friend or acquaintance?
- What are the limits of group leader self-disclosure? How could overextending the boundaries create a dual relationship?
- In a productive group, when leadership and membership roles may become blurred, what role conflicts might emerge?
- What unique boundary issues arise in marriage and family counseling?
- Are role conflicts inherent in serving as both the client's individual counselor and group counselor? In counseling both an individual family member and the entire family?

Personal Relationships in Group Counseling

How can group leaders distinguish between appropriate and inappropriate personal and social relationships with members of their groups? We think it is inappropriate for us to use our professional role to make personal and social contacts, and that it is certainly questionable to develop such relationships with current group members. In fact, we urge group counselors who look to their therapeutic groups as a source of friendships, or as a way to enrich their social lives, to examine their own personal needs and motivations. Group members should not be expected to perform the function of filling gaps in the therapist's personal and social life.

Establishing friendships with current group members can put a strain on the therapeutic relationship and can cause problems for the group leader, the member involved, and other members of the group. The group member might be inhibited from participating fully in the group for fear of jeopardizing the friendship. In addition, singling out an individual member as a friend is bound to affect the dynamics of the group. The members who are not chosen as friends are likely to feel rejected or resentful.

It is more difficult to handle the dual relationship issues that arise when personal and social relationships develop among group members. Pregroup screening can help to identify preexisting relationships among potential members that could be problematic. As Forester-Miller noted in the previous chapter, however, in small towns it may be impossible to form groups composed of people who do not already know each other. Even in urban areas where it is possible to screen for prior relationships, it is probable that as the group progresses, certain members will feel drawn to each other and may want to form personal relationships outside the group. This has its advantages and disadvantages. When members socialize outside group sessions, group cohesion might actually be increased. Yet such a practice can also destroy the cohesion of a group. If members become a social group that discusses group matters, and if they refuse to bring those matters into the group itself, the progress of the group is inevitably impeded. Other signs that indicate counterproductive socializing include the forming of cliques and excluding of certain members from social gatherings, the forming of romantic involvements without a willingness to acknowledge these involvements in the group, refusal to challenge one another in the group for fear of jeopardizing friendships, and an exclusive reliance on the group as a source of social life (Corey & Corey, 1997).

Some group leaders set ground rules at the outset that attempt to prohibit or discourage members from socializing outside of group time, and when the rationale is discussed and understood, this can be a useful approach. It is important that members understand that the primary purpose of a group experience is not for members to acquire friendships within the group but rather to teach participants attitudes and skills that they can use to form friendships in their everyday lives. Yet friendships cannot be prevented from developing, and if this occurs and affects the group's functioning it is probably best to have an open discussion in the group so that other members can share how they are being affected by these friendships.

Group Counseling for Former Clients

We know some counselors who form their groups largely from their former clients in individual therapy. They see it as a useful progression to suggest a group experience after a certain number of individual sessions. Such a practice can be useful for a client's growth and, if routinely done in this manner, seems appropriately aimed at maximizing client benefit and minimizing client expenses.

One potential problem that we see, however, is possible jealousy on the part of some clients. When they were seen individually, they had the counselor to themselves for the hour. Now, as group members, they must share their counselor with other group members. This can be therapeutically useful, but it is essential for these clients to discuss their reactions in the group setting. Further, other group members may be jealous of the person who has had private therapy with the group leader, and these reactions need to be expressed and dealt with in the group.

Admitting a Friend or Acquaintance to a Counseling Group

Admitting a friend or acquaintance is a very different matter than admitting a former client to a group. In the latter case, a professional relationship is already established. In the former case, we have the shifting of roles from a personal relationship to a professional relationship, which we think could create many difficulties for the therapist, the friend or acquaintance who becomes a group member, and possibly for others in the group. Again, the bottom line seems to be the importance of predicting potential problems when dual role relationships are being considered and discussing them fully. When there is a shifting of roles, and when this is not explored openly, problems can arise in the group. Hidden agendas will block the flow of group process.

Limits of Self-Disclosure

In the previous chapter, we discussed how overextending the boundaries of self-disclosure when counseling an individual client can create dual relationship conflicts. Here we want to note that self-disclosure brings up special problems in a group setting. As counselors, if we use the groups we lead for obtaining our own therapy, we will create confusing relationships. Are we the leader of the group, or merely another member? As leaders, we need to monitor our self-disclosure so that we are aware of what we are sharing and why we are sharing certain personal information. We need to develop guidelines that will help us determine what kinds of disclosure are helpful and what kinds might bog down the group.

This vignette reveals Glen's philosophy and practices regarding self-disclosure:

> Glen makes it a practice to be very self-disclosing in the men's groups that he facilitates in a community agency setting. He believes that one of the best ways to facilitate openness on the part of the other men is for him to model disclosure of his past and current difficulties as a man. He is also willing to take time to explore a present concern if it is getting in the way of his being present as a group leader. Although he is a skilled group leader with considerable training, he firmly believes that his own realness is what helps to create a trusting and cohesive group.

What are your thoughts about Glen's willingness to be personal in these groups? Do you see any potential ethical or clinical problems in Glen's self-disclosures about his past and present difficulties as a man? What dual relationship concerns, if any, do you have in this case?

It is not the role of group leaders to use group time to work through their personal problems; however, leaders can engage in a wide range of other self-disclosing behaviors. With few words, they can let members know that they are personally affected by the members' sharing of problems. Members can benefit from knowing that the group leader can identify with their struggles. Leaders can also express their persistent reactions to members and can offer feedback. They can model appropriate and timely self-disclosure by expressing how they are affected in the here-and-now context of the group.

In a productive group, leadership and membership roles sometimes can become blurred. However, a problem occurs when as group leaders we forget our primary role and purpose for being in the group. Our main purpose is to facilitate the growth of others, not to work through our own personal problems. If we become aware of pressing personal issues, we should consider joining a group in which we do not have leadership responsibilities.

Special Considerations for Marriage and Family Counseling

It seems to us that some boundary issues apply in a special way in marriage and family therapy. A counselor's loss of boundaries in couples or family counseling can create inappropriate alliances and render the therapy ineffective.

Consider this example:

> Paul, an intern, was counseling a couple who came to therapy to work out problems in their marriage. Paul increasingly came to view the wife as overbearing and rigid. As the supervisor observed a session, she noted that Paul's responses to the husband were generally supportive, whereas his responses to the wife's verbalizations were often challenging or nonempathic. When the supervisor met with Paul and asked him what he was experiencing in the session, Paul replied, "I don't see how he can stand being married to her!

In this example, Paul colluded with the husband, in effect lining up with him against the wife. If you were Paul's supervisor, how might you work with Paul? Might you point out that Paul had created an implicit and unacknowledged dual relationship as the husband's defender and advocate?

Dual relationships can arise for marriage and family therapists in other, more obvious ways. When the therapist has a prior relationship with either a husband or a wife, or with one member of a family, marriage and family therapists recognize the inadvisability of entering into a counseling relationship with the couple or the family. Social relationships with couples or families who are currently in counseling are generally to be avoided. When an individual has been in counseling, and then wishes to change the focus of the counseling to marriage or family therapy, some therapists refer the case to another professional. The prior individual therapeutic relationship might present some difficulties for the newly entering spouse or family members who might not feel on an equal footing.

In marital and family practice, a therapist might see a wife in individual therapy, and then at some point the husband might join the sessions for couples therapy, and at times the entire family might be seen. Some therapists may not be comfortable with this practice, and they may have difficulty in sorting out primary allegiances. In particular, confidentiality questions are likely to arise, and counselors need to be clear about their policies regarding secrets and hidden agendas.

Systems theory is based on a different orientation than individual therapy. In doing individual therapy, we may be sensitive to how an individual's changes affect his or her family, and we may explore ways in which the client's family is now influencing him or her, but the primary focus is on the individual's dynamics. From a systems perspective, one part of the system affects the whole system, and the system affects the individual. Margolin (1982) argued that complex dilemmas can arise when family members are seen together in therapy. Some interventions that serve one person's best interests might burden another family member or even be countertherapeutic. Family counselors need to make intricate judgment calls in attempting to balance their therapeutic responsibilities toward individual family members and toward the family as a whole.

Concurrent Individual and Group or Family Counseling

Are role conflicts inherent in serving as both the client's individual counselor and group or family counselor? There are many possible permutations here. Although the terms *concurrent, conjoint,* and *combined* are frequently used to describe when individual therapy and group or family therapy are offered simultaneously, Yalom (1995) has made some distinctions. According to Yalom, concurrent therapy involves two different therapists, conjoint therapy involves the same therapist with all members of the group or family, and combined therapy involves the same therapist with some of the members. Most writers have seemed to agree that when individual therapy and one of these modalities are synchronized and are working well together, the effect can be very powerful.

There are, however, some potential problems that call for careful consideration. Practitioners who see clients on an individual basis and also in a group should have a clinical justification for this practice. As we mentioned earlier, from an ethical perspective, problems arise if counselors are engaging in this practice primarily to meet their own financial or psychological needs. Gazda (1992), in the first edition of this book, also noted that there are potential problems with transference/countertransference and with dependency. He reminded us that psychodynamic therapists have expressed concern about dilution of the transference in combined or concurrent group and individual therapy, and that the complication of sibling rivalry is added when a client has to share the therapist with others in a group. He concluded that the result is often confusing when the processes of concurrent therapy are compounded with the complex workings of transference. He also pointed out the potential for combined individual and group therapy to increase client dependency on the therapist because the client must rely on the same therapist in both settings.

Yet it is possible for the same therapist to work beneficially with the same client on an individual basis and in a group setting. For example, we know a clinical social worker in a community agency who works in individual therapy with women with a history of incest and also offers a short-term support group for incest survivors. She screens members carefully and determines which clients could benefit from concurrent private therapy and participation in a support group. Clients in their individual therapy can explore in more depth certain personal issues that they may not have time to explore in the group. Concurrent therapy can work well if the therapist has a clear rationale for this form of treatment and if the therapist discusses the possible benefits and risks of this approach.

Another clinical social worker who also works in a community agency sees many of his clients on an individual basis. He also refers a number of his male clients to a men's group that he and one of his colleagues conduct in the agency. He finds that the combination of working with men in individual sessions initially, and then progressing to a group to explore common themes, to be extremely productive. In this case, it is not a situation of simultaneous individual and group counseling, but of individual therapy followed by a group. In many instances, clients can benefit from joining a group after their individual therapy is completed. The continuing support they receive can be helpful in maintaining treatment gains and is usually quite affordable.

We think that, generally, counselors are wise to avoid serving as both individual and group counselor, or as both individual and family counselor, for the same client when this situation can be avoided. Of course, in some treatment facilities, these types of dual relationships cannot be avoided. Treatment plans in inpatient settings routinely include individual and group therapy, and sometimes both modalities are provided by the same therapist. Then it is up to the practitioner to take steps to lessen the possible damaging effects of functioning in multiple roles, especially as this applies to any compromising of confidentiality. Clients have a right to know what disclosures will be kept confidential and what information might be shared with other members of a treatment team.

Perhaps the most justifiable approach to meeting the needs of clients who could benefit from both individual counseling and group or family counseling is for the services to be provided by different therapists. Many private practitioners, for instance, work with individual clients who are also concurrently attending aftercare groups at various hospitals or in the community. When concurrent individual and group or family therapy are provided by different therapists, we think the important factor is for the two therapists to work cooperatively (with the client's permission to communicate with each other), so that the goals of individual therapy and group or family therapy are understood by all parties. Decisions regarding concurrent individual therapy and group or family therapy are multifaceted; they are influenced by the setting in which the therapies occur, by the client's needs, and by the theoretical orientation of the practitioner.

Focus on Specialty Areas:
Substance Abuse Counseling
Counseling Clients Living With HIV
Rehabilitation Counseling
Forensic Psychology and Counseling

In this chapter, we continue our focus on specialty areas, examining boundary questions and concerns that arise in the fields of substance abuse counseling, counseling clients who are living with HIV, rehabilitation counseling, and forensic psychology and counseling. Our own experience with these specializations is limited, so we rely greatly on the expertise of our four guest contributors: Les J. Powell for substance abuse counseling, Craig D. Kain for counseling clients with HIV, Hal Cain for rehabilitation counseling, and Robert Haynes for forensic psychology.

SUBSTANCE ABUSE COUNSELING

Many substance abuse counselors who are themselves in recovery face some unique boundary issues in their therapeutic relationships with clients. We turn now to Les J. Powell's thoughts on these issues.

Multiple Roles Among Recovering Substance Abuse Counselors

Les J. Powell

Professionals in the field of substance abuse counseling who are recovering from a similar condition to that of their clients are described as *two-hatters* (Barker, 1996). These professionals face some unique problems, as do all counselors who are recovering from the same condition with which their clients are afflicted. A demographic survey of the members of the National Association of

Alcoholism and Drug Abuse Counselors (NAADAC) revealed that 52% of respondents categorized themselves as being in recovery from substance dependency. Further, 46% of respondents identified themselves as codependent and 53% as adult children of alcoholics (McGovern, Wright, & Wright, 1990).

These counselors often are members of recovery groups, also known as mutual-help groups. Recovery groups have become an efficient and efficacious means for recovering individuals to maintain the gains they have made. Recovery groups such as Alcoholics Anonymous (AA), Narcotics Anonymous (NA), Cocaine Anonymous (CA), Sexaholics Anonymous (SA), Rational Recovery (RR), Adult Children of Alcoholics (ACOA), and Al-Anon help people sustain a life program involving continued growth. Individuals with substance dependence are prone to relapse if they do not maintain an appropriate level of growth (AA, 1976; Gorski & Miller, 1986; White, 1993).

Individuals who belong to recovery groups have meetings in which those who are in recovery, and those who might wish to enter recovery, congregate and share their experiences, strengths, and hopes. This is accomplished by describing personal experiences of how it was, what happened, and what it is like now (AA, 1976). Often, the decision to attend self-help meetings is a lifetime commitment for the recovering individual.

Recovering substance abuse counselors may find themselves in nonfacilitated mutual self-help meetings where their clients are also present. The counseling relationship between recovering counselors and their clients may be altered if the counselors share their experiences in the meeting (Bissell & Royce, 1994). Honesty is essential in 12-step recovery programs, and clients may be less willing to share honestly in the meeting if their counselor is present (White, 1993).

Although recovering substance abuse counselors' continued growth and remission may be contingent on their attendance at self-help functions, some counselors may choose not to attend these meetings if they know that their clients also may be in attendance. Thus an ethical dilemma exists for recovering counselors who are two-hatters. If they suspect that one of their clients may attend a meeting of a mutual-help group of which they are a member, should they not attend that meeting so that the client will feel free to speak about his or her experiences, even though this attempt to avoid a dual relationship may put the counselor's own recovery in jeopardy? Should the recovering counselor find another meeting group?

"When anyone, anywhere, reaches out for help, I want the hand of AA always to be there, and for that: I am responsible" (AA, 1967, p. 332). The members of AA adhere to and abide by this statement, which is known as the responsibility pledge. Many newcomers (newly sober individuals) are taught this pledge, and other self-help groups have similar philosophies. This seemingly simple commitment may cause difficulties for an inexperienced counselor who is in recovery and is also a professional in the field of substance abuse treatment. Bissell and Royce (1994) noted that "Some treatment facilities have actually required AA members on their staffs to sponsor their own patients, a risky merging of two quite different roles that are, at best, not easy to keep separate" (p. 45). This practice can form the basis for other, potential harmful dual relationships. Too often, clients are unintentionally harmed by recovering counselors who are unprepared to differentiate between their responsibility to be sponsors and friends of other recovering people and their responsibility to their clients to maintain appropriate therapeutic boundaries. These inexperienced counselors all too often find themselves defending against negligence charges in court, or lose their certification, licensure, or career because they were ill informed about the repercussions that can follow the improper management of dual relationships.

Yet dual relationships that are encountered by recovering substance abuse counselors are not necessarily counterproductive. Bader (1994) suggested that the central questions should be whether the relationship is exploitive and whether it impairs judgment, and that the focus is most meaningfully placed on the question of exploitation rather than on the question of duality. Dual relationships that meet the recovering counselor's needs at the expense of the client may be considered exploitive. According to White (1993), "When the professional helper develops an investment and expectation in meeting his or her personal needs within the relationship with a client, the primary commitment and duty—the fiduciary contract—to care for the client has been at best weakened and at worst abandoned" (p. 152). Dual relationships that violate physical, psychological, or spiritual boundaries of the client might also be termed exploitive and/or invasive (Kasl, 1992). Kasl also stated that boundary violations occur within a relationship when the person with the most perceived power intentionally or unintentionally fails to set limits and enforce boundaries. In most circumstances, the client perceives the recovering counselor as having more power. Because clients often are unable, for many reasons, to set limits or enforce boundaries, it is the responsibility of the recovering counselor to set and enforce boundaries related to differing roles and dual relationships. As has been noted elsewhere in this book, clients may not be aware that a dual relationship exists. Therefore, it is the duty of the recovering counselor to communicate with the client and to help the client understand the differences among the roles in which they are engaged. Expectations of the recovering counselor and client may be different, depending on the role that is being assumed. For example, a client may have one set of expectations for a member of a self-help group and another set of expectations of the recovering counselor. These expectations are most appropriately discussed as they change and evolve.

The effect of a dual relationship between a recovering counselor and client in the self-help setting might be compounded in a rural community. Rural settings limit the availability of self-help meetings compared to urban settings

(Bissell & Royce, 1994). In the rural setting, recovering counselors may be more tempted not to attend self-help meetings that their clients are attending. In an urban community, the abundance of self-help meetings alleviates this problem. Further, urban settings often provide the opportunity for recovering professionals to form their own mutual-help groups.

Training and research issues. The field of substance abuse treatment is evolving as a profession. As recovering substance abuse professionals continue to pursue licensure and advanced degrees, more emphasis will be placed on their knowledge of ethical aspects of their profession, including duality of relationships (Bissell & Royce, 1994; Dove, 1995).

Research illustrating the unique dual relationships between recovering substance abuse counselors and their clients is sparse (Barker, 1996). I am presently engaged in research of this type in connection with my master's degree. This research aims to discover information that might further the education of those who are entering the substance abuse counseling field, and of those professionals who are interested in advancing their knowledge of the ethical issues involved. Substance abuse professionals in supervisory positions, educators, and inexperienced recovering substance abuse professionals might gain insight from this and other research endeavors. Information that is gained might be passed on to students, supervisors, and colleagues to help prevent harm to clients and sanctions against otherwise skilled counselors.

Summary. Recovering substance abuse professionals are well advised to develop and maintain their own personal boundaries with respect to the differing roles they assume. Recovering counselors, like all helping professionals, must have a clear understanding of their personal needs and motivations, and must apply this understanding in the development of their personal and professional boundaries. The boundaries between the roles of professional counselor and recovery group member may sometimes overlap. However, this merging of roles need not be exploitive or conflictual. Recovering counselors may reach out to their own sponsors, peers, and supervisors as ethical dilemmas are anticipated. The more that professionals utilize consultation, the less likely they are to be negligent in the performance of their professional duties.

COUNSELING CLIENTS LIVING WITH HIV

Craig D. Kain, in his following commentary on working with HIV clients, raises some issues that are similar to those just discussed by Les J. Powell in his consideration of dualities in the work of recovering substance abuse counselors. When a counselor is HIV positive and works with HIV clients, or when a counselor is in recovery from substance abuse disorder and works with clients who are also recovering, multiple role conflicts are bound to arise. Both the HIV community and the recovery community can be quite tightly knit, so that opportunities for boundary blurrings are common.

Another similarity is that HIV-positive clients are another special population whose needs can be met only if we are willing to assume some nontraditional roles, such as advocate, case manager, and change agent. Kain points out that the HIV/AIDS community is a small one, so that counselors who work with people living with HIV confront many of the same issues as do rural practitioners as well as unique issues created by the social, political, legal, and economic context in which HIV-positive clients live.

——————◆——————

Coloring Outside the Lines:
Multiple Relationships in Working With People Living With HIV

Craig D. Kain

It is important that those of us who work with HIV-positive clients demonstrate our humanness in the counseling relationship (Kain, 1996). Because HIV disease is often a dehumanizing illness, at times stripping clients of their physical ability, economic viability, and self-identity, it stands to reason that we must provide them with a genuine, human connection. This may place counselors in a quandary: how do we attend to our clients' needs for genuine human relationship while at the same time maintaining what we believe are good therapeutic practices and boundaries? In my experience, although counselors working with people living with HIV are not required to *violate* our ethical boundaries, we do need to *bend* them. We are asked to help our clients draw a picture of their life that, almost by definition, requires coloring outside the lines.

In order to better understand the quandary, we must first recognize the particular social, political, legal, and economic context in which HIV disease occurs. People living with HIV must contend with social ostracism ranging from mild disapproval to outright prejudice in the forms of racism, sexism, and homophobia. They must place their trust for a better future in a political system that influences everything from what types of research on HIV gets funded to what types of drugs get approved. People living with HIV must navigate a legal system that regulates crucial aspects of their lives, from the types of disability compensation for which they qualify to the types of visitors they may have in the hospital. Finally, HIV-positive people in this country must work their way through a system that links health care to economic status and thus often provides insufficient health care for those who lack funds. As counselors, we too must work within these contexts. We must keep them in mind because they exert an enormous influence on the decisions we make regarding the types of relationships we will have with our clients.

For these reasons as well as many others, counselors working with HIV-positive clients are often called upon to assume multiple roles (e.g., case manager, client advocate, confidant). It is important for us to remember that these roles define our relationship with our client. To me, it is not so much that we have multiple relationships, but rather that *our one relationship with our client is determined by these varied roles.*

At times we may be asked to perform tasks often considered within the scope of a case manager that cause us to have relationships with our clients outside the typical counseling session. For example, our clients may need an emergency ride to their primary physician, and we may be the only person they know to ask to arrange for it. Whether we assist the client directly (i.e., physically transport the client) or indirectly (i.e., offer to pay for a taxi), we need to recognize that we have colored outside the lines. Clients may need someone to visit them in the hospital. We may find that they do not want therapy so much as companionship and friendship. Clients may need someone to be their advocate in interactions with a government office. They may assume, often correctly, that our professional status could help them move through bureaucratic delays. In these and other similar situations our human desire to be of service to others may in our minds overshadow our professional obligations. Still, we always need to be cognizant of the ways in which we are bending our professional boundaries. We will need to discuss these with colleagues and, when appropriate, with our clients.

At times we may find ourselves being asked to counsel others in our clients' lives. We may be called upon to serve as an individual counselor to a significant other, conjoint counselor, or family counselor. Although we may try to refer to others, the crisis nature of HIV counseling often negates our best-made plans. For example, if we are asked to see clients in their homes, others attending to their care may ask to be included (or in our judgment need to be included) in treatment. When these situations occur we must make certain that all parties are aware of our multiple roles.

Our own personal roles may often come in conflict with more narrowly defined ideas of counselor-client interaction. The HIV/AIDS community is a small one. Thus if we are actively involved in AIDS education, advocacy, or fundraising, we are likely to meet clients in social situations. Given the social, economic, and political nature of HIV disease, our involvement in these activities is crucial and thus these situations are not easily avoided.

Another way in which our own personal lives may increase the number of roles we maintain with clients is if we are HIV positive. Given the limited number of social and support activities for people living with HIV we may, without anticipating it, find ourselves attending the same functions as our clients. Unlike the situations described previously, in which we maintain our expert status, in these situations we are clients. Similarly, we may unexpectedly run into a client in our physician's waiting area, especially if the physician is a well-known HIV specialist. Although this is not the same as actively seeking out a friendship with a client, it does change the nature of the counseling relationship. Can we in good conscience be in the same support group, attend the same social functions, or wait in the same reception area as our clients? The answer, as is true of many questions about HIV, is not clear cut. Pursuing other options may be a possibility for counselors in some locales, but in other areas where HIV-related services are more limited, these doctors, groups, and social functions may be the only place where HIV-positive people (clients and counselors) can obtain treatment, support, and camaraderie.

If we are faculty members in counselor education programs and also work within the HIV/AIDS community, our roles may be stretched in different ways. HIV-positive students may see our office as a "safe place" and may disclose their HIV status to us. They may ask us to keep their status confidential, which may place us in an awkward position of balancing our duty to the student with our duty to our educational institution. It is important to remember that our role as faculty member is defined differently from that of counselor or therapist. Students may not always recognize this, and it is our responsibility to inform students of any differences that may exist.

When we work with clients and students living with HIV, we constantly must be alert to how our relationships with them encompass multiple roles. To me, what is important is not whether we enter into these multiple roles (for I am convinced that doing so is an inevitable part of the work we do) but *how* we enter these roles. Do we enter into them with our eyes open or closed? Do we acknowledge these multiple roles with our clients and students, or do we try to minimize them? Do we encourage clients and students to talk with us about the effects on them (both positive and negative) of these multiple roles, or do we avoid such discussions for fear that we will be accused of overstepping our boundaries? Do we actively seek consultation when we become confused (or anticipate becoming confused) about a multiple-role situation, or do we shy away from talking with colleagues for fear of being judged unprofessional or unethical? Are we aware of our own limits when we take on new roles, in terms of our education, experience, and training to do the new tasks these roles may require? Are we equally aware of our personal limits, of our comfort in taking on new HIV-related roles, and of our emotional capacity to engage in such activities? The clearer we can be about these multiple roles with ourselves, our clients, and those to whom we turn for professional and personal guidance, the more we can rest assured that we are drawing outside the lines in the service of our clients.

REHABILITATION COUNSELING

Rehabilitation counselors facilitate the personal, social, and economic independence of persons with disabilities and, more specifically, help these persons find or return to employment. Rehabilitation counselors face some difficult issues involving role conflicts and divided loyalties because they work in both the public and private sector and serve multiple constituencies. Each of these constituencies has a vested interest in the outcome of counseling, and these interests are often competing and contradictory. For rehabilitation counselors—who may serve as counselor, gatekeeper to services, evaluator, and expert witness—the question is not one of dual roles but rather of multiple roles. Because they have multiple obligations—to the client, to their employer, to the customer (the one who pays the bill), and to society—it is especially important that they be clear about their primary loyalties. In the following contribution, Hal Cain addresses the areas in which multiple relationships and role conflicts are likely to present problems for rehabilitation counselors.

Roles and Conflicts for Rehabilitation Counselors

Hal Cain

Rehabilitation counseling is a profession within the larger context of counseling professions. Rehabilitation counselors provide services in both the public and private sectors in settings that range from inpatient hospitals to industry-based rehabilitation programs. The many roles that rehabilitation counselors assume in these settings include, but are not limited to, advocate, psychotherapist, service broker, job coach, case manager, and teacher. It is not uncommon for rehabilitation counselors to be equally involved with employers or school administrators, insurance companies, family members, and the client all at the same time.

Because the scope of practice for rehabilitation counseling is broad and the venues in which it takes place vary greatly, rehabilitation counselors, as a group, may have a greater risk potential for role conflict than other counselors. The expanding range of what constitutes rehabilitation counseling makes it impossible to identify all the potential role conflicts for practitioners. However, there are at least three major areas in which dual relationships and role conflicts are likely to present problems for rehabilitation counselors. These areas are case management, dealing with third-party payers, and advocacy.

Case management. A role often assumed by rehabilitation counselors is the coordination of clients' rehabilitation service plans. In this role, the rehabilitation counselor becomes the case manager. The dual role of case manager and counselor, which may be seen as inherent in the work of the rehabilitation counselor, carries several potential areas of role conflict.

The nature of case management dictates communication and collaboration with other service providers, intra-agency and/or interagency, and often brokering for or purchasing services from these professionals. Because a case manager is seen as a liaison between the client and other services and as the gatekeeper to these services, this position carries with it the need to be equitable in all professional relationships. A rehabilitation counselor who is also the case manager has to balance the primary client-counselor relationship with these other relationships to avoid conflicts between counseling and management responsibilities.

Having managerial powers over a client's rehabilitation services plan may be seen as advantageous for the rehabilitation counselor in that overseeing beneficial services gives the counselor greater flexibility in assuring comprehensive services geared toward positive outcomes (e.g., competitive employment, independent living, maximum medical stability). Indeed, many rehabilitation counselors function as case managers, especially in state and federal agencies, and help their clients achieve more independence through acquisition of needed services. Nevertheless, rehabilitation counselors who are case managers may also find themselves torn between the client's wishes and the client's best interests. For example, a client states during a counseling session that he is unhappy with his occupational therapist (OT) and no longer wants to attend occupational therapy. The rehabilitation counselor has observed that this client tends to avoid difficult situations and suspects that the client's displeasure with the OT is related to the OT "pushing the limits" (within acceptable practice) with the client. As a case manager, the rehabilitation counselor must recognize and respect the client's right to refuse treatment. What "hat" does the rehabilitation counselor wear in this situation? If it is the counseling hat, the counselor is most likely to work with the client on personal issues such as self-efficacy and control. But the counselor wearing a case management hat will want to see the client stay with the rehabilitation plan as written, with a focus on successful case closure. This may involve working with the client on compliance issues or a change of occupational therapists. Either way, the case manager's concern is with program issues and not intrapersonal issues. Although the two hats are not incompatible, one focuses on the treatment plan as priority and the other on individual development.

Another potential conflict resulting from the case manager/counselor dual role has to do with risk to the therapeutic relationship. Clients may lose trust in a rehabilitation counselor if they believe the counselor is more concerned with meeting the needs of others (e.g., service providers, insurance companies) involved with the rehabilitation plan. If case managers/counselors spend most of their time with clients talking about other team members' reports regarding the client's program, they run the risk of depersonalizing the counselor-client relationship. Discord in the therapeutic relationship can also be created when clients feel pressure to comply with treatment because the rehabilitation counselor, as the case manager, holds the "purse strings" to their case.

In addition to role conflicts resulting from a rehabilitation counselor's split focus, case loads may limit the amount of time spent providing direct counseling services. Many rehabilitation counselors in the public sector, and a growing number in the private sector, have case loads that make it difficult to see clients for regular counseling sessions to deal with personal issues. When case management responsibilities are added, counseling is often forced to take second priority.

Rehabilitation counselors who are in a case manager/counselor dual relationship with a client must find some way to differentiate their counseling function from their case management position. One strategy that may help avoid conflicts is to discuss with a client, up front, what these roles are and the limitations and advantages of each. Involving clients in all aspects of development of their rehabilitation plan also helps avoid misunderstandings that could lead to conflict. Clear expectations on the parts of both the rehabilitation counselor and the client will reduce the risk of role conflict.

Third-party payers. Most rehabilitation counselors, whether working in private or public sector rehabilitation, will deal with third-party payers. Third-party payers can be insurance companies, government agencies, or other funding sources that do not come directly from client fees for service. Whether the counselor is in private practice or works in an agency, role conflict in third-party payer situations stems from confusion as to who is considered the client—the payer or the person who is receiving the rehabilitation services.

The dilemmas that can lead to role conflict for rehabilitation counselors in meeting the needs of clients arise from working within the guidelines, limitations, and controls of these funding sources. For example, insurance companies usually have limits on the amount of reimbursement for therapeutic services and adaptive equipment for each rehabilitation case. If a rehabilitation counselor believes a client needs therapy or other expenditures beyond what is provided in the client's insurance policy, this creates problems. Rehabilitation counselors faced with this situation can either revise the rehabilitation plan to accommodate the policy's fiscal constraints or attempt to justify a plan that they believe will best serve the needs of the client.

When funding sources are public or private not-for-profit, limitations on clients' rehabilitation plans are sometimes due to the lack of financial resources. Administrative restrictions that may affect the quality of services provided also will cause role conflict for rehabilitation counselors who, as professionals, have a duty to exercise their best clinical judgment in carrying out their obligations to the person receiving services, that is, the client. Again, the control issue arises.

Rehabilitation counselors may find themselves in a role conflict between being an employee of the funding source and a counselor for the client. Some realities of the limits imposed due to fiscal resources cannot be avoided. Nevertheless, when artificial boundaries are set on the amount and quality of services deemed necessary by the rehabilitation counselor, ethical decisions need to be made. As an employee of the third-party payer, the rehabilitation counselor will try to contain costs. As a counselor serving the interests of the client, the rehabilitation counselor will try to obtain the optimal service mix regardless of the costs.

Providing rehabilitation counseling within the restrictions of third-party payers can be difficult. Potential role conflicts may be avoided if the rehabilitation counselor is aware of the funding limitations and can legitimately say that the client's rehabilitation plan was developed without undue restrictions from the third-party funding source. In cases where the funding source places restrictions that significantly compromise the chances of the client progressing through rehabilitation, ethically the counselor must find alternative resources or make appropriate referrals.

Advocacy. One of the forces behind rehabilitation counseling is that rehabilitation counselors are advocates for persons with disabilities. Advocating for the rights of persons with disabilities and giving input to policy change at all levels are part of a rehabilitation counselor's professional responsibilities. Role conflicts associated with being a disability rights advocate occur when rehabilitation counselors lose focus on a client's individual needs.

It is sometimes easy for rehabilitation counselors to get caught up in the disability movement and overgeneralize beyond the needs of the individual who is there for services. Rehabilitation counselors must remember that each person who comes to them for services is unique in his or her own set of issues. In addition, as advocates we sometimes tend to be overzealous in our advocacy and, in doing so, forget to teach our clients to be self-advocates.

Conclusions. The ultimate goal of rehabilitation counseling is to help individuals with disabilities achieve their full potential in life. To this end, rehabilitation counselors take a holistic approach in serving their clients. Because rehabilitation counselors assume many roles as they carry out their duties, dual relationships are virtually inevitable. Role conflicts can be minimized if rehabilitation counselors view the client-counselor relationship as the basis of quality service.

FORENSIC PSYCHOLOGY AND COUNSELING

Psychologists have long been involved in the field of forensic work, and some counselors specialize in working with criminal offenders. With the increasing number of incarcerated criminal offenders and the heightened focus on solving the problems of violent crime, workplace violence, murder and violent behavior among teenagers, and other similar concerns, more psychologists and counselors are entering the criminal justice field than ever before.

Robert Haynes draws upon his clinical forensic work experience and the 20 years he has invested in guiding clinical and counseling doctoral-level interns through an internship program in a forensic inpatient setting in the following contribution. He describes the challenges of managing multiple relationships in such a setting.

Managing Multiple Relationships in a Forensic Setting

Robert Haynes

In the forensic setting, therapeutic boundaries are often unclear and the role of the psychologist or counselor is multiple and complex. The mental health professional in a forensic setting serves in a variety of roles and may be called upon to be therapist, evaluator, security enforcer, case manager, expert witness, and predictor of future dangerousness (an imprecise science at best), all for the same client.

A common dilemma for the forensic practitioner is to determine who is the actual client (Monahan, 1980). Is it the individual client, the courts, the state, the victim, or society? For whom, and for whose good, is the practitioner working? Whose goals take priority when conducting therapy? The courts may have mandated therapy to help the client become a law-abiding citizen, but the offender may want to become less guilt ridden about committing a crime. Is it the psychotherapist's role to help the client work for what he or she wants? To challenge or confront the client? It is crucial that the therapist has a clear picture of the boundaries of the relationship and whose goals take priority, and that this understanding is clear before the therapist engages in a professional relationship with the client.

Confidentiality in the true sense is nearly impossible given that the professional is most likely working for the courts, probation, or the state. A trusting relationship is essential in therapy, but it is difficult to achieve in a forensic setting. Therapists can, however, identify with the client those topics that can remain confidential in the therapy relationship and those that cannot. It is then the client's choice whether or not to delve into areas that cannot be kept confidential. Sometimes a forensic client will venture into the nonconfidential area just to see what the therapist will do and to determine whether the therapist can be manipulated into keeping secrets. Once the therapist keeps confidential any information that should be reported, the therapist has crossed the boundary of the therapeutic relationship and will most likely see an escalation of unusual requests and demands by the client.

When I was working as a psychologist on an inpatient unit, I led group therapy sessions for many clients on the unit. Because I was the only psychologist on the unit, I was often called upon to conduct psychological evaluations of clients for the purpose of making recommendations to the court regarding the clients' readiness for release into the community. In more than one instance, I was subpoenaed to testify regarding findings of my psychological evaluation of a client who had been in one of my groups. My recommendations may well have had a large bearing on whether the client was released or confined for longer periods of time. The danger was that my evaluation may have been influenced by information I had received in the therapeutic relationship. It is challenging to keep separate the various sources of information and relationships.

Although the demands of many forensic settings require the multiple role model of practice, the practitioner can make every effort to minimize conflicts of interest. For example, the practitioner might trade the provision of psychological evaluations with another psychologist in order to avoid providing both therapy and evaluation with the same client. Therapists must be prepared to identify instances when the ethics of the situation require them to pull back from one or more roles.

Countertransference issues also affect therapeutic boundaries in working with forensic clients. It is important for forensic psychologists and counselors to understand what they can and cannot accomplish with a criminal offender. Much of our training involves learning to support the client and provide a trusting and caring relationship, and we have our own needs to be needed, to be helpful, and to nurture. These needs are often counterproductive with forensic clients and may open the door for the offender to manipulate both the therapist and the system (Meloy, Haroun, & Schiller, 1990). Support, trust, and caring may need to be moderated with caution, objectivity, and a watchful eye for manipulation. In particular, working with sociopathic offenders requires a more structured, sometimes confrontive, and always cautious approach.

It is not uncommon for helping professionals in forensic settings to feel dislike, disgust, and even repulsion toward some clients because of the heinous crimes they committed. These feelings can lead professionals to become more comfortable in the role of security enforcer and less comfortable as therapist. The practitioner must be constantly aware of the potential for such feelings and work to keep them in check. According to Mobley (1987), therapists who are most likely to be successful in working with forensic clients are those who can empathize without sympathy, confront without demeaning, care without carrying the client's burdens, direct without controlling, and see manipulation as a poor coping strategy rather than as a personal assault. They find satisfaction in erratic progress toward limited goals, can tolerate the ambiguities and conflicts of the setting, and accept their own limits so that they do not burn out.

Students and supervisees in particular may be faced with judgment calls that require an ability to foresee consequences to their decisions. To give an example, a sociopathic sex offender asked a counseling student to mail a letter to the client's seriously ill sister at the local post office rather than wait for the next day's institutional mail run. The client reported that he was his sister's only family, and that she was depending on him to help her through her life-threatening illness. Although this may appear to be a minor request, if it violates institutional rules the student who complies has crossed the line and is now assisting the client to violate the rules and work the system. The demands from this client are likely to escalate to more serious violations of institutional policy. In fact, this may be characteristic of the kind of behavior that led to the client's arrest— minor violations that escalated over time.

Not every therapist is suited to work with criminal offenders. Recommendations for psychologists and counselors working in a forensic setting include the following:

- Know your strengths and limitations in working with a forensic population.

- Be aware of how your own values and countertransference issues affect your work.

- Recognize that psychotherapy can be effective with criminal offenders but may require approaches not traditionally taught in graduate school.

- Utilize colleagues and supervisors as consultants to provide feedback regarding difficult cases and issues.

- Take care of your own mental health. Forensic work can be challenging, exhausting, and demanding.

- Remember that safety and security must be priorities, sometimes at the expense of treatment.

- Become familiar with the standards and principles that apply specifically to forensic psychology, such as the Speciality Guidelines for Forensic Psychologists (American Psychology-Law Society, & Division 41 of APA, 1991).

This chapter focused on four distinct specialty areas of practice. They are quite different from each other, yet they share these commonalities: dual and even multiple roles are inherent in the nature of the work; and practitioners need to assume some nontraditional roles if they are to serve their client populations effectively. Certainly, practitioners of many other counseling specialties confront similar issues, and we invite you to consider how the points raised by our chapter contributors might be applied to your own work. For instance, many of the issues raised by Craig D. Kain regarding work with clients living with HIV/AIDS, and by Hal Cain with respect to health care delivery in rehabilitation counseling, are equally applicable to counseling clients who are terminally ill in the hospice setting. Many counselors do not consider themselves as specialists in forensic work, yet they experience role conflicts when they find themselves involved with the legal system as part of their work with a client. An example of this kind of involvement—when a school counselor has to go to court and testify regarding child abuse or neglect—is discussed in the next chapter.

Focus on Specialty Areas:
School Counseling
Higher Education

In this chapter, we look at dual or multiple relationship dilemmas that occur in educational settings. We begin with a focus on elementary and secondary schools. Our first guest contributor to this chapter, A. Michael Dougherty, identifies some roles and duties commonly assumed by school counselors that can create dual relationship conflicts. We then move to a discussion of boundary issues in higher education, and Sue Spooner presents her views on this subject.

SCHOOL COUNSELING

Historically, school counselors have not been much concerned with dual relationship issues. Only in the most recent revision of the American School Counselors Association (ASCA) *Ethical Standards for School Counselors* (1992) has a guideline regarding dual relationships appeared. This lack of attention may be due to the fact that many dual relationship issues do not apply to working with children or to the school setting. For instance, the issue of posttherapy social relationships is more pertinent to working with adults, and the issue of bartering for goods or services does not apply to counselors who are salaried employees of a school district.

Nonetheless, we believe that school counselors need to be aware of dual relationship issues and that they do encounter multiple role conflicts in their work. These conflicts can arise in subtle and sometimes unexpected ways for school counselors. Consider these two scenarios involving Wayne and Angelica, both school counselors:

- After school, a teacher drops by Wayne's office. Wayne and the teacher are friends. Wayne casually asks, "How's it going?" The teacher's response comes out in a rush. She is feeling tremendously stressed by the demands of raising a child with a handicapping condition, caring for an aging parent, and going to graduate school. When Wayne suggests that she might want to consider seeking counseling, the teacher says, "Where on earth would I find the time or money for that! I hope you won't mind if I just 'bend your ear.'"

- Angelica is conducting a parenting skills group one evening per week. During the fourth session, one of the parents relates an anecdote about the discipline methods he uses. It seems clear to Angelica that these methods are physically abusive.

These two situations seem quite dissimilar, but they both raise potential dual relationship conflicts. In Wayne's case, the teacher hopes to receive—and clearly needs—some free counseling. It might be relatively easy for Wayne to convince himself that it is okay just to listen occasionally in his office after school, and that it is his job to serve the teachers as well as the students. Yet Wayne's friendship with the teacher prohibits him from entering into a counseling relationship.

Angelica, too, might be torn by conflicting wishes. Although she knows she is legally and ethically required to report the child abuse, she foresees the difficulty in attempting to serve both as the parent's ongoing group leader and as reporter of the abuse. She is loathe to destroy the parent's trust and perhaps to disrupt the group. She is tempted to avoid or postpone reporting in the hope that the parent will learn nonabusive discipline methods by continuing in the group.

> If you were in Wayne's place, what might you do? How might you respond to your friend's request, in a way that both preserves the friendship and assists her to get the help she needs?
>
> What might you do if you were Angelica? How could you best balance the requirements of the law, the needs of the child, the needs of the parent, and the needs of the group?

The situation in which Wayne found himself, in the first scenario, is not at all uncommon. Friendships between teachers and school counselors are a natural outgrowth of their similar interests and daily contacts. In addition, many school counselors were teachers before they became counselors, and sometimes they counsel in the same school where they taught. When the transition first occurs from teacher to counselor, difficulties can arise. Teachers who are accustomed to the open sharing that takes place among colleagues may resent that the counselor, in his or her new role, has a different perspective on student concerns and is less forthcoming with certain kinds of information due to the need to protect student confidentiality. These transitional difficulties can probably best be resolved through open communication in which the counselor clearly defines and explains the rationale that guides decisions in her or his new role.

Another problem relates to school counselors who are also still teachers. Can they balance both roles? Being a teacher might actually help them to be a better counselor, yet their role as teacher could get in the way of forming counseling relationships. We recommend that when a professional must serve simultaneously as a teacher and a counselor, every effort be made to have a caseload of counselees who are not taking classes taught by the teacher/counselor.

Inevitably, school counselors will have friends who are also parents. This can create an uncomfortable dual role conflict when a friend's child attends the counselor's school and is assigned as a counselee. The counselor must keep boundaries around the professional relationship with the child and the personal relationship with the child's parents, which can be a difficult task.

Particularly in small towns and rural communities, it is difficult for school counselors to avoid some overlap between their personal and professional lives. When the counselor's friends are also the parents or teachers of their student clients, some role conflicts may be inevitable. For example, Gerald and Marianne Corey once consulted with school counselors in Alaska. Many school counselors in that state fly from one school to another in very remote villages that are accessible only by plane. Thus the counselor serves many schools, often performs many functions, and is sometimes even a relative of many of the school children. This example reminds us that the dual relationship issues pertaining to school counseling need to be considered within the context of the community.

School counselors serve multiple constituencies. ASCA's Ethical Standards (1992) spell out the counselor's responsibilities to pupils, parents, colleagues and professional associates, school and community, self, and the profession. When school counselors try to balance their responsibilities to students with their responsibilities to parents, conflicts can arise, particularly around confidentiality issues. Counselors are legally responsible to the parents but ethically more responsible to the students. Minor clients have a right to know what information they reveal to their counselors will be kept secret and what might be shared with parents (or teachers or administrators). On way to lessen the impact of some role conflicts is to conduct sessions with the student and parents in those situations when the parent wants information about the child.

School counselors are often faced with ethical dilemmas if their roles are not clearly defined, or if school policies exist that impinge on their effectiveness. To whom does the school counselor owe primary allegiance—the student, the student's parents, the school, or the community? If counselors are expected to carry out disciplinary functions, their capacity to serve as effective personal counselors is severely restricted. If they are expected to report drug use situations to parents or administrators, this will affect their ability to form counseling relationships with many students. If counselors are required to inform parents about details in cases concerning birth control or abortion, some students may avoid their counselors. Sometimes school counselors are asked to monitor tardiness or truancy, police the restrooms or cafeteria, enforce school policies, or supervise school events. Carrying out duties associated with any of these roles can make it more difficult for counselors to establish personal counseling relationships with students.

The School Counselor as Consultant

School counselors are increasingly being expected to serve as consultants to teachers, administrators, and parents. This can create role conflicts. The counselor role assumes that the counselor's primary function is to establish a therapeutic relationship with the student's welfare as the primary consideration. Yet the consultant roles emphasizes the process of working with other professionals when this is in the interest of the client. Ferris and Linville (1985) raised some important questions: How can counselors uphold their responsibility for the student's best interest if they are working only indirectly with the student in a consultant role? What are the ethical implications of giving a measure of responsibility for intervention and treatment to consultees (parents, teachers) who are not trained as counselors?

Consulting is not the same as counseling, and the two roles should be kept separate. In their role as consultants, school counselors are most likely to encounter ethical issues pertaining to dual relationships when they are involved in situations in which boundaries are not clearly drawn. Being aware of the issues involved in the consultant/consultee/client relationship, and the rights of consultees, can enable counselors to identify and deal with ethical problems that arise. School counselors who function as consultants need to develop a well-defined set of mutually agreed-upon expectations regarding the nature of consultation. As A. Michael Dougherty noted in chapter 5, the consultant's focus must be on work-related concerns. Thus school counselors should avoid discussing the personal concerns of a teacher or an administrator during consultation with that person. They need to avoid their tendency to move toward exploring the personal problems of their consultees and monitor their interventions so that they avoid creating dependency, using manipulation, or misusing power. They should strive to maintain a collaborative relationship.

Dealing With Child Abuse

Perhaps in no arena is the potential for dual role conflicts greater than in cases of child abuse. When counselors become aware of situations involving suspected child abuse or neglect, they are required to report it. The school counselor's role, however, is rarely limited to making a report. Remley and Fry

(1993) noted that school counselors are often asked to perform a multitude of functions—including informant, counselor to the victim or perpetrator, school system employee, court witness, liaison with social services, and counselor to the family—that involve distinct and conflicting roles. These authors pointed out several conflicts that can arise.

First, the counseling relationship with the child may be endangered when a counselor files a report. A child may have conflicting reactions when the counselor reports the abuse. The counselor may be seen as an ally in putting a stop to the abuse, or the child may feel betrayed and angry, particularly if retribution occurs in the home or if the child is removed from the home and perhaps from the school as a result of the counselor's action. It is more likely, however, because most abused children are left in their parents' custody, that the counselor will have the task of providing ongoing counseling to the child. Treatment of abuse victims can be a lengthy process that severely strains the counselor's resources. A problem can also develop if the counselor does not maintain appropriate boundaries. For instance, some counselors may be tempted to befriend such children or even attempt to "adopt" them. Counselors need to recognize their limits and not allow themselves to become overly involved to the extent that they lose their capacity for objectivity.

Counselors also need to follow procedures that have been established in their school systems. Some systems require that the principal be notified before a report is made, and some systems require that teachers be informed. It is difficult to maintain confidentiality in these instances.

Once a counselor has made a report, he or she may be involved with the court system until an adjudication is made. The counselor will need to work with children's protective services caseworkers, the police, and perhaps with attorneys. If the case goes to trial, the counselor may be required to testify as a witness. The multiple roles played by school counselors involved in child abuse cases can severely test the counselor's ability to handle conflicting demands and keep the client's welfare foremost.

A. Michael Dougherty suggests that school counselors should avoid roles that conflict with their primary role as counselor. He offers counselors some strategies for taking a proactive stance in defining their roles.

Managing Role Conflicts in School Counseling

A. Michael Dougherty

School counselors are often asked as part of their everyday duties to take on roles that might possibly conflict with their primary role as counselors. I believe that school counselors should avoid roles such as disciplinarian, substitute teacher, or lunchroom/bathroom/bus monitor that conflict with their primary role as counselor to students. The unique role of the counselor in the school makes the assumption of such roles highly questionable as doing so is likely to violate some of the basic tenets of the counseling relationship (such as confidentiality). As a consequence, new counseling relationships with students may be inhibited and existing ones may be compromised.

School counselors often engage in both preventive and remedial efforts as part of their overall counseling program. Preventive aspects of the program include group guidance, consultation with teachers and administrators, advocacy, and membership on student support teams. The primary elements of the remedial role of the counselor include individual and group counseling.

Emphasis on the preventive aspects of the school counselor's role has increased during the past two decades. Preventive interventions frequently assume an acceptance of the school counselor by other staff persons as "one of us." One important way to be accepted in such a manner is to engage in the same day-to-day activities in which other staff engage. Unfortunately, many of these activities jeopardize the counseling role of the school counselor. A critical issue for school counselors, then, is how to gain acceptance by staff and at the same time avoid engaging in roles that negatively impact their counseling relationships with students. It may be tempting for school counselors to give in and take on roles such as bus duty, lunchroom duty, or bathroom monitoring, particularly when there is strong pressure from administrators and teachers for them to do so. However, when they assume these roles, they increase the probability of placing themselves in the position of disciplinarian or informant. These dual roles, even when entered into only briefly, certainly put a counselor in a conflict-of-interest situation. Consider the following scenario as an illustration:

> Maria Sanchez, a middle school counselor, is currently conducting a counseling group for children of divorce. Vanessa is one of the students in the group. Ms. Sanchez, as a member of the school staff, has accepted bathroom monitoring as part of her duties. One day, as she is monitoring the girls' bathroom, she encounters Vanessa smoking a cigarette. Ms. Sanchez must now report Vanessa to the school administration for misconduct.

Even this very simple example points out the necessity for caution on the part of school counselors in taking potentially conflicting roles with the students they counsel. By reporting Vanessa to the administration, Ms. Sanchez could seriously damage the counseling relationship. Other students may hear of this counselor who "asks you to trust her at one time and turns you in at another time," and this could keep prospective clients from seeking out Ms. Sanchez as a counselor.

School counselors often think of their roles in terms of the "three C's": counseling, consultation, and coordination. There are, however, many other potential roles that the counselor might assume. Smaller roles like taking on bus duty may seem inconsequential. However, when counselors engage in roles that are incompatible with the primary role of counselor, the resulting dual relationships with students can have an adverse impact and therefore should be avoided.

School counselors, at the outset of each school year, need clearly and publicly to state their roles to school personnel as well as to students. When staff and students understand the counselor's unique role in the school, then the counselor is much more likely to be able to avoid potentially harmful dual relationships with students. At the same time, school counselors can be accepted as "family" by staff if they take on additional duties that do not create the potential for inappropriate dual relationships, such as working in the concession stand or running afterschool parent groups.

The 1990s have brought an increased emphasis on licensure for counselors, and it is now quite common in many states for school counselors to be licensed to conduct private practice. This recent trend has created the potential for a problematic dual relationship unique to school counselors. Consider the following scenario:

> Leon, a practicing school counselor, is also a licensed professional counselor. One of Leon's specialty areas is family counseling. He maintains a small private practice and counsels with families during the evenings and on weekends. One of Leon's clients at school is Gilbert, a student with ADHD. Leon counsels with Gilbert at school on a regular basis. Gilbert's parents approach Leon about the possibility of providing family counseling services.

What are some potential problems if Leon agrees to counsel the family? Aside from the fact that it is ethically questionable for a school counselor to use his position to acquire monetary gain outside the school setting, there are relationship boundary issues that could arise. Both Leon and Gilbert will be placed in dual roles: Leon as school counselor to Gilbert as an individual and as family counselor to Gilbert's family, and Gilbert as a student being counseled and as a family member in counseling. What if the parents, during family counseling sessions, try to obtain specific information from Leon about his sessions at school with Gilbert? What if Gilbert does not want to disclose in the family sessions what he has discussed with Leon at school? Are there any circumstances under which it will be appropriate for Leon to terminate the counseling relationship with Gilbert at school and counsel him as part of the family system? Clearly, school counselors interested in opening a private practice will have to be reflective about potential ethical dilemmas and establish clear boundaries between their school counselor role and their private practice.

If you are a school counselor, are you ever asked to take on noncounseling duties that could conflict with your counselor role? How do you handle such requests? What do you see as the advantages and disadvantages of taking on extra roles and responsibilities? If you are in private practice, or are considering opening a practice, what boundaries do you need to establish to keep your two roles from coming into conflict?

To sum up, we think that perhaps the best way to minimize dual relationship conflicts is for school counselors to be clear as to their primary role and functions as counselors and to communicate this to teachers, parents, administrators, and, most important of all, to students. Demands made by principals, teachers, parents, and outside agencies can sometimes run counter to student clients' best interests. School counselors may feel as though they are placed in a no-win situation: if they object to taking on inappropriate duties such as monitoring restrooms or hallways, they risk being seen as uncooperative by administrators and as "privileged" by teachers. If they agree to take on such duties, they risk jeopardizing their counseling relationships with students. School counselors serve in multiple roles with multiple constituencies and need to have a repertoire of strategies for dealing with any conflicts that may arise. These include consulting with colleagues, clearly defining and publicizing their role and function, networking with others, and practicing personal stress management.

HIGHER EDUCATION

Many professionals who work in college and university counseling centers perform multiple functions as counselors, supervisors, administrators, course instructors, and colleagues to faculty and staff. There is considerable potential for conflict among these roles. College and university student personnel workers who work in residence halls face yet another set of dual relationship dilemmas. A number of potential conflicts seem to be inherent in the multiple roles played by those who work in higher education counseling centers and residence halls.

College and university counseling centers generally have a broad mission to provide supportive services to students, faculty, and staff. Although counseling services are provided primarily to students, what should college and university counselors do when a faculty or staff member seeks counseling from them? Role conflicts certainly are possible if the counselors accept faculty or staff members as clients when they have another, collegial relationship as well. The potential problems deserve a full and open discussion before establishing a therapeutic relationship.

What if the staff member seeking counseling is also an employee? From our perspective, there are more problems involved in counseling an employee than there are potential benefits. One of the main ethical binds in this situation pertains to the power of the counselor/employer to hire and fire and to make or deny recommendations for promotion. For example, what might you do if you were a counseling center director and counselor, and a department secretary were to ask you to provide personal counseling? One day your secretary asks you if you might be willing to talk with her about her problems with her husband. She adds that the only reason she is making this request of you is because she knows and trusts you and that it is not like her to talk to anyone about her personal life.

We can think of many risks in acceding to this request. When could the counseling sessions take place? What if the counseling went poorly? What are the implications for the work relationship? What if the secretary discloses an abusive relationship with her husband who is a practicing alcoholic? What if she begins going to a shelter when he threatens to become abusive, as you have suggested, and misses work on these occasions? Although you are sympathetic, you are upset when she falls behind in the work she does for you. How do you deal with her absenteeism when it comes time to evaluate her job performance? These are just some of the questions that might arise and that demonstrate the wisdom of avoiding establishing a therapeutic role with an employee. Although we might be willing to listen to this secretary's personal concerns as we might with a neighbor, we would exercise caution in encouraging her to go into much detail about her problems. Instead, we would encourage her to consider getting professional help from a provider in the community.

Potential role conflicts also exist when higher education counselors serve as course instructors. It is not unusual for a college or university counselor to also teach part time in the counselor education program on campus. Are there any ethical binds in this practice? We do not think it wise for counselors who are also instructors to accept a current student in one of their classes as a client in their practice at the counseling center. But what if the student is a client first who then enrolls in the instructor's class? Is the instructor/counselor free to prevent the student from enrolling in the class? What if there is only one section of the course and it is required in the student's program? In cases such as this we think that it is a good policy to seek consultation. One way to avoid some of these problems is to have clear policies in place. For instance, students who are interning in the counseling center might be prohibited from taking a class with their supervisor who also teaches in the counseling program. Although such policies could not possibly cover every contingency that might arise, their existence, if known to students, could help those students make informed choices.

On a related note, what are the potential role conflicts when the college or university counseling center serves as an internship site for students in the counselor education program? This is a fairly common practice that does not necessarily create problems. However, in the case of an intern, it is helpful to have a clear contract and understanding with the intern and with the faculty from the graduate counseling program about what is expected. The supervisory role includes evaluation, and supervisors have responsibilities not only to the interns they supervise but also to the intern's clients. As we discussed in chapter 5, supervisors serve as gatekeepers to the profession. There needs to be a full understanding of the responsibilities of the supervisor in the counseling center, of the intern, and of the faculty members of the counseling program who also provide supervision.

Are there problems in hiring an intern after he or she graduates? If the intern proves to be an exceptionally competent counselor and could fit well into a vacant position, we do not see an ethical problem in hiring this person. However, once the former intern is hired, he or she is no longer a supervisee but a colleague. This shift in roles can involve a difficult transition for both the former supervisor and the former intern and might necessitate some special sensitivity, awareness, and open discussion.

We know several counselors who work in university counseling centers who also have part-time independent private practices. Is it ever acceptable for these counselors to refer counseling center clients to themselves in their private practice? To refer to their colleagues who may also have independent private practices?

Our immediate reaction is that it is not acceptable for college and university counselors to refer student clients to themselves. It is important for these counselors to follow the policies of the counseling center where they work, as these policies are likely to address the issue. This may not always be a simple matter, however. Consider the situation in which the college or university counseling center has a limitation on the number of times (say, six sessions) that a student can be seen by a counselor. Assume that at the sixth session the student says, "I feel that I am just beginning to make some progress, yet I realize that the college has a policy that ongoing counseling cannot be provided by the counseling center. I know that you have a private practice, and I am willing to see you there. I feel that we have an excellent working relationship, and I really do not want to stop at this point."

If you were this counselor, how might you respond? What might you say to the counselor if he or she were to consult you for advice on this matter? What if the counselor suggested a referral and the student resisted, making it clear that he wanted to continue seeing the counselor with whom he began? What if the geographic location was one in which there were no other therapists within a range of 100 miles?

These questions show how complex this situation is. Although college and university counselors generally should not accept a student client into their private practices, an emergency situation could arise. For instance, a suicidal client might be seen by the college counselor for the limited number of sessions allowed and might refuse a referral to another provider. The counselor might assess the risk in continuing to attempt to refer the client as being higher than the risk involved in seeing the client in his or her private practice. In addition, some nonemergency situations call for common sense judgments. Perhaps a client needs only one or two additional sessions to complete his or her work in counseling. Referring the client to another counselor does not seem to be the best option, especially because starting over with a new counselor might involve additional expense to the client. In these cases, we recommend that counselors discuss the situation with the center director to see whether exceptions can be made.

Whether or not higher education counselors have their own private practices, it is likely that they will need to refer some clients whose needs they cannot meet due to constraints of the setting. How do these counselors develop a referral base? A counselor who does not have a private practice may have a colleague in the counseling center who does. We believe it is prudent policy to avoid referring to this colleague. Rather, the referral base should include practitioners in the community for whom no conflict of interest exists. Competent community practitioners should be afforded an opportunity to apply to be included on the referral list. Limiting the list too narrowly to one's friends or associates could raise the issue of restraint of trade.

Sue Spooner makes the point that referral sources are not always readily available. She argues for common sense and some flexibility in role definitions, combined with education and awareness, as keys to avoiding many of the serious complications of dual relationships.

Dual Relationship Issues in Higher Education

Sue Spooner

The potential for dual relationships has been present in higher education for most of this century, if not longer. It exists all across the student affairs realm and beyond, in both the academic and business affairs segments of any campus. Counselor educators and counseling center staff members are obvious targets of approach by staff, students, and colleagues when they consider seeking help for personal or other problems. Other student affairs staff members may or may not be trained as counselors, but if they are viewed as approachable they are also sought out by members of the college or university community who want help with personal concerns. This need not always be problematic (indeed, in the case of a student seeking help from the counseling center, it is desirable), but it calls for a special awareness of the issues inherent in offering something as simple as a listening ear to someone who is not a "client." Personal topics arise in the course of casual conversations, in formal supervisory sessions, and in consultations about professional and work-related concerns. Sometimes the lines of demarcation are not entirely clear. In a supervisory session, one might learn that an employee has developed a serious problem with alcohol abuse. Referral is both appropriate and helpful, but so is follow-up. Maintaining the level of trust necessary to accomplish a successful referral calls for good counseling skills, and when these skills exist, we ought to use them.

For those professionals whose skills are fully integrated into their personal styles, it is ridiculous and probably impossible to require that they refrain from responding in a therapeutic way to concerns raised by colleagues, staff, or students. Creating a climate of guilt and anxiety over the use of one's ingrained skills seems counterproductive. It is simplistic to suggest that one should always refer such requests to someone outside the institution. In practice, this is not always feasible. When an institution is situated in a small town, or in a rural environment, the only resources may be those present on the campus itself. In locations where private practitioners are available, the cost may not be covered by insurance and may be too expensive for the help seeker. The colleague who approaches us may have had great difficulty in finding the courage to do so, and is indicating a degree of confidence in us that is not only flattering but bodes well for a successful outcome.

The residence hall environment is particularly illustrative of the dual relationship issues that arise in the student affairs domain. Residence life staffs tend to become melded into tightly knit working units. They work closely together 24 hours a day, so that their personal lives and their jobs blend into each other almost seamlessly. They know the intimate details of each other's lives, and they share both social and professional concerns with equal freedom. Romantic relationships among staff are common, and they also sometimes occur between students who are staff and residents who are students. Although we may officially frown on such relationships, it is unlikely that they can be eliminated or even limited. Our approach should be to educate staff to the issues surrounding such relationships, with an emphasis on the ethical guidelines to which they should adhere.

Resident life staff typically are aware of problems their students and other staff members have with drugs and alcohol, with school work, with family ties, and with myriad other elements of the lives of the young professionals and the young adult students they serve. They are frequently the best sources of help, at least initially, for both students and colleagues experiencing problems. They also know about referral and tend to use their referral sources wisely and well.

Much the same can be said for other areas of student affairs in which dual relationships may exist. The supervisor-subordinate relationship between boss and employee, the student activities staffer who develops close relationships with student leaders, and the academic adviser who must frequently deal not only with academic planning but also with the personal elements of a student's life all contain the potential for the complications of dual relationships. The key is not to avoid them at all costs but to be aware of the issues and conflicts that can arise and be prepared to deal with them as ethically and professionally as possible.

The climate of higher education has changed noticeably over the last decade. There is less casual sex, both among peers and between students and staff. There is a greater awareness about sexually transmitted diseases, and especially about the issues surrounding sexual harassment. This is not to say that these behaviors do not occur, but generally there is more deliberation before choosing to engage in them. Faculty and staff are more cautious in their relationships with students. Nevertheless, where young staff and the raging hormones of traditional-age students come together, human nature exerts a powerful influence. The office romance is also still with us. When the boss is dating or even living with another staff member, there are endless difficulties, not the least of which ensue when the relationship gets into trouble. Biased employee evaluations, preferential or prejudicial treatment over work assignments, and even fights in the office over problems in the relationship are just some of the complications that arise from such dual relationships. It is wise to discourage them, but it is impossible to prevent them. In most cases, it is agreed that the practice of staff entering into romantic relationships with students is—and should be—prohibited, as specified in our ethical codes. But what of the adult student who has an entire life apart from her or his status as a student? When consenting adults enter into mutually chosen relationships, it is unlikely that we can enforce the prohibition.

Certainly, the professional counselor and the counselor educator have some extra cautions with which to cope. Anyone who has been a sexual partner cannot later become a client. Even after the counseling or teaching relationship has ended, becoming sexually or just personally involved presents risks. Referring a client to oneself, if one has a private practice outside the campus, offers a fertile area for ethical conflicts. As most counseling center directors will tell us, being both an administrator and a counselor is fraught with potential dual roles, most of which cannot be avoided. Counseling center staff frequently teach in the counselor education program and perhaps in the undergraduate program as well. When a student wants to become a client, this is clearly prohibited, but the help seeker needs to be assisted though the referral process. Seeking social outlets with colleagues is a normal and common part of the campus culture but also offers potential problems when friendship and supervision conflict.

In certain cases, the existence of friendships across student service areas can be beneficial. The young professional who works in student activities may be best friends with a staff member in career services. They are apt to discuss situations that arise for either of them around students, other staff, and the general ebb and flow of the institution. Perhaps a student who is deeply involved in activities could use the help of the career services office to weave those experiences into a better resume. A referral is more apt to happen when the staffers have a good relationship. The academic adviser who knows and trusts a colleague on the counseling center staff is more likely to refer to that counselor a student whose personal problems are drawing energy from needed study. We can all help each other as professionals to recognize our limitations and to react appropriately in situations calling for attention to our ethical codes.

Another area in which some change has occurred is in our understanding about boundaries. In the 1960s and 1970s, the term had not been applied to human development. Now, we have a somewhat better understanding of the need to develop a sense of our various roles and to set boundaries between them. If we are clearer about who we are, in the core sense, and how that personhood carries into each segment of our lives, we can better manage to avoid the serious problems of dual relationships, even if we cannot or do not want to avoid them entirely. Consideration of dual relationships needs to become an element of staff training for all areas in student affairs, with presentation of the applicable content from the American College Personnel Association (ACPA) Ethical Principles (1995), the National Association of Student Personnel Administrators (NASPA) Standards of Practice (1996), and the ACA Code of Ethics. Even though not all student affairs staff are trained as counselors, there can be a high payoff in exposure to these documents and in an examination of how they apply to the work environment and our personal lives.

Returning to the case of the colleague or supervisee who presents us with a problem or concern, consciously or unconsciously seeking our help, first there is the question of how long and how deeply to become involved. That decision must be based on knowledge of one's own limitations, the seriousness of the situation, and whether other help is available. Some of us feel obligated to offer help when asked but limit the help to a more consultative mode, suggesting alternatives and resources. Faculty members should not enter into long-term psychotherapeutic relationships with colleagues, but neither should they ignore or rebuff any cry for help. Maintaining a list of referral sources is an obvious but easily overlooked necessity. Other common sense approaches include helping those in supervisory roles understand the conflicts they encounter, encouraging all staff training to include codes of ethics, and taking care that activities that involve intense self-disclosure are led by those who are properly trained to lead them and who do not have supervisory responsibility for the participants.

Education for staff, students, and colleagues should be ongoing. Awareness of the hazards of dual relationships while recognizing their inevitability should go far toward eliminating serious complications from the many roles that student services personnel in higher education play on a day-to-day basis.

Clearly, the potential for multiple role conflicts exists in educational institutions across the entire spectrum from elementary schools through graduate programs. As both of our contributors to this chapter have noted, awareness and training are key elements in our ability to recognize potential problems and to deal with them in an appropriate manner. We think Sue Spooner's point is especially cogent for practitioners of every counseling specialty: that the clearer we can be about who we are, in the core sense, and how that personhood carries into every aspect of our professional and personal lives, the better we will be able to manage multiple relationship dilemmas.

This chapter concludes our examination of multiple role and relationship issues in counseling practice. We realize that there are many specialty areas that might just as easily been included in addition to those that appeared. It has not been our aim to present inclusive coverage of specialties, but rather we hope that we have raised representative issues in a way that all readers can relate to them and apply them in their work.

11

Key Themes, Questions, and Decision Making

In this concluding chapter, we highlight some key concepts or themes that have emerged throughout the book and present questions for reflection and integration. We also offer a model of a decision-making process that we find helpful when confronted with potential multiple relationships.

Ten themes (or concepts) have been woven throughout the tapestry of this work:

1. **Multiple relationship issues affect virtually all mental health practitioners, regardless of their work setting or clientele.** No helping professional remains untouched by potential multiple role conflicts and dilemmas. We have examined how dual or multiple relationship issues impact professionals in many settings and in a number of specialty areas of practice. We explored these issues as they apply to working with individual clients, couples or families, and groups. We also looked at the complex questions that arise when relationships are tripartite, such as those involving supervisor/supervisee/client and consultant/consultee/ client system.

   Although we have attempted to cover a broad range of issues, we realize that there are a number of special areas of concern that we have not addressed. Despite the fact that we have not been able to discuss multiple relationship concerns in all counseling specializations, we feel confident in concluding that dual and multiple role conflicts are indeed pervasive in the mental health professions.

2. **All professional codes of ethics caution against dual relationships, but the newer codes acknowledge the complex nature of these relationships.** Codes of ethics surely are helpful when we look for guidance regarding multiple relationship dilemmas, and they should be consulted. However, it seems clear to us that codes of ethics cannot provide all the answers to the questions we face. A crucial ethical princi-

ple that applies to all potential multiple relationships is to do no harm. As professionals, it is our ethical responsibility to devise safeguards to prevent harm to clients, students, or supervisees who may be involved in dual or multiple relationships with us. At the same time, it is imperative that we involve the clients, students, and supervisees in open discussion of the possible risks and benefits of any dual relationship we consider entering. For students, seasoned practitioners, and clients alike, learning to deal with role conflicts can help us appreciate the complexity in human relationships.

3. **Not all multiple relationships can be avoided, nor are they necessarily always harmful.** Multiple relationships are fraught with complexities and ambiguities. They are unavoidable in some situations, and they sometimes contain potential both for risk and for benefit to clients. We have seen that some forms of role blending can be beneficial, such as the mentoring relationships between professor and student or the teaching of group counseling courses by combining didactic and experiential learning experiences.

4. **Multiple role relationships challenge us to monitor ourselves and to examine our motivations for our practices.** As practitioners, we need to engage in an ongoing process of self-reflection. It is all too easy to deceive ourselves into thinking that we have the best interests of our clients in mind. One example that we offered was that of a private practitioner who encourages clients who are in individual therapy to join a group that the practitioner is forming. This may not be what the clients need, and if we are not honest with ourselves, we run the risk of exploiting our clients. It is essential that we ask ourselves, whenever a multiple role issue arises, whose needs are being met.

5. **Whenever we consider becoming involved in a dual or multiple relationship, we would be wise to seek consultation from trusted colleagues or a supervisor.** Willingness to seek consultation is a sign of professionalism. We may also save ourselves a costly and painful malpractice judgment if we are able to demonstrate that we acted in good faith and sought consultation. Colleagues can help us to gain another perspective on potential problem areas that we may have overlooked. They can also help us maintain our objectivity and can enhance our ability to appraise situations honestly.

6. **There are few absolute answers that can neatly resolve dual or multiple relationship dilemmas.** Rather than thinking in terms of "finding the answer," it may be better to consider that there may be more than one acceptable way to respond to ethical dilemmas in multiple relationships. Answers that may be appropriate for us may not be appropriate for you in your situation. Simply because we have differing views about a specific

issue does not mean that one of us is right and the other is wrong. The therapeutic styles and preferences of the practitioner and the unique needs of each client must be taken into account. Thus we need to be able to tolerate ambiguity, and we will not find security in the absolute answers that some others may be quick to offer us.

7. **The cautions for entering into dual or multiple relationships should be for the benefit of our clients or others served rather than to protect ourselves from censure.** Although it does appear that mental health professionals are increasingly being sued for malpractice, we hope that we will not be so driven by fear of lawsuits (or by fear of having an ethics complaint lodged against us) that we fail to consider what our clients need and the role of our ethical reasoning skills when we are faced with potential multiple roles and relationships. In the final analysis, there is no substitute for our professional judgment, integrity, and good will.

8. **In determining whether to proceed with a dual or multiple relationship, consider whether the potential benefit of the relationship outweighs the potential for harm.** Generally, dual relationships should be entered into only when the risks of harm are small or when there are strongly offsetting ethical and clinical benefits for the consumer. It is prudent to consider the risks to the client and the professional involved as well as the possible effects on other consumers, other professionals, the profession itself, and society. Although we may identify benefits to certain multiple roles, we must be cautious in proceeding.

9. **It is the responsibility of counselor preparation programs to introduce boundary issues and explore multiple relationship questions. It is important to teach students ways of thinking about alternative courses of action.** When students first enter their graduate programs in the helping professions, they may have given little thought to the complexities involved in multiple relationships. We hope that the issues we have raised will be discussed extensively in ethics courses and in such courses as group supervision, practicum, and internship. When students are involved in supervised field placements, they are bound to encounter some dilemmas related to maintaining boundaries with their clients. As counselor educators and supervisors, we should encourage students to bring their concerns about these dilemmas to us for discussion. We can also introduce issues through case vignettes and role-playing exercises. We hope that we will do more than provide students with a list of do's and don'ts and will challenge students to think through their own positions on issues.

10. **Counselor education programs have a responsibility to develop their own guidelines, policies, and procedures for dealing with multiple roles and role conflicts within the program.** We think that faculty should be

engaged in continuing discussion about ways to prevent harmful dual relationships within the training program. As educators and supervisors, if we cannot deal with multiple relationships effectively, what chance will we have to teach students how to deal with these issues? If we are not modeling effective ways of thinking about and dealing with boundary issues, how can we expect our students to grapple constructively with them? Faculty groups, with student representation, can develop practical guidelines and procedures in a proactive manner.

Questions for Reflection and Integration

Throughout this book, in each chapter, we have tried to involve you, our readers. We have asked questions that we hope have encouraged you to think about the issues we have raised. Here in the last chapter, we include a summary list of some of the questions that have recurred in various forms. As you review this list, we ask you to consider your own stance toward the issues and the ways they affect your work as a professional.

- Are **sexual relationships with former clients** (or students or supervisees) ever ethically acceptable? If so, do you think it is a good idea to establish a minimum 2-year time period between terminating the professional relationship and beginning the personal one? What about **social relationships or friendships with former clients?** Collegial or peer relationships with former students or supervisees?

- How should the mental health professions deal with the issue of **sexual attraction** between counselors and clients? How can counselor education programs prepare prospective counselors so that they are able to distinguish clearly between feeling a sexual attraction and acting on that attraction?

- What steps can the profession take to **prevent sexual improprieties** with clients, students, or supervisees? What is your own role in prevention?

- Do the **codes of ethics** that govern your professional identity, work setting, and clientele address boundary issues and multiple relationships in a way that is helpful to you? If you want to see changes in your codes, how do you want them to read?

- If you are a **graduate student**, what kinds of training do you want to receive in order to feel prepared to cope with relationship boundary issues? What kinds of relationships do you want—and not want—to have with your professors?

- What are the appropriate boundaries of a **supervisor's role**? Can supervision address personal concerns of the supervisee without creating a dual role conflict? Where should the boundaries be drawn between counseling and supervision?

- Is **bartering** with clients for goods or services or **accepting a gift** from a client ever acceptable to you in your practice? If so, under what circumstances?

- What do you see as the appropriate limits of **counselor self-disclosure**? What boundary issues might be created for you in your work if you were to overextend these limits?

- What special role conflicts do you encounter when you function as a **supervisor or consultant**? To whom do you owe your first obligation— to your supervisee or consultee, or to the client who is ultimately served? What role conflicts do you encounter in attempting to balance these obligations?

- If you function in **multiple roles** in your work—in any combination of such roles as counselor, supervisor, administrator, teacher, client advocate, case manager, colleague, or group leader—what role conflicts do you most frequently encounter? How do you resolve them?

A Decision-Making Model

One picture that has emerged for us, as a result of examining and pondering these questions, is a model of a decision-making process that can be useful when confronted with dual or multiple relationship dilemmas.

It seems clear to us that some dual or multiple relationships, built into the counselor's job description or dictated by the unique needs of clients, are indeed unavoidable. Examples include the rehabilitation counselor who must manage the client's case budget; the counselor in a rural community whose clients are also her banker, beautician, and pharmacist; and the school counselor who must report child abuse and then continue to function as the child's counselor and liaison with child protective services. In these and similar instances, the professional's obligation is to take all possible steps to minimize the risks of harm. The client's informed consent is an ethically important first step that entails a full and open discussion with the client in which the risks are explored. Further, counselors who are engaged in unavoidable dual or multiple relationships are advised to seek consultation both at the time the relationship is entered and periodically throughout its duration. Ongoing self-monitoring and documentation are additional prudent measures. When unavoidable dual or multiple relationships become problematic, it is wise to obtain supervision.

Other types of role blending are avoidable, and in these cases the professional has a choice as to whether or not to engage in blended or multiple roles.

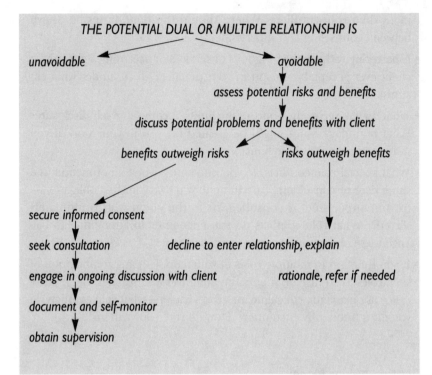

THE POTENTIAL DUAL OR MULTIPLE RELATIONSHIP IS

unavoidable   avoidable

assess potential risks and benefits

discuss potential problems and benefits with client

benefits outweigh risks   risks outweigh benefits

secure informed consent

seek consultation   decline to enter relationship, explain

engage in ongoing discussion with client   rationale, refer if needed

document and self-monitor

obtain supervision

Here it is essential that potential risks and benefits be carefully weighed. A judgment needs to be made regarding factors that create a potential for harm, including differences in expectations, divergent responsibilities, and the power differential. In some instances, when the potential benefits are great and the risks are small, the professional may decide to proceed. Examples include serving as a mentor to a student, teaching a group counseling class in a way that combines didactic and experiential learnings, and working with a client who has AIDS, and the client's family, in a nontraditional, out-of-office environment.

In yet other cases, a careful consideration of potential risks will lead the professional to conclude that it is best not to enter into a dual or multiple relationship. Although the temptation to do so might be well motivated, the risk of harm is strong. Examples include entering into a close, personal friendship with a current client, student, or supervisee and entering into a business relationship with a client. When a potential dual or multiple relationship can and should be avoided, professionals need to take steps to ensure that clients understand the rationale for not proceeding with the problematic aspect of the relationship. For instance, in the first example, this might involve acknowledging the attractiveness of the idea of a friendship, discussing the risks to the counseling relationship if a friendship were to develop, and mutually agreeing on what the boundaries of the professional relationship will be.

Although the decision-making model helps to clarify our thinking, each of us will encounter situations in our work that will raise difficult questions for which the answers remain elusive. Our expectation is that we have stimulated thinking and self-examination. In our view, the ability of mental health professionals to reason through ethical issues can be strongly tested by conflicting roles and multiple relationship situations. As is the case with learning to make ethical decisions in other areas of professional practice, many of these situations defy easy answers. To some degree, the personal style of each counselor needs to be taken into consideration in resolving multiple relationship dilemmas. Some practitioners may be comfortable practicing in the context of multiple roles, but others may need to establish more singular, clear-cut boundaries.

Closing Thoughts

We stated in the final chapter of the first edition of this book that coauthoring a work about dual relationships was a learning experience for each of us. This has been equally true in the revision process. We discovered new slants on issues that we had not previously considered, rethought old issues in the context of revisions in ethical standards and more recent literature, and learned a great deal from our guest contributors.

Certainties are rare in the helping professions. We make no claim to having discovered answers to complex and difficult questions about professional relationship boundaries. Rather, we hope to have raised some important issues, to have explored a range of viewpoints, and to have discussed our own positions. We hope that the various chapters have provided material for thoughtful reflection and a springboard for ongoing discussion. We expect that ethically conscientious professionals will continue to struggle with the multiple relationship dilemmas that they face and the multiple roles they will be expected to balance in their work. In the absence of certainties, we must rely on our reasoned professional judgment, openness to discussing issues with clients (or students or supervisees) who are equally affected by decisions made, and consultation with colleagues.

References

Akamatsu, T. J. (1988). Intimate relationships with former clients: National survey of attitudes and behavior among practitioners. *Professional Psychology: Research and Practice, 19*(4), 454-458.

Alcoholics Anonymous. (1967). *As Bill sees it.* New York: Alcoholics Anonymous World Services.

Alcoholics Anonymous. (1976). *Alcoholics Anonymous* (3rd ed.). New York: Alcoholics Anonymous World Services.

Allen, V. B. (1986). A historical perspective on the AACD Ethics Committee. *Journal of Counseling and Development, 64,* 293.

American Association for Marriage and Family Therapy. (1991). *AAMFT code of ethics.* Washington, DC: Author.

American College Personnel Association. (1995). Statement of ethical principles. In *ACPA membership directory,* 1995-96 (pp. 14-17). Washington, DC: Author.

American Counseling Association. (1995). *Code of ethics and standards of practice.* Alexandria, VA: Author.

American Counseling Association Ethics Committee. (1995). *A practitioner's guide to ethical decision making.* Alexandria, VA: Author.

American Psychological Association. (1987). *If sex enters into the psychotherapy relationship.* Washington, DC: Author.

American Psychological Association. (1992). *Ethical principles of psychologists and code of conduct.* Washington, DC: Author.

American Psychological Association Ethics Committee. (1987). Report of the ethics committee: 1986. *American Psychologist, 42,* 730-734.

American Psychology-Law Society & Division 41 of the American Psychological Association. (1991). *Specialty guidelines for forensic psychologists.* Lincoln: University of Nebraska, Department of Psychology.

American School Counselors Association. (1992). Ethical standards for school counselors. *The ASCA Counselor, 29*(3), 13-16.

Anderson, S. K., & Kitchener, K. S. (1996). Nonromantic, nonsexual post-therapy relationships between psychologists and former clients: An exploratory study of critical incidents. *Professional Psychology: Research and Practice, 27,* 59-66.

Anonymous. (1991). Sexual harassment: A female counseling student's experience. *Journal of Counseling and Development, 69,* 502-506.

Association for Counselor Education and Supervision. (1993, Summer). Ethical guidelines for counseling supervisors. *ACES Spectrum, 53*(4).

Association for Specialists in Group Work. (1991). Professional standards for the training of group workers. *Together,* 9-14.

Atkinson, D. R., Morten, G., & Sue, D. W. (Eds.). (1993). *Counseling American minorities: A cross-cultural perspective* (4th ed.). Dubuque, IA: Brown and Benchmark.

Atkinson, D. R., Thompson, C. E., & Grant, S. K. (1993). A three-dimensional model for counseling racial/ethnic minorities. *The Counseling Psychologist, 21*(2), 257-277.

Austin, K. M., Moline, M. E., & Williams, G. T. (1990). *Confronting malpractice: Legal and ethical dilemmas in psychotherapy.* Newbury Park, CA: Sage.

Bader, E. (1994). Dual relationships: Legal and ethical trends. *Transactional Analysis Journal, 24*(1), 64-66.

Bajt, T. R., & Pope, K. S. (1989). Therapist-patient sexual intimacy involving children and adolescents. *American Psychologist, 44,* 55.

Barker, M. (1996). The ethical dilemma of the two-hatter. *The Counselor, 14*(3), 15-16.

Bartell, P. A., & Rubin, L. J. (1990). Dangerous liaisons: Sexual intimacies in supervision. *Professional Psychology: Research and Practice, 21*(6), 442-450.

Bates, C. M., & Brodsky, A. M. (1989). *Sex in the therapy hour: A case of professional incest.* New York: Guilford Press.

Beauchamp, T. (1982). *Philosophical ethics: An introduction to moral philosophy.* New York: McGraw-Hill.

Berman, J. R. (1985). Ethical feminist perspectives on dual relationships with clients. In L. B. Rosewater & L. E. Walker, *Handbook of feminist therapy: Women's issues in psychotherapy* (pp. 287-296). New York: Springer.

Bernard, J. M., & Goodyear, R. K. (1992). *Fundamentals of clinical supervision.* Boston: Allyn and Bacon.

Biaggo, M., & Greene, B. (1995). Overlapping dual relationships. In E. Rave & C. Larsen, *Ethical decision making in therapy: Feminist perspectives* (pp. 88-123). New York: Guilford Press.

Bissell, L. C., & Royce, J. E. (1994). *Ethics for addiction professionals* (2nd ed.). Center City, MN: Hazelden Foundation.

Bograd, M. (1993, January/February). The duel over dual relationships. *The California Therapist,* pp. 7-16.

Bok, S. (1979). *Lying: Moral choice in public and private life.* New York: Vintage Books.

Borders, L. D., Cashwell, C. S., & Rotter, J. C. (1995). Supervision of counselor licensure applicants: A comparative study. *Counselor Education and Supervision, 35,* 54-69.

Borys, D. S. (1988). *Dual relationships between therapist and client: A national survey of clinicians' attitudes and practices.* Unpublished doctoral dissertation, University of California, Los Angeles.

Borys, D. S., & Pope, K. S. (1989). Dual relationships between therapist and client. A national study of psychologists, psychiatrists, and social workers. *Professional Psychology: Research and Practice, 20*(5), 283-293.

Bowman, V. E., Hatley, L. D., & Bowman, R. L. (1995). Faculty-student relationships: The dual role controversy. *Counselor Education and Supervision, 34*, 232-242.

Brown, L. (1994). Boundaries in feminist therapy: A conceptual formulation. *Women and Therapy, 15*(1), 29-38.

Brown, R., & Prager, L. (1985). Ethical issues in graduate education, faculty and student responsibilities. *Journal of Higher Education, 56*(4), 403-418.

California Department of Consumer Affairs. (1990). *Professional therapy never includes sex.* Sacramento, CA: Author.

Carter, R. T. (1995). *The influence of race and racial identity in psychotherapy.* New York: Wiley.

Corey, M. S., & Corey, G. (1997). *Groups: Process and practice* (5th ed.). Pacific Grove, CA: Brooks/Cole.

Corey, G., Corey, M. S., & Callanan, P. (1993). *Issues and ethics in the helping professions* (4th ed.). Pacific Grove, CA: Brooks/Cole.

Dougherty, A. M. (1995). *Consultation: Practice and perspectives in school and community settings* (2nd ed.). Pacific Grove, CA: Brooks/Cole.

Dove, W. R. (1995). Ethics training for the alcohol/drug abuse professional. *Alcoholism Treatment Quarterly, 12*(4), 19-30.

Egan, G. (1994). *The skilled helper: A problem-management approach to helping* (5th ed.). Pacific Grove, CA: Brooks/Cole.

Emerson, S., & Markos, P. A. (1996). Signs and symptoms of the impaired counselor. *Journal of Humanistic Education and Development, 34*, 108-117.

Ferris, P.A., & Linville, M. E. (1985). The child's rights: Whose responsibility? *Elementary School Guidance and Counseling, 19,* 172-180.

Forester-Miller, H., & Duncan, J. A. (1990). The ethics of dual relationships in the training of group counselors. *Journal for Specialists in Group Work, 20,* 222-231.

Forester-Miller, H., & Remley, T.P. *Perceived effectiveness of graduate courses that prepare counselors for group work.* Unpublished manuscript. North Carolina Central University, Durham.

Foster, S. (1996, January). The consequences of violating the "forbidden zone." *Counseling Today,* p. 24.

Freeman, L., & Roy, J. (1976). *Betrayal.* New York: Stein & Day.

Gabbard, G. O. (Ed.). (1989). *Sexual exploitation in professional relationships.* Washington, DC: American Psychiatric Association.

Gabbard, G. O. (1995, April). What are boundaries in psychotherapy? *The Menninger Letter, 3*(4), 1-2.

Gainsley, J. (1996). In the field: Groups in rural Sumter County. *Together, 24*(3), 9.

Gartrell, N., Herman, J., Olarte, S., Feldstein, M., & Localio, R. (1987). Reporting practices of psychologists who knew of sexual misconduct by colleagues. *American Journal of Orthopsychiatry, 57*(2), 287-295.

Gazda, G. M. (1992). Dual role relationships in group counseling. In B. Herlihy & G. Corey, *Dual relationships in counseling* (pp. 200-202). Alexandria, VA: American Association for Counseling and Development.

Gibson, W. T., & Pope, K. S. (1993). The ethics of counseling: A national survey of certified counselors. *Journal of Counseling and Development, 71,* 330-336.

Gill-Wigal, J., & Heaton, J. A. (1996, Summer). Managing sexual attraction in the therapeutic relationship. *Directions in Mental Health Counseling, 6,* 3-14.

Glaser, R. D., & Thorpe, J. S. (1986). Unethical intimacy: A survey of sexual contact and advances between psychology educators and female graduate students. *American Psychologist, 41*, 43-51.

Glosoff, H. L., & Herlihy, B. (1995, Winter). Teaching, training, and supervision standards in the 1995 ACA Code of Ethics: What's new, what's different? *ACES Spectrum*, pp. 10-13.

Glosoff, H. L., Corey, G., & Herlihy, B. (1996). Dual relationships. In B. Herlihy & G. Corey, *ACA ethical standards casebook* (5th ed., pp. 251-257). Alexandria, VA: American Counseling Association.

Gorski, T. T., & Miller, M. (1986). *Staying sober.* Independence, MO: Herald House/Independence Press.

Gottlieb, M. C. (1990). Accusations of sexual misconduct: Assisting in the complaint process. *Professional Psychology: Research and Practice, 21*(6), 455-461.

Gottlieb, M. C. (1994). Ethical decision making, boundaries, and treatment effectiveness: A reprise. *Ethics and Behavior, 4*(3), 287-293.

Greenburg, S. L., Lewis, G. J., & Johnson, M. (1985). Peer consultation groups for private practitioners. *Professional Psychology: Research and Practice, 16*(3), 437-447.

Greenspan, M. (1986). Should therapists be personal? Self-disclosure and therapeutic distance in feminist therapy. *Women and Therapy, 5*, 5-17.

Gutheil, T. G., & Gabbard, G. O. (1993). The concept of boundaries in clinical practice: Theoretical and risk-management dimensions. *American Journal of Psychiatry, 150*(2), 188-196.

Hammel, G.A., Olkin, R., & Taube, D.O. (1996). Student-educator sex in clinical and counseling psychology doctoral training. *Professional Psychology: Research and Practice, 27*(1), 93-97.

Hararr, W. R., VandeCreek, L., & Knapp, S. (1990). Ethical and legal aspects of clinical supervision. *Professional Psychology: Research and Practice, 21*, 37-41.

Hedges, L. E. (1993, July/August). In praise of dual relationships. Part II: Essential dual relatedness in developmental psychotherapy. *The California Therapist*, pp. 42-46.

Herlihy, B. (1996). When a colleague is impaired: The individual counselor's response. *Journal of Humanistic Education and Development, 34*, 118-127.

Herlihy, B., & Corey, G. (1992). *Dual relationships in counseling.* Alexandria, VA: American Association for Counseling and Development.

Herlihy, B., & Corey, G. (1994). Codes of ethics as catalysts for improving practice. *Ethical Issues in Professional Counseling, 2*(3), 2-12.

Herlihy, B., & Corey, G. (1996). *ACA ethical standards casebook* (5th ed.). Alexandria, VA: American Counseling Association.

Herlihy, B., & Golden, L. (1990). *Ethical standards casebook* (4th ed.). Alexandria, VA: American Association for Counseling and Development.

Hill, M. (1990). On creating a theory of feminist therapy. *Women and Therapy, 9*(1/2), 53-65.

Hill, M., Glaser, K., & Harden, J. (1995). A feminist model for ethical decision making. In E.J. Rave & C. C. Larsen (Eds.), *Ethical decision making in therapy: Feminist perspectives* (pp. 18-37). New York: Guilford Press.

Hillerbrand, E. T., & Stone, G. L. (1986). Ethics and clients: A challenging mixture for counselors. *Journal of Counseling and Development, 64*, 419-420.

Holroyd, J. C., & Brodsky, A. M. (1977). Psychologists' attitudes and practices regarding erotic and nonerotic physical contact with patients. *American Psychologist, 32*, 843-849.

Hotelling, K. (1988). Ethical, legal, and administrative options to address sexual relationships between counselor and client. *Journal of Counseling and Development, 67*, 233-237.

James, J. (1996, May 11). University to adopt rules that put limits on dating. *Register-Guard*, Eugene, OR, pp. 1, 6A.

Kain, C. D. (1996). *Positive: HIV affirmative counseling.* Alexandria, VA: American Counseling Association.

Karenga, M. (1984). *Selections from the Husia.* Los Angeles: Kawaida Productions.

Kasl, C. D. (1992). *Many roads, one journey: Moving beyond the 12 steps.* New York: HarperCollins.

Kitchener, K. S. (1984). Intuition, critical evaluation, and ethical principles: The foundation for ethical decisions in counseling psychology. *The Counseling Psychologist, 12,* 43-56.

Kitchener, K. S. (1988). Dual relationships: What makes them so problematic? *Journal of Counseling and Development, 67,* 217-221.

Kitchener, K. S. (1992). Posttherapy relationships: Ever or never? In B. Herlihy & G. Corey, *Dual relationships in counseling* (pp. 145-148). Alexandria, VA: American Association for Counseling and Development.

Kitchener, K.S., & Harding, S. S. (1990). Dual role relationships. In B. Herlihy & L. Golden, *Ethical standards casebook* (4th ed., pp. 146-154). Alexandria, VA: American Association for Counseling and Development.

Ladany, N., & Friedlander, M. L. (1995). The relationship between the supervisory working alliance and trainees' experience of role conflict and role ambiguity. *Counselor Education and Supervision, 34,* 220-231.

Lamb, D. (1992). Relationships with former clients: Ethical, legal, and clinical considerations. *Register Report, 18,* 13-14.

Leatherman, C. (1993). In the debate over faculty-student dating, the talk turns to ethics, sex, even love. *Chronicle of Higher Education, 24*(37), A15-A17.

Lloyd, A. P. (1992). Dual relationship problems in counselor education. In B. Herlihy & G. Corey, *Dual relationships in counseling* (pp. 59-64). Alexandria, VA: American Association for Counseling and Development.

Margolin, G. (1982). Ethical and legal considerations in marital and family therapy. *American Psychologist, 37*(7), 788-801.

McCarthy, P., Sugden, S., Koker, M., Lamendola, F., Maurer, S., & Renninger, S. (1995). A practical guide to informed consent in clinical supervision. *Counselor Education and Supervision, 35,* 130-138.

McGovern, T., Wright, L., & Wright, N. M. (1990, May/June). National understanding of the NAADAC code of ethics. *The Counselor*, pp. 37-38.

Meara, N., Schmidt, L., & Day, J. (1996). Principles and virtues: A foundation for ethical decisions, policies, and character. *The Counseling Psychologist, 24*, 4-77.

Meloy, J. R., Haroun, A., & Schiller, E. F. (1990). *Clinical guidelines for involuntary outpatient treatment.* Sarasota, FL: Professional Resource Exchange.

Merta, R. J., & Sisson, J. A. (1991). The experiential group: An ethical and professional dilemma. *Journal for Specialists in Group Work, 16*, 236-245.

Merta, R. J., Johnson, P., & McNeil, K. (1995). Updated research on group work: Educators, course work, theory, and teaching methods. *Journal for Specialists in Group Work, 20*, 143-150.

Merta, R. J., Wolfgang, L., & McNeil, K. (1993). Five models for using the experiential group in the preparation of group counselors. *Journal for Specialists in Group Work, 18*, 200-207.

Miller, G. (1996). The supervision of students by students. In B. Herlihy & G. Corey, *ACA ethical standards casebook* (5th ed., pp. 281-284). Alexandria, VA: American Counseling Association.

Miller, G. M., & Larrabee, M. J. (1995). Sexual intimacy in counselor education and supervision: A national survey. *Counselor Education and Supervision, 34*, 332-343.

Mobley, M. J. (1987). Psychotherapy with criminal offenders. In I. Weiner & A. Hess (Eds.), *Handbook of forensic psychology.* New York: Wiley.

Monahan, J. (Ed.). (1980). *Who is the client?* Washington, DC: American Psychological Association.

National Association of Social Workers. (1996). *Code of ethics.* Washington, DC: Author.

National Association of Student Personnel Administrators. (1996). Standards of professional practice. In *NASPA membership handbook* (pp. 19-20). Washington, DC: Author.

Nerison, R. M. (1992). *Dual client-therapist relationships: Incidence and consequences to clients.* Unpublished doctoral dissertation, University of Iowa.

Neukrug, E. S., Healy, M., & Herlihy, B. (1992). Ethical practices of licensed professional counselors: An updated survey of state licensing boards. *Counselor Education and Supervision, 32,* 130-141.

Nobles, W. (1986). *African psychology: Toward its reclamation, reascension, and revitalization.* Oakland, CA: Institute for Black Family Life and Culture.

Noel, B., & Watterson, K. (1992). *You must be dreaming.* New York: Poseidon.

Olarte, S. W. (1997). Sexual boundary violations. In *Hatherleigh Guide to Ethics in Therapy.* New York: Hatherleigh.

Pellegrino, E., & Thomasma, D. (1993). *The virtues in medical practice.* New York: Oxford University Press.

Pierce, K. A., & Baldwin, C. (1990). Participation versus privacy in the training of group counselors. *Journal for Specialists in Group Work, 15,* 149-158.

Plaisel, E. (1985). *Therapist.* New York: St. Martin's/Marek.

Pope, K. S. (1985). Dual relationships: A violation of ethical, legal, and clinical standards. *California State Psychologist, 20*(3), 3-6.

Pope, K. S. (1988). How clients are harmed by sexual contact with mental health professionals: The syndrome and its prevalence. *Journal of Counseling and Development, 67,* 222-226.

Pope, K. S. (1994). *Sexual involvement with therapists: Patient assessment, subsequent therapy, forensics.* Washington, DC: American Psychological Association.

Pope, K. S., & Bouhoutsos, J. C. (1986). *Sexual intimacy between therapists and patients.* New York: Praeger Press.

Pope, K. S., & Tabachnick, B. G. (1993). Therapists' anger, hate, fear, and sexual feelings: National survey of therapist responses, client characteristics, critical events, formal complaints, and training. *Professional Psychology: Research and Practice, 24,* 142-152.

Pope, K. S., & Vasquez, M. J. T. (1991). *Ethics in psychotherapy and counseling.* San Francisco: Jossey-Bass.

Pope, K. S., & Vetter, V. (1991). Prior therapist-patient sexual involvement among patients seen by psychologists. *Psychotherapy, 28,* 429-438.

Pope, K. S., Keith-Spiegel, P., & Tabachnick, B. G. (1986). Sexual attraction to clients: The human therapist and the (sometimes) inhuman training system. *American Psychologist, 41*(2), 147-158.

Pope, K.S., Levenson, H., & Schover, L. (1979). Sexual intimacy in psychology training. *American Psychologist, 34,* 682-689.

Pope, K. S., Sonne, J., & Holroyd, J. (1993). *Sexual feelings in psychotherapy: Explorations for therapists and therapists in training.* Washington, DC: American Psychological Association.

Pope, K.S., Tabacknick, B. G., & Keith-Spiegel, P. (1987). Ethics of practice: The beliefs and behaviors of psychologists as therapists. *American Psychologist, 42,* 993-1006.

Rave, E. J., & Larsen, C. C. (1995). *Ethical decision making in therapy: Feminist perspectives.* New York: Guilford Press.

Remley, T. P., & Fry, L. J. (1993). Reporting suspected child abuse: Conflicting roles for the counselor. *School Counselor, 40,* 253-259.

Rest, J. (1982). The major components of morality. In W. Kurtines & J. Gerwitz, *Moral behavior and moral development* (pp. 24-40). New York: Wiley.

Richards, D. (1990). *Building and managing your private practice.* Alexandria, VA: American Association for Counseling and Development.

Ridley, C. R. (1995). *Overcoming unintentional racism in counseling and therapy.* Thousand Oaks, CA: Sage.

Riger, S. (1991). Gender dilemmas in sexual harassment policies and procedures. *American Psychologist, 46*(5), 497-505.

Robinson, W., & Reid, P. (1985). Sexual intimacies in psychology revisited. *Professional Psychology: Research and Practice, 16,* 512-520.

Rutter, P. (1989). *Sex in the forbidden zone.* Los Angeles: Jeremy Tarcher.

Salisbury, W. A., & Kinnier, R. T. (1996). Posttermination friendship between counselors and clients. *Journal of Counseling and Development, 74,* 495-500.

Schafer, C. (1990, March 1). Ethics: Dual relationships come under scrutiny. *Guidepost,* pp. 1, 3, 16.

Schoener, G., & Gonsiorek, J. (1988). Assessment and development of rehabilitation plans for counselors who have sexually exploited their clients. *Journal of Counseling and Development, 67,* 227-232.

Sherry, P. (1991). Ethical issues in the conduct of supervision. *The Counseling Psychologist, 19*(4), 566-584.

Shimberg, B. (1986). Preventing sexual exploitation of clients by counselors: A plea for protection. *Journal of Counseling and Development, 65,* 119-120.

Simon, R. I. (1989). Sexual exploitation of patients: How it begins before it happens. *Psychiatry Annals, 19,* 104-112.

Simon, R. I. (1991). Psychological injury caused by boundary violations: Precursors to therapist-patient sex. *Psychiatry Annals, 21,* 614-619.

Simon, R. I. (1992). Treatment boundary violations: Clinical, ethical, and legal considerations. *Bulletin of the American Academy of Psychiatry and the Law, 20,* 269-288.

Simon, S. (1987). *Clinical psychiatry and the law.* Washington, DC: American Psychiatric Press.

Sleek, S. (1994, December). Ethical dilemmas plague rural practice. *APA Monitor,* pp. 26-27.

Slimp, P. A., & Burian, B. K. (1994). Multiple role relationships during internship: Consequences and recommendations. *Professional Psychology: Research and Practice, 25*(1), 39-45.

Smith, D., & Fitzpatrick, M. (1995). Patient-therapist boundary issues: An integrative review of theory and research. *Professional Psychology: Research and Practice, 26*(5), 499-506.

Stadler, H. (1986a). To counsel or not to counsel: The ethical dilemma of dual relationships. *Journal of Counseling and Human Service Professions, 1*(1), 134-140.

Stadler, H. (1986b, September). Making hard choices: Clarifying controversial ethical issues. *Counseling and Human Development, 1,* 1-10.

Stadler, H. (1989). Child abuse reporting: A strategy for acting on ethical responsibilities. *The Counseling Psychologist, 17,* 102-110.

Stadler, H. (1992). Counseling relationships between students and educators. In B. Herlihy & G. Corey, *Dual relationships in counseling* (pp. 52-56). Alexandria, VA: American Association for Counseling and Development.

St. Germaine, J. (1993). Dual relationships: What's wrong with them? *American Counselor, 2*(3), 25-30.

Stoltenberg, C. D., & Delworth, U. (1987). *Supervising counselors and therapists: A developmental approach.* San Francisco: Jossey-Bass.

Sue, D. W. (1996). Ethical issues in multicultural counseling. In B. Herlihy & G. Corey, *ACA ethical standards casebook* (5th ed., pp. 193-197). Alexandria, VA: American Counseling Association.

Sue, D. W., & Sue, D. (1990). *Counseling the culturally different: Theory and practice.* New York: Wiley.

Sue, S., & Zane, N. (1987). The role of culture and cultural techniques in psychotherapy: A critique and reformulation. *American Psychologist, 42,* 37-45.

Sue, D. W., Ivey, A. E., & Pedersen, P. B. (1996). *A theory of multicultural counseling and psychotherapy.* Pacific Grove, CA: Brooks/Cole.

Sumerel, M. B., & Borders, L. D. (1996). Addressing personal issues in supervision: Impact of counselors' experience level on various aspects of the supervisory relationship. *Counselor Education and Supervision, 35,* 268-285.

Tabachnick, B. G., Keith-Spiegel, P., & Pope, K. S. (1991). Ethics of teaching: Beliefs and behaviors of psychologists as educators. *American Psychologist, 46*(5), 506-515.

Thoreson, R. W., Shaughnessy, P., & Frazier, P. A. (1995). Sexual contact during and after professional relationships: Practices and attitudes of female counselors. *Journal of Counseling and Development, 74*, 84-89.

Thoreson, R. W., Shaughnessy, P., Heppner, P. P., & Cook, S. W. (1993). Sexual contact during and after the professional relationship: Attitudes and practices of male counselors. *Journal of Counseling and Development, 71*, 429-434.

Tomm, K. (1993, January/February). The ethics of dual relationships. *The California Therapist*, pp. 7-19.

Twemlow, S., & Gabbard, G. O. (1989). The love-sick therapist. In G. O. Gabbard (Ed.), *Sexual exploitation in professional relationships* (pp. 71-87). Washington, DC: American Psychiatric Press.

Tyler, J. M., & Tyler, C. (1994). Ethics in supervision: Managing supervisee rights and supervisor responsibilities. *Directions in Mental Health Counseling, 4*(11), 4-25.

Usher, C. H., & Borders, L. D. (1993). Practicing counselors' preferences for supervisory style and supervisory emphasis. *Counselor Education and Supervision, 33*, 66-79.

Vasquez, M. J. T. (1988). Counselor-client sexual contact: Implications for ethics training. *Journal of Counseling and Development, 67*, 238-241.

Vasquez, M. J. T. (1991). Sexual intimacies with clients after termination: Should a prohibition be explicit? *Ethics and Behavior, 1*(1), 45-61.

Vinson, J. S. (1987). Use of complaint procedures in cases of therapist-patient sexual contact. *Professional Psychology: Research and Practice, 18*, 159-164.

Walden, S. L. (1996). *Public knowledge of counseling ethics.* Unpublished doctoral dissertation, Kent State University.

Walker, E., & Young, T. D. (1986). *A killing cure.* New York: Holt, Rinehart & Winston.

Whiston, S. C., & Emerson, S. (1989). Ethical implications for supervisors in counseling of trainees. *Counselor Education and Supervision, 28*, 318-325.

White, W. (1993). *Critical incidents: Ethical issues in substance abuse prevention and treatment.* Bloomington, IL: Lighthouse Training Institute.

Wilson, J. (1993). *The moral sense.* New York: Free Press.

Wise, P. S., Lowery, S., & Silverglade, L. (1989). Personal counseling for counselors in training: Guidelines for supervisors. *Counselor Education and Supervision, 28,* 326-336.

Yalom, I. D. (1995). *Theory and practice of group psychotherapy* (4th ed.). New York: Basic Books.

Index

A

ACA Code of Ethics (1995), 2, 3, 85
  bartering practices, 42, 96, 100
  counseling friends, 97
  counselor educators, 49-50, 52, 53, 54,
    56-57, 58
  culturally appropriate practice in, 42
  ethics of sexual dual relationships, 18
  ethics for sexual relationships with former
    clients, 18-19
  ethics on unavoidability of dual
    relationships, 7
  higher education, 156
  pro bono services, 117
  supervisors, 66-67, 68, 73
  training group counselors, 87-88
ACA Ethics Committee
  consumer member on, 44
  counselor educators, 50
  ethical decision-making model, 45-46
Adler, Alfred, 118
Adult Children of Alcoholics (ACOA), 128
adviser, counselor as, 106
advocate, counselor as, 105
African American clients, 107-8
  African-centered view of dual
    relationships, 109-11
AIDS/HIV, counseling clients living
  with, 130-34

Al-Anon, 128
Alcoholics Anonymous (AA), 128, 129
ambivalence, 24, 36
American Association for Marriage and
    Family Therapy (AAMFT)
  code of ethics of, 2, 3-4
  counselor educators, 50
  ethics of sexual dual relationships, 18
  ethics for sexual relationships with former
    clients, 19
American College Personnel Association
    (ACPA), Ethical Principles, 156
American Counseling Association (ACA)
  Ethical Standards Casebook, 36, 55
  male ACA members and sexual contact
    with clients, 22
  See also ACA Code of Ethics (1995); ACA
    Ethics Committee
American Psychological Association (APA), 29
  APA Insurance Trust and sexual
    malpractice suits, 23
  code of ethics of, 2, 3
  counselor educators, 50, 51
  ethics of sexual dual relationships, 18
  ethics for sexual relationships with former
    clients, 19
  ethics on unavoidability of dual
    relationships, 7, 8
  nonpsychologist on APA Ethics
    Committee, 44

American School Counselors Association (ASCA), *Ethical Standards for School Counselors*, 143, 145
Anderson, S. K.
  relationships with former clients, 104
  sexual intimacy between therapists and clients, 22
Anonymous (1991), 37-38
Asian clients, 107-8
Association for Counselor Education and Supervision (ACES), *Ethical Guidelines for Counseling Supervisors*, 66, 67, 68, 73, 77
Association for Specialists in Group Work (ASGW), 89
  Professional Standards for the Training of Group Workers, 87
Atkinson, D. R., 105, 108
Austin, K. M., 23

B

Bader, E., 129
Baldwin, C., 85
Bartell, P. A., 30
bartering, 42
  for goods and services, 96-97, 98, 99-100
Bates, C. M., 24, 38
Berman, J. R., 116, 119
Bernard, J. M., 77
Betrayal (Freeman and Roy), 38
Biaggo, M., 117, 119
Bissell, L. C., 128-29
Bograd, M., 6
Book of Declarations of Virtues, 110
Borders, L. DiAnne
  subtle boundary issues in supervision, 73-75
  supervisory relationship, 65, 71
Borys, D.S.
  accepting gifts from clients, 100
  consumer perspectives, 36
  counseling friend/acquaintance, 97-98
  exploiting the client, 10
  self-disclosure, 101
  social relationships with clients, 102
Bowman, R. L., 54-55
Bowman, V. E.
  faculty and student dual relationships, 54-55
  supervisor/supervisee sexual relationships, 68
Brodsky, A. M., 38
  psychologists and sexual contact with

clients, 22
  sexual dual relationships, 24
Brown, L., 95, 116
Brown, R., 56
Burian, B. K., 65, 72

C

Cain, Hal, rehabilitation counseling, 127, 134-37, 141
California Department of Consumer Affairs, 29
California State University, 51
Callanan, P., 6
change agent, counselor in role of, 105
child abuse, 146-47
client's perspective
  attitudes and beliefs of consumers, 35-36
  client's experiences with dual relationships, 36-39
  implications, 39-40
  inclusion of the client perspective in ethical practice, 40-47
Cocaine Anonymous (CA), 128
college and university counseling centers. *See* higher education
consultants
  college faculty members as, 58
  ethnic minority clients and counselor/consultant, 105-6
  school counselor as consultant, 146
consultation, 78-79
  dual role conflicts in, 80-82
consumers
  dual relationship risks to, 12
  dual relationships and effects on other, 13
  sexual dual relationships and consumer education, 29
Cook, S. W., 22
Corey, G.
  counselor educators, 56
  ethics codes, 6
  private practice, 118-19
  school counselors, 145
Corey, M. S.
  ethics codes, 6
  school counselors, 145
counseling clients living with HIV, 130-34
counseling in the community, 95
  accepting gifts from clients, 100-101
  African-centered view of dual

relationships, 109-11

alternative counselor roles in working with diverse clients, 104-6

bartering for good and services, 96-97, 99-100

counseling a friend/acquaintance, 97-98

former clients, 103-4

issues in rural practice, 98

limits of self-disclosure, 101-2, 107

multicultural perspectives on multiple relationships, 106-9

rural communities and dual relationships, 99-100, 108, 121, 129-30

social relationships with clients, 102-3

Counseling Today, 19

counselor

problematic dual relationships and role of, 8

recovering substance abuse counselors, 127-30

sexual dual relationships and counselor education, 30-31

counselor educators, 9, 49-50

client perspective and, 46

dual relationships between students, 55

dual relationships in counselor education, 56-60, 61-64

relationship boundaries between students and professors, 53- 55

role conflicts for, 51-53

sexual dual relationships, 50-51

student perspective, 61-64

teaching students about boundary issues, 60-61

countertransference/transference issues

client perspectives and, 43

in supervision, 77-78

crossings, boundary, 9

culturally appropriate practice, client perspective and, 42

decision-making models, 163-65

ACA's ethical, 45-46

for supervisors, 75-76

D

Delworth, U., 71

diverse clients, working with, 104-6

Dougherty, Michael

consultation issues, 65, 80-82, 146

school counseling, 143, 147-50

dual or multiple relationships, 1-3

conflicting views in, 5-7

decision-making model, 163-65

ethical standards, 3-4

harmful and benign, 5

key themes, 159-62

potential for harm, 10-11

questions for reflection and integration, 162-63

recognizing, 4-5

risks in, 12-13

safeguards to minimize risks, 13-14

subtle but important distinctions, 8-10

unavoidability of, 7-8

Duncan, J.A., 88

E

Egan, G., 76

Emerson, S., 76

empowerment, client, 41-42

ethical decision-making model, 45-46

ethical standards

codes of ethics as guidelines, 6

codes of ethics of professional associations, 3-4

ethics on unavoidability of dual relationships, 7-8

implications of codes of ethics, 7

sexual dual relationships, 18

ethics codes

African-centered, 110

client participation in creation of, 44

supervision guidelines and, 66-68

ethnic minority clients, 104-6

F

facilitators, counselors as, 106

faculty-student sexual relationships.
See counselor educators

family counseling.
See group and family counseling

Feminist Model for ethical decision making, 45-46

Feminist Therapy Code of Ethics, 118

Ferris, P. A., 146

fiduciary relationships, 39

financial issues

in private practice, 116-17

rehabilitation counseling and third-party

payers, 136-37
forensic psychology and counseling, 138-41
Forester-Miller, Holly
  bartering, 97
  dual relationships in training group
    workers, 86, 87-89
  group counselor training, 83-84
  rural communities and dual relationships,
    95, 99-100, 108, 121
former clients
  group counseling for, 122
  sexual relationships with, 18-21
  social relationships with, 103-4
  as source of referrals, 13
Foster, S., 24
Freeman, L., 38
Friedlander, M. L., 71, 77
friends/acquaintances
  admittance to counseling group, 122
  counseling, 97-98
Fry, L. J., 146-47

G

Gainsley, J., 99
Gazda, G. M., 125
geographical and cultural issues, in private
    practice, 116
Gibson, W. T.
  consumer perspectives, 36
  ethics survey, 4
gift giving, 42
  accepting gifts from clients, 100-101
Gill-Wigal, J., 28
Glaser, R. D., 50
Glosoff, Harriet L., private practice, 113, 114-
    20
Gonsiorek, J., categories of counselors who
    sexually exploit their clients, 22-23
Goodyear, R. K., 77
Gottlieb, M. C., 30
Grant, S. K., 105, 108
Greene, B., 117, 119
group counselor training, 83-84
  combining experiential and didactic
    approaches, 84
  dual relationships in, 87-89
  ethical use of experiential approaches to
    training, 85-86
  experiential group, 90-92

group and family counseling, 120
  admitting a friend/acquaintance to a coun-
    seling group, 122
  concurrent individual and group or family
    counseling, 125-26
  group counseling for former clients, 122
  group counseling in rural communities,
    100, 108, 121, 129-30
  limits of self-disclosure, 122-23
  personal relationships in group counseling,
    120-21
  special considerations for marriage and
    family counseling, 123-25
Guidepost, 22

H

Hammel, G. A., 51
Hararr, W. R., 71-72
Harding, S. S.
  assessing the potential for harm, 10-11
  bartering, 96
  counseling relationships and friendships,
    97
Hatley, L. D., 54-55
Haynes, Robert, forensic psychology, 127,
    138-41
healer, referral to an indigenous, 106
Healy, M., 12
Heaton, J. A., 28
Hedges, L. E., 7
Heppner, P. P., 22
Herlihy, B.
  counselor educators, 56
  isolation in private practice, 115
  state licensing board survey, 12
higher education, 150-53
  dual relationship issues in, 153-57
Hill, M., 114, 117
Hillerbrand, E. T., 45
Hispanic/Latino clients, 107-8
HIV/AIDS, counseling clients living with,
    130-34
Holroyd, J. C.
  psychologists and sexual contact with
    clients, 22
  sexual attraction towards a client, 27
Hotelling, K., 29

I

If Sex Enters Into the Psychotherapy Relationship (brochure), 29
inherent duality, 9, 65
interpersonal boundaries, 9
isolation
    private practice and, 114-15
    sexual dual relationships and client, 24

J

Johnson, P., 85

K

Kain, Craig D., counseling clients living with HIV, 127, 130-34, 141
Karenga, M., 110
Kasl, C. D., 129
Keith-Spiegel, P., 30-31
A Killing Cure (Walker and Young), 38
Kinnier, R. T.
    consumer perspectives, 36
    relationships with former clients, 104
    sexual intimacies with former clients, 20
Kitchener, K. S.
    assessing the potential for harm, 10-11
    bartering, 96
    counseling relationships and friendships, 97
    counselor educators, 57
    relationships with former clients, 103-4
    sexual intimacy between therapists and clients, 22
Knapp, S., 71-72

L

Ladany, N., 71, 77
Larrabee, M. J.
    faculty-student sexual relationships, 51
    supervisor/supervisee sexual relationships, 68
legal issues
    malpractice actions against therapists, 12
    sexual malpractice suits, 23-24
    supervisee incompetence, 78
licensure boards, state counseling
    dual relationship complaints to, 12
    professional disclosure statements, 44
Linville, M. E., 146

Lloyd, A. P., 53-54
Lowery, S., 70

M

McCarthy, P., 77
McNeil, K., 84, 85
malpractice suits
    malpractice actions against therapists, 12
    sexual, 23-24
Margolin, G., 124
marriage counseling, 123-25
Meara, N., 59
mentoring relationships, 8-9, 54
Merta, R. J.
    experiential group, 90-92
    training group counselors, 84, 85, 89
Miller, G. M.
    dual relationships between students, 55
    faculty-student sexual relationships, 51
    supervisor/supervisee sexual relationships, 68
Mobley, M. J., 140
Moline, M. E., 23
Morten, G., 105, 108
multiculturalism
    multicultural counseling movement, 107
    multicultural perspectives on multiple relationships, 106-9
Muratori, Michelle C., counselor education, 49, 54, 61-64
mutual-help groups, 128

N

Narcotics Anonymous (NA), 128
National Association of Alcoholism and Drug Abuse Counselors (NAADAC), 127-28
National Association of Social Workers (NASW)
    code of ethics of, 2, 3
    ethics of sexual dual relationships, 18
    ethics for sexual relationships with former clients, 19
National Association of Student Personnel Administrators (NASPA), Standards of Practice, 156
Nerison, R. M., consumer perspectives study, 35-36, 37, 38-39, 40
Neukrug, E. S., 12
Noel, B., 38

noncounselor role, mentoring and, 8
nonsexual dual relationships, 2-3, 4, 12
    client's perspectives and, 36, 38-39

O

occupational therapist (OT), 135
office romance, 155

P

paraprofessionals, 13
Parham, Thomas A., African-centered view of
    dual relationships, 95, 109-11
peer role relationships, 58
Pellegrino, E., 59
Pierce, K. A., 85
Plaisel, E., 38
Pope, K. S.
    consumer perspectives, 36, 40
    counselor education, 30-31
    ethics survey, 4
    isolation in private practice, 115
    malpractice suits for sexual impropriety, 23
    problems in dual relationships, 5-6
    sexual attraction towards a client, 27, 28
    therapist-patient sex syndrome, 24-25
Powell, Les J., substance abuse counseling,
    127-30
A Practitioner's Guide to Ethical Decision Making
    (ACA), 45
Prager, L., 56
private practice, 113-14
    multiple relationship issues in, 114-20
Professional Therapy Never Includes Sex
    (booklet), 29
professionals
    dual relationship risks to, 12
    dual relationships and effects on other, 13
    sexual relationships and monitoring
        professional practice, 31-32
prudence, 59

R

Rational Recovery (RR), 128
recovery groups, 128
rehabilitation counseling, 134-37
Remley, T. P., 89, 146-47
Rest, J., 57

Richards, D., 113
role blending, 8, 10, 54
Roy, J., 38
Royce, J. E., 128-29
Rubin, L. J., 30
rural communities, counseling in, 98-100,
    108, 121, 129-30
Rutter, P., 17

S

St. Germaine, J., 6
Salisbury, W. A.
    consumer perspectives, 36
    relationships with former clients, 104
    sexual intimacies with former clients, 20
Schoener, Gary
    categories of counselors who sexually
        exploit their clients, 22-23
    posttermination romantic relationship, 19
school counseling, 143-46
    dealing with child abuse, 146-47
    managing role conflicts in, 147-50
    school counselor as consultant, 146
self-disclosure, 101-2, 107, 122-23
Sex in the Therapy Hour: A Case of Professional
    Incest (Bates and Brodsky), 38
Sexaholics Anonymous (SA), 128
sexual dual relationships, 17
    counselor educators and, 50-51
    ethical standards, 18
    harm to clients, 24-26
    incidence, 21-22
    legal sanctions, 23-24
    the offending therapist, 22-23
    prevention and remediation, 28-32
    sexual attraction to clients, 26-28
    sexual relationships with former clients, 18-21
    in supervision, 68
Sexual Feelings in Psychotherapy: Explorations for
    Therapists and Therapists in Training
    (Pope, Sonne, and Holroyd), 27, 28
sexual harassment, 37-38
Shaughnessy, P., 22
Silverglade, L., 70
Sisson, J.A., 90-91
Sleek, S., 98
Slimp, P. A., 65, 72
social relationships
    with clients, 102-3

with former clients, 103-4
with supervisees, 71-72
Sonne, J., 27
Spooner, Sue, dual relationship issues in
higher education, 153- 57
Stadler, Holly A., counselor education, 49, 55,
56-60
Stoltenberg, C. D., 71
Stone, G. L., 45
student-faculty sexual relationships.
See counselor educators
substance abuse counseling, 127-30
Sue, Derald Wing
ethnically diverse client groups, 105
gift giving, 100
multicultural perspectives on multiple
relationships, 95, 106-9
Sumerel, M. B., 71
supervision, 65-66
boundary between counseling and, 68-71
countertransference issues, 77-78
decision-making models for supervisors, 75-76
ethics codes and guidelines, 66-68
informed consent in, 76-77
inherent duality, 9, 65
sexual dual relationships in, 68
social and business relationships with
supervisees, 71-72
subtle boundary issues in, 73-75
supervisee incompetence, ethical and legal
considerations, 78

T

Tabachnick, B. G., 30-31
Therapist (Plaisel), 38
therapist-patient sex syndrome, 24-25, 37
therapists, male and female
categories of counselors who sexually
exploit their clients, 22-23
sexual intimacies with former clients,
21-22, 23
third-party payers, 136-37
Thomasma, D., 59
Thompson, C. E., 105, 108
Thoreson, R. W.
counselor education, 31
male ACA members and sexual contact
with clients, 22
Thorpe, J. S., 50

Tomm, K., 6-7
transference/countertransference issues
client perspectives and, 43
in supervision, 77-78

U

university and college counseling centers.
See higher education
University of Iowa, 51
University of Oregon, 51
University of Virginia, 51
Usher, C. H., 71

V

VandeCreek, L., 71-72
Vasquez, M. J. T.
counselor education, 30
isolation in private practice, 115
malpractice suits for sexual impropriety, 23
problems in dual relationships, 5-6
sexual attraction towards a client, 28
victims, sexual dual relationships and support
for the, 29-30
violations
boundary, 9
repeat violations of ethical standards, 12

W

Walden, Susan L.
client perspective in ethical practice, 35,
40-47
ethical counselor behavior, 36
Walker, E., 38
Watterson, K., 38
Whiston, S. C., 76
White, W., 129
Williams, G. T., 23
Wise, P. S., 70
Wolfgang, L., 84
women, reluctance to file complaints,
29-30, 37-38

Y

Yalom, I. D., 125
You Must Be Dreaming (Noel and Watterson), 38
Young, T. D., 38